Economics of the Public Sector

Economics of the Public Sector

Edited by
John Hardiman

Larsen & Keller
www.larsen-keller.com

Economics of the Public Sector
Edited by John Hardiman
ISBN: 978-1-63549-659-8 (Hardback)

Larsen & Keller
Published by Larsen and Keller Education,
5 Penn Plaza,
19th Floor,
New York, NY 10001, USA

Cataloging-in-Publication Data

Economics of the public sector / edited by John Hardiman.
p. cm.
Includes bibliographical references and index.
ISBN 978-1-63549-659-8
1. Finance, Public. 2. Fiscal policy. 3. Economic policy. 4. Public administration--Decision making.
I. Hardiman, John.
HJ141 .E26 2018
336--dc23

Printed and bound in China.

For more information regarding Larsen and Keller Education and its products, please visit the publisher's website www.larsen-keller.com

Table of Contents

Preface

Public economics refers to the process of using fields like equity and economic efficiency to study the importance and use of government policy and interference of government in economic markets. The most important topics included in this field are analysis of market, government failure, public finance, taxation and its effects, public policy design, etc. While understanding the long-term perspectives of the topics, the text makes an effort in highlighting their impact as a modern tool for the growth of the discipline. This textbook is a complete source of knowledge on the present status of this important field. It is meant for students who are looking for an elaborate reference text on public economics.

To facilitate a deeper understanding of the contents of this book a short introduction of every chapter is written below:

Chapter 1- The government plays a key role in making policies through concepts such as economic efficiency and equity. Taxation, subsidies, fiscal policies, national budget, government debt, etc. are some of the key topics of this subject. This is an introductory chapter which will introduce briefly all the significant aspects of public economics.

Chapter 2- The concepts of public economics can be divided into theoretical tools and empirical tools. The ability of a product to satisfy a customer is known as utility. Theoretical tools rationalize economic decision making while empirical tools substantiate theory with economic data. This chapter discusses in detail the theories and methodologies related to public economics.

Chapter 3- The cost or benefit an individual incurs whose causality is indirectly related to the individual is known as externality. It can be divided into negative externality or positive externality. The major components of externality are discussed in this chapter.

Chapter 4- An important question in public economics revolves around the concept of public goods. Should public goods be accounted as part of subsidies and benefits provided by the government? Public economics is best understood in confluence with the major topics listed in the following chapter.

Chapter 5- Government intervention in the provision of public goods is based on certain theories. Median voter theory provides data that represents the majority of median voters, who are those whose preference towards a public good is at the middle level. There are certain shortcomings of this theory as it views voter preference as one-dimensional. This chapter discusses the methods of government intervention in a critical manner providing key analysis to the subject matter.

I owe the completion of this book to the never-ending support of my family, who supported me throughout the project.

Editor

1

A Brief Introduction to Public Economics

The government plays a key role in making policies through concepts such as economic efficiency and equity. Taxation, subsidies, fiscal policies, national budget, government debt, etc. are some of the key topics of this subject. This is an introductory chapter which will introduce briefly all the significant aspects of public economics.

Public Economics

Public economics (or economics of the public sector) is the study of government policy through the lens of economic efficiency and equity.

At its most basic level, public economics provides a framework for thinking about whether or not the government should participate in economic markets and to what extent it should do so. In order to do this, microeconomic theory is utilized to assess whether the private market is likely to provide efficient outcomes in the absence of governmental interference. Inherently, this study involves the analysis of government taxation and expenditures. This subject encompasses a host of topics including market failures, externalities, and the creation and implementation of government policy. Public economics builds on the theory of welfare economics and is ultimately used as a tool to improve social welfare.

Broad methods and topics include:

- the theory and application of public finance
- analysis and design of public policy
- distributional effects of taxation and government expenditures
- analysis of market failure and government failure.

Emphasis is on analytical and scientific methods and normative-ethical analysis, as distinguished from ideology. Examples of topics covered are tax incidence, optimal taxation, and the theory of public goods.

Subject Range

The Journal of Economic Literature (JEL) classification codes are one way categorizing the range of economics subjects. There, Public Economics, one of 19 primary classifications, has 8 categories. They are listed below with JEL-code links to corresponding available article-preview links of The New Palgrave Dictionary of Economics Online (2008) and with similar footnote links for each respective *sub*category if available:

JEL: H (all) – Public Economics

JEL: H0 – General

JEL: H1 – Structure and Scope of Government

JEL: H2 – Taxation, Subsidies, and Revenue

JEL: H3 – Fiscal Policies and Behavior of Economic Agents

JEL: H4 – Publicly Provided Goods

JEL: H5 – National Government Expenditures and Related Policies

JEL: H6 – National Budget, Deficit, and Debt

JEL: H7 – State and Local Government; Intergovernmental Relations

JEL: H8 – Miscellaneous Issues.

Taxation

Diamond–Mirrlees Efficiency Theorem

In 1971, Peter A. Diamond and James A. Mirrlees published a seminal paper which showed that even when lump-sum taxation is not available, production efficiency is still desirable. This finding is known as the Diamond–Mirrlees efficiency theorem, and it is widely credited with having modernized Ramsey's analysis by considering the problem of income distribution with the problem of raising revenue. Joseph E. Stiglitz and Partha Dasgupta (1971) have criticized this theorem as not being robust on the grounds that production efficiency will not necessarily be desirable if certain tax instruments cannot be used.

Pigouvian Taxes

A.C. Pigou (1877-1959).

One of the achievements for which the great English economist A.C. Pigou is known, was his work on the divergences between marginal private costs and marginal social costs (externalities). In his book, *The Economics of Welfare* (1932), Pigou describes how these divergences come about:

...one person A, in the course of rendering some service, for which payment is made, to a second person B, incidentally also renders services or disservices to other persons (not producers of like services), of such a sort that payment cannot be extracted from the benefited parties or compensation enforced on behalf of the injured parties.

In particular, Pigou is known for his advocacy of what are known as corrective taxes, or Pigouvian taxes:

It is plain that divergences between private and social net product of the kinds we have so far been considering cannot, like divergences due to tenancy laws, be mitigated by a modification of the contractual relation between any two contracting parties, because the divergence arises out of a service or disservice to persons other than the contracting parties. It is, however, possible for the State, if it so chooses, to remove the divergence in any field by "extraordinary encouragements" or "extraordinary restraints" upon investments in that field. The most obvious forms which these encouragements and restraints may assume are, of course, those of bounties and taxes.

Pigou describes as positive externalities, examples such as resources invested in private parks that improve the surrounding air, and scientific research from which discoveries of high practical utility often grow. Alternatively, he describes negative externalities, such as the factory that destroys a great part of the amenities of neighboring sites.

In 1960, the economist Ronald H. Coase proposed an alternative scheme whereby negative externalities are dealt with through the appropriate assignment of property rights. This result is known as the Coase theorem.

Public Goods

Public goods, or collective consumption goods, exhibit two properties; non-rivalry and non-excludability. Something is non-rivaled if one person's consumption of it does not deprive another person, (to a point) a firework display is non-rivaled - since one person watching a firework display does not prevent another person from doing so. Something is non-excludable if its use cannot be limited to a certain group of people. Again, since one cannot prevent people from viewing a firework display it is non-excludable. Conceptually, another example of public good is the service that is provided by law enforcement organizations, such as sheriffs and police. Typically, cities and towns are served by only one police department, and the police department serves all of the people within its jurisdiction.

Cost–benefit Analysis

Jules Dupuit (1804-1866).

While the origins of cost–benefit analysis can be traced back to Jules Dupuit's classic article "On the Measurement of the Utility of Public Works" (1844), much of the subsequent scholarly development occurred in the United States and arose from the challenges of water-resource development. In 1950, the U.S. Federal Interagency River Basin Committee's Subcommittee on Benefits and Costs published a report entitled, *Proposed Practices for Economic Analysis of River Basin Projects* (also known as the *Green Book*), which became noteworthy for bringing in the language of welfare economics. In 1958, Otto Eckstein published *Water-Resource Development: The Economics of Project Evaluation*, and Roland McKean published his *Efficiency in Government Through Systems Analysis: With Emphasis on Water Resources Development*. The latter book is also considered a classic in the field of operations research. In subsequent years, several other important works appeared: Jack Hirshleifer, James DeHaven, and Jerome W. Milliman published a volume entitled *Water Supply: Economics, Technology, and Policy* (1960); and a group of Harvard scholars including Robert Dorfman, Stephen Marglin, and others published *Design of Water-Resource Systems: New Techniques for Relating Economic Objectives, Engineering Analysis, and Governmental Planning* (1962).

Definition of Public

- Governments are organizations formed to exercise authority over the actions of persons who live together in society and to manage the provision of essential services.
- The everyday life of citizens is affected by public policies decisions made by Governments.
- In the study of public economics we are concerned about the Role of the government.
- When should the government intervene in the economy?
- How might the government intervene?
- What is the effect of those interventions on economic outcomes?
- Why do governments choose to intervene in the way that they do?

Why do we Need Governments?

The existence of governments stems from the necessity of finding a mechanism to undertake decisions that affect a group of people.

How does a group of people come to decide on an issue that affects them all BUT in different ways. For example heterogeneity of preferences might lead some people to benefit from a policy & some to lose.

[Amartya Sen (Nobel Price 1998): "the choices of the people, by the people, for the people" is broadly speaking the subject of "social choice"].

What do Governments do?

- Direct state involvement in economic activity.
- Governments provide several goods and services. Some of those goods are "public" other are "private". We will later discuss the difference between private and public goods and the rationale for their government provision.
  - Expenditure side: provision (and in some cases production) of goods and services.
  - Revenue Side: price setting, determining taxes & subsidies. In addition, determine price of goods produced by state run enterprises.
  - Regulation eg. Laws and assignment of property rights.
- Revenue and expenditure / represent the traditional partition for economists in public economics.

Taxation

Governments have near monopoly power to tax, subsidize and regulate.

Taxes, subsidies and regulation alter individual incomes and incentives via budget constraint.

What is the Role of Government?

Expenditure Side

What services should the government provide?

- Organization of economic activity
- Contract enforcement
- Collection of revenue

Taxation Side

How should the government raise its money?

- Efficient mean of collection revenue (least cost way).

When Should the Government Intervene in the Economy?

- Think of the economy as a series of trades between producers and consumers. A trade is efficient if it makes at least one party better off without making the other party worse off. In micro economics you may have learnt that competitive market equilibrium is the most efficient outcome for the society. It is the outcome that maximizes the gains from efficient trades, the one where supply & demand curves intersect.
- If the competitive market equilibrium is the most efficient outcome for the society why do governments intervene in the operation of some of these markets?

- Two main justifications for government intervention are:
  - Market failures
  - Redistribution

Market Failures

- Market failures cause a market to not deliver an efficient outcome.
- Example: Consider Car Insurance in India.[There are a large number of road accidents in India caused by rash driving. However, even though insurance is available with every purchase of car these days not many people buy insurance to drive a car.]
- This by itself, however, does not reflect market failure. It just means that many people do not value the insurance enough to buy it at current market prices. As far as the individual decision (bold) maker is concerned you can still argue that it is an efficient outcome for him/her.
- However, is this equilibrium the most efficient outcome for the society?
- Suppose that I am uninsured and am a rash driver all the same. However, even if I don't care about an accident that would affect me, I might be dangerous to fellow drivers and pedestrians on the road. Hence the total economic cost incurred might be much higher than that incurred by myself. The gains from owning the insurance would be much higher than the cost of the insurance borne by myself. That is why having car insurance should be compulsory.
- However, when I make my insurance decision I don't consider the total social value but only the value to myself. So that I don't buy the insurance. Thus the competitive outcome does not maximize total social efficiency in this case.
- Lack of insurance could cause *negative externalities* from–the uninsured may not take account of their impact on others.
  - Government may induce individuals to buy insurance.
- If competitive equilibrium does not lead to efficiency maximizing outcome, there is potential for efficiency improvement through government intervention. The government can compare the social cost and benefit as a third party and induce me to buy the insurance for myself.
- However, this is an example of negative externality. It is not necessary that the government intervention would always increase efficiency when private market outcome is not efficient.

Market Failure

In economics, market failure is a situation in which the allocation of goods and services is not efficient. That is, there exists another conceivable outcome where an individual may be made better-off without making someone else worse-off. Market failures can be viewed as scenarios where individuals' pursuit of pure self-interest leads to results that are not efficient – that can be improved upon from the societal point of view. The first known use of the term by economists was in 1958, but the concept has been traced back to the Victorian philosopher Henry Sidgwick.

Market failures are often associated with time-inconsistent preferences, information asymmetries, non-competitive markets, principal–agent problems, externalities, or public goods. The existence of a market failure is often the reason that self-regulatory organizations, governments or supra-national institutions intervene in a particular market. Economists, especially microeconomists, are often concerned with the causes of market failure and possible means of correction. Such analysis plays an important role in many types of public policy decisions and studies. However, government policy interventions, such as taxes, subsidies, bailouts, wage and price controls, and regulations (including poorly implemented attempts to correct market failure), may also lead to an inefficient allocation of resources, sometimes called government failure.

Given the tension between, on the one hand, the undeniable costs to society caused by market failure, and on the other hand, the potential that attempts to mitigate these costs could lead to even greater costs from "government failure", there is sometimes a choice between imperfect outcomes, i.e. imperfect market outcomes with or without government interventions. But either way, if a market failure exists the outcome is not Pareto efficient. Most mainstream economists believe that there are circumstances (like building codes or endangered species) in which it is possible for government or other organizations to improve the inefficient market outcome. Several heterodox schools of thought disagree with this as a matter of principle.

An *ecological* market failure exists when human activity in a market economy is exhausting critical non-renewable resources, disrupting fragile ecosystems services, or overloading biospheric waste absorption capacities. In none of these cases does the criterion of Pareto efficiency obtain.

Categories

Different economists have different views about what events are the sources of market failure. Mainstream economic analysis widely accepts a market failure (relative to Pareto efficiency) can occur for three main reasons: if the market is "monopolised" or a small group of businesses hold significant market power, if production of the good or service results in an externality, or if the good or service is a "public good".

The Nature of the Market

Agents in a market can gain market power, allowing them to block other mutually beneficial gains from trade from occurring. This can lead to inefficiency due to imperfect competition, which can take many different forms, such as monopolies, monopsonies, or monopolistic competition, if the agent does not implement perfect price discrimination. In a monopoly, the market equilibrium will no longer be Pareto optimal. The monopoly will use its market power to restrict output below the quantity at which the marginal social benefit is equal to the marginal social cost of the last unit produced, so as to keep prices and profits high. An issue for this analysis is whether a situation of market power or monopoly is likely to persist if unaddressed by policy, or whether competitive or technological change will undermine it over time.

It is then a further question about what circumstances allow a monopoly to arise. In some cases, monopolies can maintain themselves where there are "barriers to entry" that prevent other companies from effectively entering and competing in an industry or market. Or there could exist significant first-mover advantages in the market that make it difficult for other firms to compete. In another way, a natural monopoly is an extreme case of the failure of competition as a restraint on producers. A natural monopoly is a firm whose per-unit cost decreases as it increases output; in this situation it is most efficient (from a cost perspective) to have only a single producer of a good.

The Nature of the Goods

Non-excludability

Some markets can fail due to the nature of the goods being exchanged. For instance, goods can display the attributes of public goods or common goods, wherein sellers are unable to exclude non-buyers from using a product, as in the development of inventions that may spread freely once revealed. This can cause underinvestment because developers cannot capture enough of the benefits from success to make the development effort worthwhile. This can also lead to resource depletion in the case of common-pool resources, where, because use of the resource is rival but non-excludable, there is no incentive for users to conserve the resource. An example of this is a lake with a natural supply of fish: if people catch the fish faster than they can reproduce, then the fish population will dwindle until there are no fish left for future generations.

Externalities

A good or service could also have significant externalities, where gains or losses associated with the product, production or consumption of a product because it differs from the private cost. These externalities can be innate to the methods of production or other conditions important to the market. For example, when a firm is producing steel, it absorbs labor, capital and other inputs, it must pay for these in the appropriate markets, and these costs will be reflected in the market price for steel. If the firm also pollutes the atmosphere when it makes steel, however, and if it is not forced to pay for the use of this resource, then this cost will be borne not by the firm but by society. Hence, the market price for steel will fail to incorporate the full opportunity cost to society of producing. In this case, the market equilibrium in the steel industry will not be optimal. More steel will be produced than would occur were the firm to have to pay for all of its costs of production. Consequently, the marginal social cost of the last unit produced will exceed its marginal social benefit.

Traffic congestion is an example of market failure that incorporates both non-excludability and externality. Public roads are common resources that are available for the entire population's use (non-excludable), and act as a complement to cars (the more roads there are, the more useful cars become). Because there is very low cost but high benefit to individual drivers in using the roads, the roads become congested, decreasing their usefulness to society. Furthermore, driving can impose hidden costs on society through pollution (externality). Solutions for this include public transportation, congestion pricing, tolls, and other ways of making the driver include the social cost in the decision to drive.

Perhaps the best example of the inefficiency associated with common/public goods and externalities is the environmental harm caused by pollution and overexploitation of natural resources.

The Nature of the Exchange

Some markets can fail due to the nature of their exchange. Markets may have significant transaction costs, agency problems, or informational asymmetry. Such incomplete markets may result in economic inefficiency but also a possibility of improving efficiency through market, legal, and regulatory remedies. From contract theory, decisions in transactions where one party has more or better information than the other is an asymmetry. This creates an imbalance of power in transactions which can sometimes cause the transactions to go awry. Examples of this problem are adverse selection and moral hazard. Most commonly, information asymmetries are studied in the context of principal–agent problems. George Akerlof, Michael Spence, and Joseph E. Stiglitz developed the idea and shared the 2001 Nobel Prize in Economics.

Bounded Rationality

In *Models of Man*, Herbert A. Simon points out that most people are only partly rational, and are emotional/irrational in the remaining part of their actions. In another work, he states "boundedly rational agents experience limits in formulating and solving complex problems and in processing (receiving, storing, retrieving, transmitting) information" (Williamson, p. 553, citing Simon). Simon describes a number of dimensions along which "classical" models of rationality can be made somewhat more realistic, while sticking within the vein of fairly rigorous formalization. These include:

- limiting what sorts of utility functions there might be.
- recognizing the costs of gathering and processing information.
- the possibility of having a "vector" or "multi-valued" utility function.

Simon suggests that economic agents employ the use of heuristics to make decisions rather than a strict rigid rule of optimization. They do this because of the complexity of the situation, and their inability to process and compute the expected utility of every alternative action. Deliberation costs might be high and there are often other, concurrent economic activities also requiring decisions.

Coase Theorem

The Coase theorem, developed by Ronald Coase and labeled as such by George Stigler, states that private transactions are efficient as long as property rights exist, only a small number of parties are involved, and transactions costs are low. Additionally, this efficiency will take place regardless of who owns the property rights. This theory comes from a section of Coase's Nobel prize-winning work *The Problem of Social Cost*. While the assumptions of low transactions costs and a small number of parties involved may not always be applicable in real-world markets, Coase's work changed the long-held belief that the owner of property rights was a major determining factor in whether or not a market would fail.

A market is an institution in which individuals or firms exchange not just commodities, but the *rights* to use them in particular ways for particular amounts of time. Markets are institutions which organize the *exchange of control* of commodities, where the nature of the control is defined by the property rights attached to the commodities.

As a result, agents' control over the uses of their commodities can be imperfect, because the system of rights which defines that control is incomplete. Typically, this falls into two generalized rights – *excludability* and *transferability*. Excludability deals with the ability of agents to control who uses their commodity, and for how long – and the related costs associated with doing so. Transferability reflects the right of agents to transfer the rights of use from one agent to another, for instance by selling or leasing a commodity, and the costs associated with doing so. If a given system of rights does not fully guarantee these at minimal (or no) cost, then the resulting distribution can be inefficient. Considerations such as these form an important part of the work of institutional economics. Nonetheless, views still differ on whether something displaying these attributes is meaningful without the information provided by the market price system.

Interpretations and Policy Examples

The above causes represent the mainstream view of what market failures mean and of their importance in the economy. This analysis follows the lead of the neoclassical school, and relies on the notion of Pareto efficiency – and specifically considers market failures absent considerations of the "public interest", or equity, citing definitional concerns. This form of analysis has also been adopted by the Keynesian or new Keynesian schools in modern macroeconomics, applying it to Walrasian models of general equilibrium in order to deal with failures to attain full employment, or the non-adjustment of prices and wages.

Policies to prevent market failure are already commonly implemented in the economy. For example, to prevent information asymmetry, members of the New York Stock Exchange agree to abide by its rules in order to promote a fair and orderly market in the trading of listed securities. The members of the NYSE presumably believe that each member is individually better off if every member adheres to its rules – even if they have to forego money-making opportunities that would violate those rules.

As an example of externalities, municipal governments enforce building codes and license tradesmen to mitigate the incentive to use cheaper (but more dangerous) construction practices, ensuring that the total cost of new construction includes the (otherwise external) cost of preventing future tragedies. The voters who elect municipal officials presumably feel that they are individually better off if everyone complies with the local codes, even if those codes may increase the cost of construction in their communities.

CITES is an international treaty to protect the world's common interest in preserving endangered species – a classic "public good" – against the private interests of poachers, developers and other market participants who might otherwise reap monetary benefits without bearing the known and unknown costs that extinction could create. Even without knowing the true cost of extinction, the signatory countries believe that the societal costs far outweigh the possible private gains that they have agreed to forego.

Some remedies for market failure can resemble other market failures. For example, the issue of systematic underinvestment in research is addressed by the patent system that creates artificial monopolies for successful inventions.

Objections

Public Choice

Economists such as Milton Friedman from the Chicago school and others from the Public Choice school, argue that market failure does not necessarily imply that government should attempt to solve market failures, because the costs of government failure might be worse than those of the market failure it attempts to fix. This failure of government is seen as the result of the inherent problems of democracy and other forms of government perceived by this school and also of the power of special-interest groups (rent seekers) both in the private sector and in the government bureaucracy. Conditions that many would regard as negative are often seen as an effect of subversion of the free market by coercive government intervention. Beyond philosophical objections, a further issue is the practical difficulty that any single decision maker may face in trying to understand (and perhaps predict) the numerous interactions that occur between producers and consumers in any market.

Austrian

Some advocates of *laissez-faire* capitalism, including many economists of the Austrian School, argue that there is no such phenomenon as "market failure". Israel Kirzner states that, "Efficiency for a social system means the efficiency with which it permits its individual members to achieve their individual goals." Inefficiency only arises when means are chosen by individuals that are inconsistent with their desired goals. This definition of efficiency differs from that of Pareto efficiency, and forms the basis of the theoretical argument against the existence of market failures. However, providing that the conditions of the first welfare theorem are met, these two definitions agree, and give identical results. Austrians argue that the market tends to eliminate its inefficiencies through the process of entrepreneurship driven by the profit motive; something the government has great difficulty detecting, or correcting.

Marxian

Objections also exist on more fundamental bases, such as that of equity, or Marxian analysis. Colloquial uses of the term "market failure" reflect the notion of a market "failing" to provide some desired attribute different from efficiency – for instance, high levels of inequality can be considered a "market failure", yet are not Pareto inefficient, and so would not be considered a market failure by mainstream economics. In addition, many Marxian economists would argue that the system of individual property rights is a fundamental problem in itself, and that resources should be allocated in another way entirely. This is different from concepts of "market failure" which focuses on specific situations – typically seen as "abnormal" – where markets have inefficient outcomes. Marxists, in contrast, would say that markets have inefficient and democratically unwanted outcomes – viewing market failure as an inherent feature of any capitalist economy – and typically omit it from discussion, preferring to ration finite goods not exclusively through a price mechanism, but based upon need as determined by society expressed through the community.

Ecological

In ecological economics, the concept of externalities is considered a misnomer, since market agents are viewed as making their incomes and profits by systematically 'shifting' the social and ecological costs of their activities onto other agents, including future generations. Hence, externalities is a *modus operandi* of the market, not a failure: The market cannot exist without constantly 'failing'.

The fair and even allocation of non-renewable resources over time is a market failure issue of concern to ecological economics. This issue is also known as 'intergenerational fairness'. It is argued that the market mechanism fails when it comes to allocating the Earth's finite mineral stock fairly and evenly among present and future generations, as future generations are not, and cannot be, present on today's market. In effect, today's market prices do not, and cannot, reflect the preferences of the yet unborn. This is an instance of a market failure passed unrecognized by most mainstream economists, as the concept of Pareto efficiency is entirely static (timeless). Imposing government restrictions on the general level of activity in the economy may be the only way of bringing about a more fair and even intergenerational allocation of the mineral stock. Hence, Nicholas Georgescu-Roegen and Herman Daly, the two leading theorists in the field, have both called for the imposition of such restrictions: Georgescu-Roegen has proposed a minimal bioeconomic program, and Daly has proposed a comprehensive steady-state economy. However, Georgescu-Roegen, Daly, and other economists in the field agree that on a finite Earth, geologic limits will inevitably strain most fairness in the longer run, regardless of any present government restrictions: *Any* rate of extraction and use of the finite stock of non-renewable mineral resources will diminish the remaining stock left over for future generations to use.

Another ecological market failure is presented by the overutilisation of an otherwise renewable resource at a point in time, or within a short period of time. Such overutilisation usually occurs when the resource in question has poorly defined (or non-existing) property rights attached to it while too many market agents engage in activity simultaneously for the resource to be able to sustain it all. Examples range from over-fishing of fisheries and over-grazing of pastures to over-crowding of recreational areas in congested cities. This type of ecological market failure is generally known as the 'tragedy of the commons'. In this type of market failure, the principle of Pareto efficiency is violated the utmost, as *all* agents in the market are left worse off, while nobody are benefitting. It has been argued that the best way to remedy a 'tragedy of the commons'-type of ecological market failure is to establish enforceable property rights politically – only, this may be easier said than done.

The issue of anthropogenic global warming presents an overwhelming example of a 'tragedy of the commons'-type of ecological market failure: The Earth's atmosphere may be regarded as a 'global common' exhibiting poorly defined (non-existing) property rights, and the waste absorption capacity of the atmosphere with regard to carbon dioxide is presently being heavily overloaded by a too large volume of emissions from the world economy. Historically, the fossil fuel dependence of the Industrial Revolution has unintentionally thrown mankind out of ecological equilibrium with the rest of the Earth's biosphere (including the atmosphere), and the market has failed to correct the situation ever since. Quite the opposite: The unrestricted market has been exacerbating this global state of ecological *dis*-equilibrium, and is expected to continue doing so well into the foreseeable future. This particular market failure may be remedied to some extent at the political level by the establishment of an international (or regional) cap and trade property rights system, where carbon dioxide emission permits are bought and sold among market agents.

The term 'uneconomic growth' describes a pervasive ecological market failure: The ecological costs of further economic growth in a so-called 'full-world economy' like the present world economy may exceed the immediate social benefits derived from this growth.

Economic Interventionism

Economic interventionism (sometimes state interventionism) is an economic policy perspective favoring government intervention in the market process to correct the market failures and promote the general welfare of the people. An economic intervention is an action taken by a government or international institution in a market economy in an effort to impact the economy beyond the basic regulation of fraud and enforcement of contracts and provision of public goods. Economic intervention can be aimed at a variety of political or economic objectives, such as promoting economic growth, increasing employment, raising wages, raising or reducing prices, promoting income equality, managing the money supply and interest rates, increasing profits, or addressing market failures.

Red tape binds 19th century documents, the origin of phrase "red tape" to criticize economic interventionist laws and regulations

The term *intervention* assumes on a philosophical level that the state and economy should be inherently separated from each other; therefore the terminology applies to capitalist market-based economies where government action interrupts the market forces at play through regulations, economic policies or subsidies (however state-owned enterprises that operate in the market do not constitute an intervention). The term "intervention" is typically used by advocates of laissez-faire and free markets.

Capitalist market economies that feature high degrees of state intervention are often referred to as mixed economies.

Types of Interventions

Economic interventions common in contemporary market-based economies include targeted taxes, targeted tax credits, minimum wage legislation, union shop rules, contracting preferences, direct subsidies to certain classes of producers, price supports, price caps, production quotas, import quotas, and tariffs. Demand management and Keynesian economics are sometimes cited as mild forms of economic planning, designed to overcome cyclical instability inherent in market economies, or to make market economies function properly in a desired fashion.

Government regulation over markets and/or firms can also be a type of intervention when it inhibits, corrects or distorts the market mechanism in setting the price of a good or service.

Indicative planning in market economies is sometimes considered to be a form of intervention when it greatly influences the setting of prices in markets.

Political Perspectives

Libertarians and other advocates of free market or laissez-faire economics generally view government interventions as harmful, due to the law of unintended consequences, belief in government's inability to effectively manage economic concerns, and other considerations. Government officials tend to be naturally disposed to seek more power and authority, and the money that usually goes with those things, and this quest often takes the form of economic interventionism which they then seek to justify. Many modern liberals (in the United States) and contemporary social democrats (in Europe) are inclined to support interventionism, seeing state economic interventions as an important means of promoting greater income equality and social welfare.

On the other hand, Marxists often feel that government welfare programs might interfere with the goal of overthrowing capitalism and replacing it with socialism, because a welfare state makes capitalism more tolerable to the average worker. Socialists often criticize interventionism (as supported by social democrats and social liberals) as being untenable and liable to cause more economic distortion in the long-run. From this perspective, any attempt to "patch up" capitalism's contradictions would lead to distortions in the economy elsewhere, so that the only real and lasting solution is to entirely replace capitalism with a socialist economy.

Political conservatives of the nationalist variety also frequently support economic interventionism as a means of protecting the power and wealth of a country or its people, particularly via advantages granted to industries seen as nationally vital.

Effects

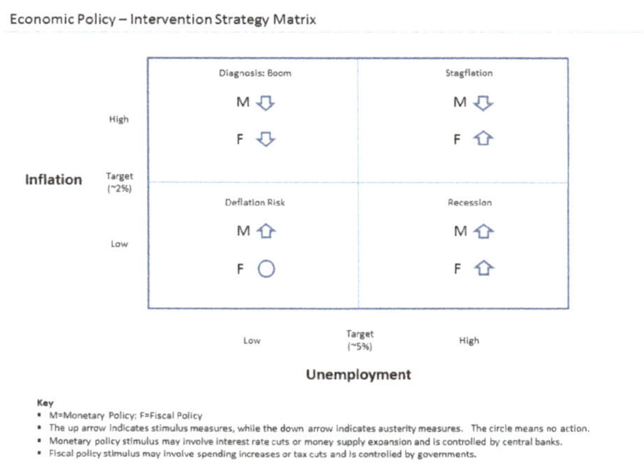

Typical intervention strategies under different conditions

The effects of government economic interventionism are widely disputed.

Regulatory authorities do not consistently close markets, yet as seen in economic liberalization efforts by states and various institutions (International Monetary Fund and World Bank) in Latin America, "...financial liberalization and privatization coincided with democratization". One study suggests that after the lost decade an increasing "diffusion of regulatory authorities" emerged, these actors engaged in restructuring the economies within Latin America. Latin America through the 1980s had undergone a debt crisis and *hyperinflation* (during 1989 and 1990). These international stakeholders restricted the state's economic leverage, and bound it in contract to co-operate.

Multiple projects and years of failed attempts, for the Argentine state to comply, the renewal and intervention seemed stalled. Two key intervention factors that instigated economic progress in Argentina, were substantially increasing privatization and the establishment of a currency board. As one can see this exemplifies global institutions including the International Monetary Fund and the World Bank instigate and propagate openness to increase foreign investments and economic development within places including Latin America.

In Western countries, government officials theoretically weigh the cost benefit for an intervention for the population or they succumb beneath coercion by a third private party and must take action. Also intervention for economic development is at the discretion and self-interest of the stake holders, the multifarious interpretations of *progress* and development theory could mean. To illustrate this during the 2008 debt crisis; the government and international institutions did not prop Lehman Brothers up therefore allowing them to file bankruptcy. Days later when AIG waned towards collapsing, the state spent public money to keep it from falling. These corporations have interconnected interests with the state. Therefore, their incentive is to influence the government to designate regulatory policies that will not inhibit their accumulation of assets.

In Japan, Abenomics is a form of intervention with respect to Prime Minister Shinzo Abe's desire to restore the country's former glory in the midst of a globalized economy.

U.S. Government Interventions

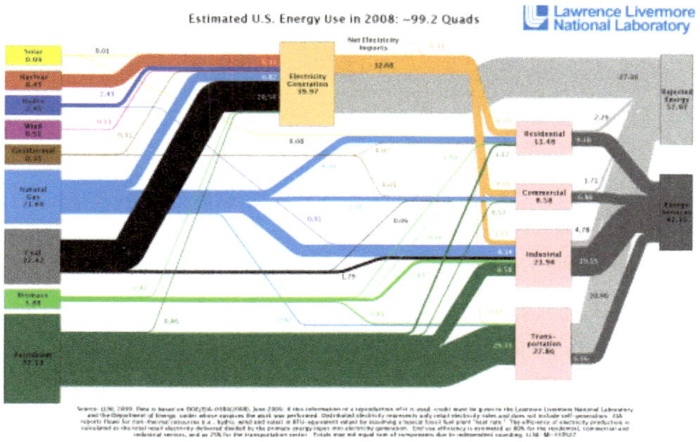

U.S. energy sources and sinks

President Richard Nixon signed amendments to the Clean Air Act in 1970, that expanded it to mandate state and federal regulation of both automobiles and industry. It was later further amended in 1977 and 1990.

> "One of the first modern environmental protection laws enacted in the United States was the National Environmental Policy Act of 1969 (NEPA), which requires the government to consider the impact of its actions or policies on the environment. NEPA remains one of the most commonly used environmental laws in the nation. In addition to NEPA, there are numerous pollution-control statutes that apply to such specific environmental media as air and water. The best known of these laws are the Clean Air Act (CAA), Clean Water Act (CWA), and the Comprehensive Environmental Response, Compensation, and Liability Act (CERCLA) commonly referred to as Superfund. Among the many other important

pollution control laws are the Resource Conservation and Recovery Act (RCRA), Toxic Substances Control Act (TSCA), Oil Pollution Prevention Act (OPP), Emergency Planning and Community Right-to-Know Act (EPCRA), and the Pollution Prevention Act (PPA)."

United States pollution control statutes tend to be numerous and diverse, and many of the environmental statutes passed by Congress are aimed at pollution prevention, they often need to be expanded and updated before their impact is fully realized. Pollution-control laws are generally too broad to be managed by existing legal bodies, so Congress must find or create an agency for each that will be able to implement the mandated mission effectively.

During World War I, U.S government intervention mandated that the manufacturing of cars be replaced with machinery to successfully fight the war. Today government intervention could be used to break the U.S dependence on oil by mandating U.S automakers to produce electric cars such as the Chevrolet Volt. Recently, Michigan Gov. Jennifer Granholm (D) said, "We need help from Congress," namely, renewing the clean energy manufacturing tax credit and the tax incentives that make plug-ins cheaper to buy for consumers. It is possible that government mandated carbon taxes could be used to improve technology and make cars like the Volt more affordable to consumers. Unfortunately, current bills suggest carbon prices would only add a few cents to the price of gasoline, which has negligible effects, compared to what's needed to change fuel consumption. Washington is beginning to invest in car manufacturing industry by partially provinding $6 billion in battery-related public and private investments since 2008, and the White House has taken credit for putting a down payment on the U.S. battery industry that may reduce battery prices in the coming years. Currently, opponents believe that the carbon dioxide emissions tax, that the U.S. government introduced, on new cars that is unfair on consumers and looks like a revenue-raising fiscal intervention instead of limiting harm caused to the environment. A national fuel tax means everyone, no matter what vehicle they drive, will pay the tax. The amount of tax each individual or company pays will be proportional to the emissions they generate. The more they drive, the more that they would need to pay. This tax is supported by the motor manufacturers, however stipulations confirmed by the National Treasury, state that minibuses and midibuses will receive a special exclusion from the emissions tax on cars and light commercial vehicles, which comes into effect from September 1, 2010. This exclusion is because these taxi vehicles are used for public transport, which opponents of the tax disagree with.

During George W. Bush's 2000 campaign, he promised to commit $2 billion over 10 years to advance clean coal technology through research and development initiatives. According to Bush supporters, he fulfilled that promise in his fiscal year 2008 budget request, allocating $426 million for the Clean Coal Technology Program. During his administration, Congress passed the Energy Policy Act of 2005, funding research into carbon-capture technology to remove and bury the carbon in coal after it is burned. The coal industry received $9 billion in subsidies under the act, as part of an initiative supposedly to reduce U.S. dependence on foreign oil and reduce carbon emissions. This included $6.2 billion for new power plants, $1.1 billion in tax breaks to install pollution-control technology and another $1.1 billion to make coal a cost efficient fuel. The act also allowed redefinitions of coal processing, such as spraying on diesel or starch, to qualify them as "non-traditional," allowing coal producers to avoid paying $1.3 billion in taxes per year.

The Waxman-Markey bill, also called the American Clean Energy and Security Act, passed by the House Energy and Commerce Committee in 2010, targets dramatic CO2 reductions after 2020, when the price of the permits would rise to further limit consumers' demand for CO2-intensive goods and services. The legislation is targeting 83 percent reduction in CO2 emissions from 2005 levels in the year 2050. A study by the EPA estimates that the price of the permit would rise from about $20 a ton in 2020 to more than $75 a ton in 2050.

The US Office of Management and Budget (OMB) shows that federal subsidies for coal in the United States were planned to be reduced significantly between 2011 and 2020, provided the budget passed through Congress and reduces four coal tax preferences: Expensing of Exploration and Development Costs, Percent Depletion for Hard Mineral Fossil Fuels, Royalty Taxation, and Domestic Manufacturing Deduction for Hard Mineral Fossil Fuels. The fiscal 2011 budget proposed by the Obama administration would cut approximately $2.3 billion in coal subsidies during the next decade.

Justification for the State

The justification of the state refers to the source of legitimate authority for the state or government. Typically, such a justification explains why the state should exist, and to some degree scopes the role of government - what a legitimate state should or should not be able to do.

There is no single, universally accepted justification of the state. In fact, anarchists believe that there is no justification for the state at all, and that human societies would be better off without it. However, most political ideologies have their own justifications, and thus their own vision of what constitutes a legitimate state. Indeed, a person's opinions regarding the role of government often determine the rest of their political ideology. Thus, discrepancy of opinion in a wide array of political matters is often directly traceable back to a discrepancy of opinion in the justification for the state.

The constitutions of various countries codify views as to the purposes, powers, and forms of their governments, but they tend to do so in rather vague terms, which particular laws, courts, and actions of politicians subsequently flesh out. In general, various countries have translated vague talk about the purposes of their governments into particular state laws, bureaucracies, enforcement actions, etc.

The following are just a few examples.

Transcendent Sovereignty

In feudal Europe, the most widespread justification of the state was the divine right of kings, which stated that monarchs draw their power from God, and the state should only be an apparatus that puts the monarch's will into practice. The legitimacy of the state's lands was derived from the lands being the personal possession of the monarch. The divine right theory, combined with primogeniture, became a theory of hereditary monarchy in the nation states of the early modern period. The Holy Roman Empire was not a state in that sense, and was not a true theocracy.

The political ideas current in China at that time involved the idea of the mandate of heaven. It was similar to the divine right in that it placed the ruler in a divine position, as the link between Heaven and Earth, but it differed from the divine right of kings in that it did not assume that the connection between a dynasty and the state was permanent. Inherent in the concept was that a ruler held the mandate of heaven only as long as he provided good government. If he did not, heaven would withdraw its mandate and whoever restored order would hold the new mandate. This is true theocracy; the power and wisdom to govern is granted by God, not by human political schemes, and can be equally removed by God. This is also the idea presented in the Judeo-Christian Bible from the time Israel requests "a king like the nations" through to Christ himself telling his contemporary leaders that they only had power because God gave it to them. The classic Biblical example is Nebuchadnezzar who created the Babylonian empire because God ordained his power, but who later ate grass like a cow for seven years because he deified himself instead of acknowledging God. Nebuchadnezzar is restored when he again acknowledges God is the true sovereign.

The Social Contract

In the period of the eighteenth century, usually called the Enlightenment, a new justification of the European state developed. Jean-Jacques Rousseau's social contract theory states that governments draw their power from the governed, its 'sovereign' people (usually a certain ethnic group, and the state's limits are legitimated theoretically as that people's lands, although that is often not, rarely exactly, the case), that no person should have absolute power, and that a *legitimate* state is one which meets the needs and wishes of its citizens. These include security, peace, economic development and the resolution of conflict. Also, the social contract requires that an individual gives up some of his natural rights in order to maintain social order via the rule of law. Eventually, the divine right of kings fell out of favor and this idea ascended; it formed the basis for modern democracy.

Public Goods

This is an example of the theoretical thinking shifting the emphasis from faith and theoretical principles such as sovereignty to the socio-economic logic, as Karl Marx did. Thus modern political theorists typically legitimize the state with two major ideas: redistribution and the provision of public goods. In *The Limits of Government*, philosopher David Schmidtz takes on the second of these ideas. While a market system may allow self-interested to create and allocate many goods optimally, there exists a class of "collective" - or "public goods" that are not produced adequately in a market system. These collective goods are goods that all individuals want but for whose production it is often not individually rational for people voluntarily to do their part to secure a collectively rational outcome. The state can step in and force us all to contribute toward the production of these goods, and we can all thereby be made better off. There are actually many different opinions when it comes to this topic.

Political Ideologies

It is on those questions that one can find the differences between conservatism, socialism, liberalism, libertarianism, fascism, especially the latter, and other political ideologies. There are also two ideologies - anarchism and communism - which argue that the existence of the state is ultimately unjustified and harmful. For this reason, the kind of society they aim to establish would be stateless.

Anarchism claims that the community of those fighting to create a new society must themselves constitute a stateless society. Communism wishes to immediately or eventually replace the communities, unities and divisions that things such as work, money, exchange, borders, nations, governments, police, religion, and race create with the universal community possible when these things are replaced.

State socialism states that the degree to which a state is working class is the degree to which it fights government, class, work, and rule. The degree to which it wins such a fight is held to be the degree to which it is communist instead of capitalist, socialist, or the state. Anarcho-capitalism argues that taxes are theft, that government and the business community complicit in governance is organized crime and is equivalent to the criminal underworld, and that defense of life and property is just another industry, which must be privatized. Anarcho-communism and anarcho-collectivism says that taxes, being theft, are just property, which is also theft, and that the state is inherently capitalist and will never result in a transition to communism, and says that those fighting against capitalism and the state to produce a communist society must themselves already form such a community. However, the majority of viewpoints agree that the existence of *some* kind of government is morally justified. What they disagree about is the proper role and the proper form of that government.

There are several ways to conceive of the differences between these different political views. For example, one might ask *in what areas* should the government have jurisdiction, to *what extent* it may intervene in those areas, or even what constitutes *intervention* in the first place. Some institutions can be said to exist only because the government provides the framework for their existence; for instance, Marxists argue that the institution of private property only exists due to government. The intervention debate can be framed in terms of big government versus small government.

Government Intervention

If the government wants to intervene in a market, there are a number of options:

- Using the *price mechanism* with taxes or subsidies
  - Example: Tax credits that lower the "effective price" of health insurance premium or housing.
- *Mandate* that either individuals or firms provide the good
  - Example: Mandates that require employers to provide health insurance.
- *Public Provision*
  - Provision of various public goods or services to targeted groups.
  - Example: Provision of free food in schools, The National Rural Employment Generation Scheme in India.
- *Public Financing of Private Provision*
  - Example: Public funded schools that are privately managed.

Effects of Interventions

Empirical public economics focuses on assessing the "direct" and "indirect" effects of government actions.

Direct Effects

Direct effects of government actions assume "no behavioral responses" and examine the intended consequences of those actions.

Indirect Effects

Indirect effects arise because some people change their behavior in response to an intervention.

- For example consider the NREGS program, which guarantees 100 days of free employment.
  - Direct effect of NREGS is the in text of the policy: Generating employment for the poor and effectively improving their lives through income generation.
  - Indirect effect: Some people dropout of the labor force and join the MNREGS program. This might have created labor shortage in other areas like agriculture.

Key question: How many of these people would be affected directly and indirectly?

The theory does not provide guidance on magnitudes of these changes or effects. Hence empirical public economics gathers data and uses statistical models to assess how individuals and firms would respond to alternate policy interventions.

Why do Governments do what they do?

- Governments do not simply behave as benign actors who intervene only because of market failure and redistribution.
- For example, substantial variation across countries in health care delivery suggests efficiency and redistribution are not the only considerations.
- How should government intervene is a normative question, concerned with how things should be done.
- Why do government do what they do is on the other hand a positive question. While we want government to intervene only in cases of market failures or redistribution, that is not the case in reality. There are various other political economy considerations.
- Tools of *political economy* help us understand how governments make public policy decisions.
  - Just as there are a host of market failures that can interfere with the welfare maximizing outcome of the private market, there are a host of government failures that can lead to inappropriate government interventions.

The Size and Growth of Government

- The size of the government is often measured relative to some benchmark, the most common one being GDP.
  - Few commonly used measures are the radio of government expenditure to GDP& the ratio of fiscal deficit to GDP.
- Size of the centre versus the states is a measure of Decentralization.
  - How much power is given to the states?

The Size and Shape of Governments

A mixed economy has 1/4 - 1/2 of all economic activity done through the government.

In most countries government plays a prominent role in the allocation of resources Ownership, (re)distribution and consumption

Done through taxes, subsidies, regulation, public provision and so on.

However, the size of the government and the extent to which it produces goods varies from one country to another.

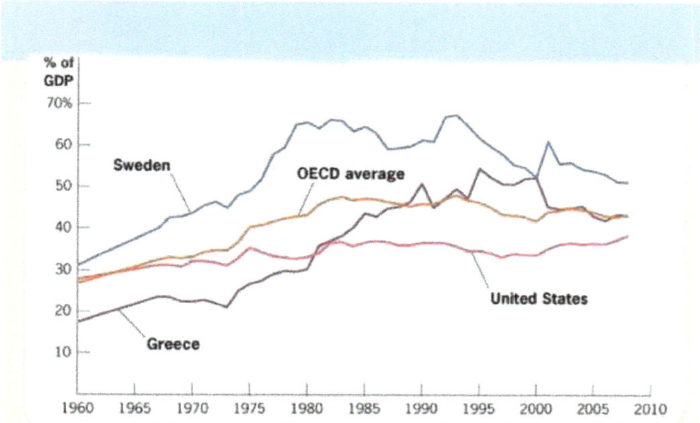

Total Government Spending Across Developed Nations, 1960–2008 • Government spending as a share of GDP has grown throughout the developed world, but the pace of growth has varied. The United States has seen a modest growth in its government share over this period, while government spending in Greece has more than tripled as a share of the economy.

Source: Organization for Economic Cooperation and Development (2008). Annex Table 30.

- In India high rates of economic growth have concurred with high fiscal deficits for two decades (unbold & uncapitalize).
  - The average rate of growth of real GDP from 1982 to 2002 was 5.8 percent. In turn, the average ratio of the fiscal deficit of the Government to GDP was 8.3 percent.
  - The tables below show some relevant figures. Table shows the distribution of government expenditure in various categories. Tables highlight the expenditures made by the central and state government in education and health. And roughly 13% is spent on health by the government in various European countries.

- Expenditure on education as a fraction of GDP has remained constant but literacy has improved by almost 13 percentage points. However, since GDP has grown over this period, total outlay in education has also grown.
- Health spending as a fraction of GDP also remained constant but IMR has improved, though marginally when you compare to similar countries.

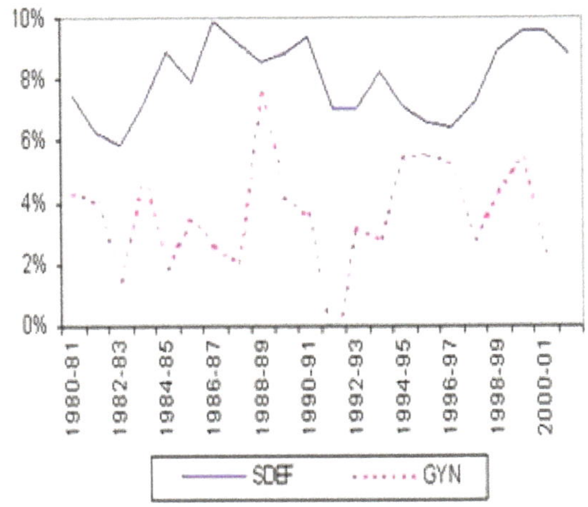

Rate of Economic growth and ratio fiscal deficit to GDP

Composition of Government Expenditure

Composition of Government Expenditure Ratio to total expenditure				
	1999-2000	2003-04	2004-05	2005-06
Agriculture & cooperation	2.31	0.58	0.73	0.95
Rural Development	2.77	3.70	3.09	3.84
Rural Sector	5.08	4.28	3.82	4.79
Food & Public Distribution	3.77	6.07	5.82	5.56
Health	0.71	0.63	0.69	0.80
Family welfare	1.19	1.06	1.19	1.35
Elementary Education	1.25	1.29	1.78	2.62
Secondary & Higher Education	1.95	1.13	1.16	1.21
Drinking Water Supply	0.69	0.66	0.74	0.99
Welfare	9.56	10.84	11.38	12.53
Urban Development	0.58	0.87	0.69	0.66
Petroleum & Natural Gas	0.04	1.64	0.79	0.77
Power	1.01	0.45	0.55	0.64
Roads & Highways	2.21	1.73	1.71	2.59
Civil Aviation	0.07	0.06	0.08	0.13
Telecom	0.01	0.23	1.21	0.60
Railways	0.99	1.65	1.88	1.36
Infrastructure	4.92	6.63	6.91	6.75
Other Exp.	80.43	78.24	77.87	75.93

Expenditure on Education Ratio of Expenditure to GDP(%)				
	L.R. %	Centre: Elementary Education	Centre: Total education	Centre + States: Education
1991	52.2	0.04	0.29	3.06
1996	58.4	0.12	0.31	2.74
2001	65.4	0.14	0.38	2.98

Expenditure on Health Ratio of Expenditure to GDP(%)					
I.M.R Centre: Centre: (per 1000) Health health				Public Centre Public H Water S	
1991	80	0.08	0.03	1.15	
1996	72	0.09	0.04	1.05	
2001	66	0.09	0.04	1.17	
RE Revised estimates BE Budget Estimates LR Literacy rate IMR infant mortality rate					

Distribution of Revenue Sources

- So far we discussed the expenditure side. On the revenue side, taxes comprise an important component of revenue. The different categories of taxes are:
  - *Individual income tax*
  - *Tax on goods and services.*
  - *Tax on international trade.*
  - *Social Security taxes (non-existent in India).*
- Table: shows the distribution of taxes under various categories across different countries.

Tax and Revenue Structure of Central Governments in Selected Countries								
	Tax revenue (% of GDP)	Taxes on goods and services (% value added of industry and services)	Taxes on goods and services (% of current Revenue)	Taxes on income, Profits and capital gains(% of current revenue)	Taxes on Internatio-nal Trade(% of current revenue)	Social security Taxes(% of current revenue	Other taxes(% of current revenue	Total revenue as percentage of current revenue
1990								
India	10.1	7.4	36.1	15.0	28.8	0.0	0.5	80.4
United States	17.4	0.7	3.2	51.6	1.6	34.6	1.1	92.1
New Zealand	35.9	13.2	27.1	53.1	2.1	0.0	3.1	85.4

Canada	18.6	4.0	16.7	51.2	2.8	16.0	0.0	91.8
South Africa	24.3	10.3	33.6	50.8	3.6	1.8	2.4	92.5
China	4.0	1.5	17.6	31.2	13.8	0.0	0.0	83.6
2001								
India	10.0	5.6	29.2	28.6	18.5	0.0	0.2	76.4
United States	20.2	0.8	3.2	57.5	1.0	30.0	1.4	93.9
New Zealand	28.4	-	26.9	64.1	1.73	0.0	1.1	93.8
Canada	19.3	-	16.5	52.4	1.3	21.2	0.0	91.4
South Africa	26.5	10.8	32.6	54.2	2.9	1.8	3.5	95.2
China	6.8	6.5	74.5	6.4	9.5	0.0	3.6	94.0

References

- Daly, Herman E.; Farley, Joshua (2011). Ecological Economics. Principles and Applications. (PDF contains full textbook) (2nd ed.). Washington: Island Press. ISBN 9781597266819
- De Beaufort Wijnholds, J. Onno. "The Argentine Drama: A View from the IMF Board" (PDF). The Crisis That Was Not Prevented: Argentina, the IMF, and Globalisation. FONDAD. Retrieved 2 February 2012
- Roy E. Cordato (1980). "The Austrian Theory of Efficiency and the Role of Government" (PDF). The Journal of Libertarian Studies. 4 (4): 393–403
- Martínez-Alier, Juan (1987). Ecological Economics: Energy, Environment and Society. Oxford: Basil Blackwell. ISBN 0631171460
- Ellen Frankel, Paul (1980). "Laissez Faire in Nineteenth Century Britain: Fact or Myth". Literature of Liberty. iii (4): 5–38. Retrieved 5 February 2012
- Georgescu-Roegen, Nicholas (1975). "Energy and Economic Myths" (PDF). Southern Economic Journal. Tennessee: Southern Economic Association. 41 (3): 347–81. doi:10.2307/1056148
- Daly, Herman E., ed. (1980). Economics, Ecology, Ethics. Essays Towards a Steady-State Economy. (PDF contains only the introductory chapter of the book) (2nd ed.). San Francisco: W.H. Freeman and Company. ISBN 0716711788

2

Public Economics: Concepts and Theories

The concepts of public economics can be divided into theoretical tools and empirical tools. The ability of a product to satisfy a customer is known as utility. Theoretical tools rationalize economic decision making while empirical tools substantiate theory with economic data. This chapter discusses in detail the theories and methodologies related to public economics.

Tools of Public Economics

Suppose that you are a member of the economic advisory board of the PM and the PM must decide on the amount of cash transfer that is to be made to the NREGS program. The chief economic advisor believes that by providing cash to very low income families, it only encourages them to stay at home rather than go to work. To provide incentives to these people the government must cut back on the cash benefits. The PM disagrees; he thinks that poor families who are at home in villages are incapable of finding a job that pays them high enough to encourage them to work. So if the state cuts the cash benefits it will only penalize these poor households. You being a researcher are being asked to inform this debate by assessing the degree to which cutting cash benefits to low income families will encourage them to work by evaluating the cut.

Such an evaluation would require you to use both theoretical and empirical tools of economics.

- *Theoretical tools* are a set of tools used to understand economic decision making.

  They are primarily graphical and mathematical.

- *Empirical tools* allow you to examine the theory with data.

  - First we would discuss a few theoretical tools derived from microeconomics that are most commonly used in public policy analysis. Theoretical Tools: Recap of utility maximization.

Constrained Utility Maximization

- Constrained utility maximization: individuals have well defined utility functions.

In modeling preferences, we do not impose any budget constraint. Simply ask what people prefer, ignoring what they can afford.

- Constrained utility maximization: all decisions are made in order to maximize the well-being of the individual, subject to his available resources.

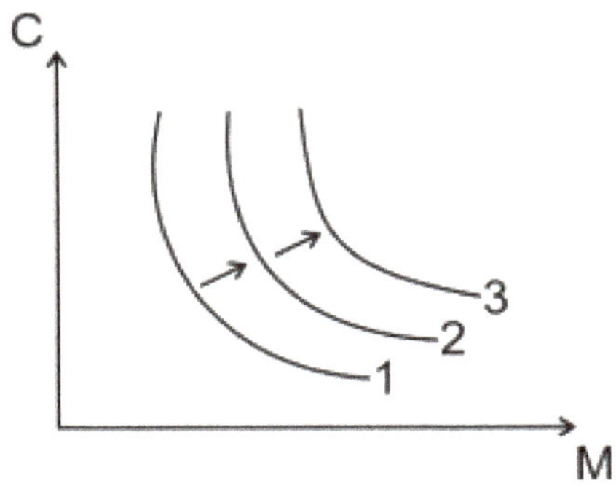

Assumption0: Individuals prefer higher Indifference Curves:

↓

Non Satiation

↓

10th pizza is not as good as 1st.
But having the 10th pizza is better than not having it

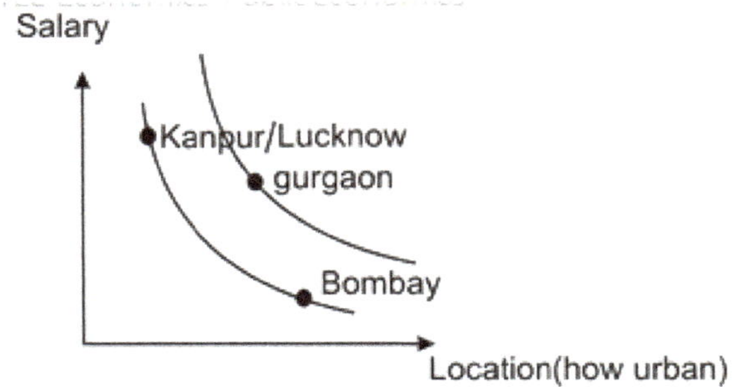

Higher salary in Kanpur is enough to compensate him for a city life in Bombay.
but he may prefer Gurgaon to either: the salary is higher than in Bombay but city (how urban) is more fun than Kanpur.

→ Convexity of preferences

- Recall that *Marginal utility* is defined as the additional increment to utility from consuming an additional unit of a good.
- *Diminishing marginal utility* means each additional unit makes the individual less happy than the previous unit.
  - Let us consider 2 goods M and C and the utility function $U = Q_M Q_C$,, the marginal utility is:

$$MU_{QM} \frac{\partial U}{\partial Q_M} = Q_C$$

Utility

In economics, utility is a measure of preferences over some set of goods (including services: something that satisfies human wants); it represents satisfaction experienced by the consumer of a good. The concept is an important underpinning of rational choice theory in economics and game theory: since one cannot directly measure benefit, satisfaction or happiness from a good or service, economists instead have devised ways of representing and measuring utility in terms of measurable economic choices. Economists have attempted to perfect highly abstract methods of comparing utilities by observing and calculating economic choices; in the simplest sense, economists consider utility to be revealed in people's willingness to pay different amounts for different goods.

Applications

Utility is usually applied by economists in such constructs as the indifference curve, which plot the combination of commodities that an individual or a society would accept to maintain a given level of satisfaction. Utility and indifference curves are used by economists to understand the underpinnings of demand curves, which are half of the supply and demand analysis that is used to analyze the workings of goods markets.

Individual utility and social utility can be construed as the value of a utility function and a social welfare function respectively. When coupled with production or commodity constraints, under some assumptions these functions can be used to analyze Pareto efficiency, such as illustrated by Edgeworth boxes in contract curves. Such efficiency is a central concept in welfare economics.

In finance, utility is applied to generate an individual's price for an asset called the indifference price. Utility functions are also related to risk measures, with the most common example being the entropic risk measure.

Revealed Preference

It was recognized that utility could not be measured or observed directly, so instead economists devised a way to infer underlying relative utilities from observed choice. These 'revealed preferences', as they were named by Paul Samuelson, were revealed e.g. in people's willingness to pay:

Utility is taken to be correlative to Desire or Want. It has been already argued that desires cannot be measured directly, but only indirectly, by the outward phenomena to which they give rise: and that in those cases with which economics is chiefly concerned the measure is found in the price which a person is willing to pay for the fulfillment or satisfaction of his desire.

Functions

There has been some controversy over the question whether the utility of a commodity can be measured or not. At one time, it was assumed that the consumer was able to say exactly how much utility he got from the commodity. The economists who made this assumption belonged to the 'cardinalist school' of economics. Today utility functions, expressing utility as a function of the amounts of the various goods consumed, are treated as either *cardinal* or *ordinal*, depending on whether they are or are not interpreted as providing more information than simply the rank ordering of preferences over bundles of goods, such as information on the strength of preferences.

Cardinal

When cardinal utility is used, the magnitude of utility differences is treated as an ethically or behaviorally significant quantity. For example, suppose a cup of orange juice has utility of 120 utils, a cup of tea has a utility of 80 utils, and a cup of water has a utility of 40 utils. With cardinal utility, it can be concluded that the cup of orange juice is better than the cup of tea by exactly the same amount by which the cup of tea is better than the cup of water. One cannot conclude, however, that the cup of tea is two thirds as good as the cup of juice, because this conclusion would depend not only on magnitudes of utility differences, but also on the "zero" of utility. For example, if the "zero" of utility was located at -40, then a cup of orange juice would be 160 utils more than zero, a cup of tea 120 utils more than zero.

Neoclassical economics has largely retreated from using cardinal utility functions as the basis of economic behavior. A notable exception is in the context of analyzing choice under conditions of risk.

Sometimes cardinal utility is used to aggregate utilities across persons, to create a social welfare function.

Ordinal

When ordinal utilities are used, differences in utils (values taken on by the utility function) are treated as ethically or behaviorally meaningless: the utility index encodes a full behavioral ordering between members of a choice set, but tells nothing about the related *strength of preferences*. In the above example, it would only be possible to say that juice is preferred to tea to water, but no more.

Ordinal utility functions are unique up to increasing monotone transformations. For example, if a function $u(x)$ is taken as ordinal, it is equivalent to the function $u(x)^3$, because taking the 3rd power is an increasing monotone transformation. This means that the ordinal preference induced by these functions is the same. In contrast, cardinal utilities are unique only up to increasing linear transformations, so if $u(x)$ is taken as cardinal, it is not equivalent to $u(x)^3$.

Preferences

Although preferences are the conventional foundation of microeconomics, it is often convenient to represent preferences with a utility function and analyze human behavior indirectly with utility functions. Let X be the consumption set, the set of all mutually-exclusive baskets the consumer could conceivably consume. The consumer's utility function $u : X \to \mathbb{R}$ ranks each package in the consumption set. If the consumer strictly prefers x to y or is indifferent between them, then $u(x) \geq u(y)$.

For example, suppose a consumer's consumption set is X = {nothing, 1 apple,1 orange, 1 apple and 1 orange, 2 apples, 2 oranges}, and its utility function is u(nothing) = 0, u(1 apple) = 1, u(1 orange) = 2, u(1 apple and 1 orange) = 4, u(2 apples) = 2 and u(2 oranges) = 3. Then this consumer prefers 1 orange to 1 apple, but prefers one of each to 2 oranges.

In micro-economic models, there are usually a finite set of L commodities, and a consumer may consume an arbitrary amount of each commodity. This gives a consumption set of $\mathbb{R}^L_+$, and each package $x \in \mathbb{R}^L_+$ is a vector containing the amounts of each commodity. In the previous example, we might say there are two commodities: apples and oranges. If we say apples is the first commodity, and oranges the second, then the consumption set $X = \mathbb{R}^2_+$ and $u(0, 0) = 0$, $u(1, 0) = 1$, $u(0, 1) = 2$, $u(1, 1) = 4$, $u(2, 0) = 2$, $u(0, 2) = 3$ as before. Note that for u to be a utility function on X, it must be defined for every package in X.

A utility function $u : X \to \mathbb{R}$ represents a preference relation $\preceq$ on X iff for every $x, y \in X$,

$u(x) \leq u(y)$ implies $x \preceq y$.. If u represents $\preceq$ then this implies $\preceq$ is complete and transitive, and hence rational.

Examples

In order to simplify calculations, various alternative assumptions have been made concerning details of human preferences, and these imply various alternative utility functions such as:

- CES (*constant elasticity of substitution*, or *isoelastic*) utility
- Isoelastic utility
- Exponential utility
- Quasilinear utility
- Homothetic preferences
- Stone–Geary utility function
- Gorman polar form
  - Greenwood–Hercowitz–Huffman preferences
  - King–Plosser–Rebelo preferences
- Hyperbolic absolute risk aversion

Most utility functions used in modeling or theory are well-behaved. They are usually monotonic and quasi-concave. However, it is possible for preferences not to be representable by a utility function. An example is lexicographic preferences which are not continuous and cannot be represented by a continuous utility function.

Expected

The expected utility theory deals with the analysis of choices among risky projects with multiple (possibly multidimensional) outcomes.

The St. Petersburg paradox was first proposed by Nicholas Bernoulli in 1713 and solved by Daniel Bernoulli in 1738. D. Bernoulli argued that the paradox could be resolved if decision-makers displayed risk aversion and argued for a logarithmic cardinal utility function.

The first important use of the expected utility theory was that of John von Neumann and Oskar Morgenstern, who used the assumption of expected utility maximization in their formulation of game theory.

Von Neumann–Morgenstern

Von Neumann and Morgenstern addressed situations in which the outcomes of choices are not known with certainty, but have probabilities attached to them.

A notation for a *lottery* is as follows: if options A and B have probability p and $1 - p$ in the lottery, we write it as a linear combination:

$$L = pA + (1 - p)B$$

More generally, for a lottery with many possible options:

$$L = \sum_i p_i A_i,$$

where $\sum_i p_i = 1$..

By making some reasonable assumptions about the way choices behave, von Neumann and Morgenstern showed that if an agent can choose between the lotteries, then this agent has a utility function such that the desirability of an arbitrary lottery can be calculated as a linear combination of the utilities of its parts, with the weights being their probabilities of occurring.

This is called the *expected utility theorem*. The required assumptions are four axioms about the properties of the agent's preference relation over 'simple lotteries', which are lotteries with just two options. Writing $B \preceq A$ to mean 'A is weakly preferred to B' ('A is preferred at least as much as B'), the axioms are:

1. completeness: For any two simple lotteries L and M, either $L \preceq M$ or $M \preceq L$ (or both, in which case they are viewed as equally desirable).
2. transitivity: for any three lotteries L, M, N, if $L \preceq M$ and $M \preceq N$, then $L \preceq N$.
3. convexity/continuity (Archimedean property): If $L \preceq M \preceq N$, then there is a p between 0 and 1 such that the lottery $pL + (1 - p)N$ is equally desirable as M.
4. independence: for any three lotteries L, M, N and any probability p, $L \preceq M$ if and only if $pL + (1 - p)N \preceq pM + (1 - p)N$. Intuitively, if the lottery formed by the probabilistic combination of L and N is no more preferable than the lottery formed by the same probabilistic combination of M and N, then and only then $L \preceq M$.

Axioms 3 and 4 enable us to decide about the relative utilities of two assets or lotteries.

In more formal language: A von Neumann–Morgenstern utility function is a function from choices to the real numbers:

$$u : X \to \mathbb{R}$$

which assigns a real number to every outcome in a way that captures the agent's preferences over simple lotteries. Under the four assumptions mentioned above, the agent will prefer a lottery L_2 to a lottery L_1 if and only if, for the utility function characterizing that agent, the expected utility of L_2 is greater than the expected utility of L_1:

$$L_1 \preceq L_2 \text{ iff } u(L_1) \leq u(L_2).$$

Repeating in category language: u is a morphism between the category of preferences with uncertainty and the category of reals as an additive group.

Of all the axioms, independence is the most often discarded. A variety of generalized expected utility theories have arisen, most of which drop or relax the independence axiom.

As Probability of Success

Castagnoli and LiCalzi and Bordley and LiCalzi (2000) provided another interpretation for Von Neumann and Morgenstern's theory. Specifically for any utility function, there exists a hypothetical reference lottery with the expected utility of an arbitrary lottery being its probability of performing no worse than the reference lottery. Suppose success is defined as getting an outcome no worse than the outcome of the reference lottery. Then this mathematical equivalence means that maximizing expected utility is equivalent to maximizing the probability of success. In many contexts, this makes the concept of utility easier to justify and to apply. For example, a firm's utility might be the probability of meeting uncertain future customer expectations.

Indirect

An indirect utility function gives the optimal attainable value of a given utility function, which depends on the prices of the goods and the income or wealth level that the individual possesses.

Money

One use of the indirect utility concept is the notion of the utility of money. The (indirect) utility function for money is a nonlinear function that is bounded and asymmetric about the origin. The utility function is concave in the positive region, reflecting the phenomenon of diminishing marginal utility. The boundedness reflects the fact that beyond a certain point money ceases being useful at all, as the size of any economy at any point in time is itself bounded. The asymmetry about the origin reflects the fact that gaining and losing money can have radically different implications both for individuals and businesses. The non-linearity of the utility function for money has profound implications in decision making processes: in situations where outcomes of choices influence utility through gains or losses of money, which are the norm in most business settings, the optimal choice for a given decision depends on the possible outcomes of all other decisions in the same time-period.

Discussion and Criticism

Cambridge economist Joan Robinson famously criticized utility for being a circular concept: "Utility is the quality in commodities that makes individuals want to buy them, and the fact that individuals want to buy commodities shows that they have utility" Robinson also pointed out that because the theory assumes that preferences are fixed this means that utility is not a testable assumption. This is so because if we take changes in peoples' behavior in relation to a change in prices or a change in the underlying budget constraint we can never be sure to what extent the change in behavior was due to the change in price or budget constraint and how much was due to a change in preferences. This criticism is similar to that of the philosopher Hans Albert who argued that the ceteris paribus conditions on which the marginalist theory of demand rested rendered the theory itself an empty tautology and completely closed to experimental testing. In essence, demand and supply curve (theoretical line of quantity of a product which would have been offered or requested for given price) is purely ontological and could never been demonstrated empirically.

Another criticism comes from the assertion that neither cardinal nor ordinal utility is empirically observable in the real world. In the case of cardinal utility it is impossible to measure the level of satisfaction "quantitatively" when someone consumes or purchases an apple. In case of ordinal utility, it is impossible to determine what choices were made when someone purchases, for example, an orange. Any act would involve preference over a vast set of choices (such as apple, orange juice, other vegetable, vitamin C tablets, exercise, not purchasing, etc.).

Other questions of what arguments ought to enter into a utility function are difficult to answer, yet seem necessary to understanding utility. Whether people gain utility from coherence of wants, beliefs or a sense of duty is key to understanding their behavior in the utility organon. Likewise, choosing between alternatives is itself a process of determining what to consider as alternatives, a question of choice within uncertainty.

An evolutionary psychology perspective is that utility may be better viewed as due to preferences that maximized evolutionary fitness in the ancestral environment but not necessarily in the current one.

Marginal Utility

In economics, utility is the satisfaction or benefit derived by consuming a product, thus the marginal utility of a good or service is the change in the utility from increase or decrease in the consumption of that good or service. Economists sometimes speak of a law of diminishing marginal utility, meaning that the first unit of consumption of a good or service yields more utility than the second and subsequent units, with a continuing reduction for greater amounts. Therefore, the fall in marginal utility as consumption increases is known as diminishing marginal utility. Mathematically:

$$MU_1 > MU_2 > MU_3 \ldots\ldots > MU_n$$

The marginal decision rule states that a good or service should be consumed at a quantity at which the marginal utility is equal to the marginal cost.

Marginality

The term *marginal* refers to a small change, starting from some baseline level. As Philip Wicksteed explained the term,

> "Marginal considerations are considerations which concern a slight increase or diminution of the stock of anything which we possess or are considering"

Frequently the marginal change is assumed to start from the endowment, meaning the total resources available for consumption. This endowment is determined by many things including physical laws (which constrain how forms of energy and matter may be transformed), accidents of nature (which determine the presence of natural resources), and the outcomes of past decisions made by the individual himself or herself and by others.

For reasons of tractability, it is often assumed in neoclassical analysis that goods and services are continuously divisible. Under this assumption, marginal concepts, including marginal utility, may be expressed in terms of differential calculus. Marginal utility can then be defined as the first derivative of Total Utility—the total satisfaction obtained from consumption of a good or service—with respect to the amount of consumption of that good or service.

In practice the smallest relevant division may be quite large. Sometimes economic analysis concerns the marginal values associated with a change of one unit of a discrete good or service, such as a motor vehicle or a haircut. For a motor vehicle, the total number of motor vehicles produced is large enough for a continuous assumption to be reasonable: this may not be true for, say, an aircraft carrier.

Utility

Depending on which theory of *utility* is used, the interpretation of marginal utility can be meaningful or not. Economists have commonly described utility as if it were *quantifiable*, that is, as if different levels of utility could be compared along a numerical scale. This has affected the development and reception of theories of marginal utility. Quantitative concepts of utility allow familiar arithmetic operations, and further assumptions of continuity and differentiability greatly increase tractability.

Contemporary mainstream economic theory frequently defers metaphysical questions, and merely notes or assumes that preference structures conforming to certain rules can be usefully *proxied* by associating goods, services, or their uses with quantities, and *defines* "utility" as such a quantification.

Another conception is Benthamite philosophy, which equated usefulness with the production of pleasure and avoidance of pain, assumed subject to arithmetic operation. British economists, under the influence of this philosophy (especially by way of John Stuart Mill), viewed utility as "the feelings of pleasure and pain" and further as a "*quantity* of feeling" (emphasis added).

Though generally pursued outside of the mainstream methods, there are conceptions of utility that do not rely on quantification. For example, the Austrian school generally attributes value to *the satisfaction of wants*, and sometimes rejects even the *possibility* of quantification. It has been argued that the Austrian framework makes it possible to consider rational preferences that would otherwise be excluded.

In any standard framework, the same object may have different marginal utilities for different people, reflecting different preferences or individual circumstances.

Diminishing Marginal Utility

The concept that marginal utilities diminish across the ranges relevant to decision-making is called the "law of diminishing marginal utility" (and is also known as Gossen's First Law). This refers to the increase in utility an individual gains from increasing their consumption of a particular good. "The law of diminishing marginal utility is at the heart of the explanation of numerous economic phenomena, including time preference and the value of goods (...) The law says, first, that the marginal utility of each homogenous unit decreases as the supply of units increases (and vice versa); second, that the marginal utility of a larger-sized unit is greater than the marginal utility of a smaller-sized unit (and vice versa). The first law denotes the law of diminishing marginal utility, the second law denotes the law of increasing total utility."

The law of diminishing marginal utility is similar to the law of diminishing returns which states that as the amount of one factor of production increases as all other factors of production are held the same, the marginal return (extra output gained by adding an extra unit) decreases.

As the rate of commodity acquisition increases, *marginal* utility decreases. If commodity consumption continues to rise, marginal utility at some point may fall to zero, reaching maximum total utility. Further increase in consumption of units of commodities causes marginal utility to become negative; this signifies dissatisfaction. For example,

- beyond some point, further doses of antibiotics would kill no pathogens at all, and might even become harmful to the body.
- to satiate thirst a person drinks water but beyond a point, consumption of more water might make the person vomit, hence leading to negative marginal and thus diminished total utility.
- it takes a certain amount of food energy to sustain a population, yet beyond a point, more calories cannot be consumed and are simply discarded (or cause disease).

Diminishing marginal utility is traditionally a microeconomic concept and often holds for an individual, although the marginal utility of a good or service might be *increasing* as well. For example:

- bed sheets, which up to some number may only provide warmth, but after that point may be useful to allow one to effect an escape by being tied together into a rope;
- tickets, for travel or theatre, where a second ticket might allow one to take a date on an otherwise uninteresting outing;
- dosages of antibiotics, where having too few pills would leave bacteria with greater resistance, but a full supply could effect a cure.
- the third leg is more useful than the first two when building a chair.

As suggested elsewhere in this article, occasionally one may come across a situation in which marginal utility increases even at a macroeconomic level. For example, the provision of a service may only be viable if it accessible to most or all of the population, and the marginal utility of a raw material required to provide such a service will increase at the "tipping point" at which this occurs. This is similar to the position with very large items such as aircraft carriers: the numbers of these items involved are so small that marginal utility is no longer a helpful concept, as there is merely a simple "yes" or "no" decision.

Independence from Presumptions of Self-interested Behavior

While the above example of water rations conforms to ordinary notions of self-interested behavior, the concept and logic of marginal utility are independent of the presumption that people pursue self-interest. For example, one can conceive of an individual who gave highest priority to the rose bush, next highest to the dog, and last to himself. In that case, if the individual has three rations of water, then the marginal utility of any one of those rations is that of watering the person. With just two rations, the person is left unwatered and the marginal utility of either ration is that of watering the dog. Likewise, a person could give highest priority to the needs of one of her neighbors, next to another, and so forth, placing her own welfare last; the concept of diminishing marginal utility would still apply.

Marginalist Theory

Marginalism explains choice with the hypothesis that people decide whether to effect any given change based on the marginal utility of that change, with rival alternatives being chosen based upon which has the greatest marginal utility.

Market Price and Diminishing Marginal Utility

If an individual possesses a good or service whose marginal utility to him is less than that of some other good or service for which he could trade it, then it is in his interest to effect that trade. Of course, as one thing is sold and another is bought, the respective marginal gains or losses from further trades will change. If the marginal utility of one thing is diminishing, and the other is not increasing, all else being equal, an individual will demand an increasing ratio of that which is acquired to that which is sacrificed. (One important way in which all else might not be equal is when the use of the one good or service complements that of the other. In such cases, exchange ratios might be constant.) If any trader can better his position by offering a trade more favorable to complementary traders, then he will do so.

In an economy with money, the marginal utility of a quantity is simply that of the best good or service that it could purchase. In this way it is useful for explaining supply and demand, as well as essential aspects of models of imperfect competition.

Adam Smith

The Paradox of Water and Diamonds

The "paradox of water and diamonds", usually most commonly associated with Adam Smith, though recognized by earlier thinkers, is the apparent contradiction that water possesses a value far lower than diamonds, even though water is far more vital to a human being.

Price is determined by both marginal utility and marginal cost, and here the key to the "paradox" is that the marginal cost of water is far lower than that of diamonds.

That is not to say that the price of any good or service is simply a function of the marginal utility that it has for any one individual nor for some ostensibly typical individual. Rather, individuals are willing to trade based upon the respective marginal utilities of the goods that they have or desire (with these marginal utilities being distinct for each potential trader), and prices thus develop constrained by these marginal utilities.

Quantified Marginal Utility

Under the special case in which usefulness can be quantified, the change in utility of moving from state S_1 to state S_2 is

$$\Delta U = U(S_2) - U(S_1)$$

Moreover, if S_1 and S_2 are distinguishable by values of just one variable g which is itself quantified, then it becomes possible to speak of the ratio of the marginal utility of the change in g to the size of that change:

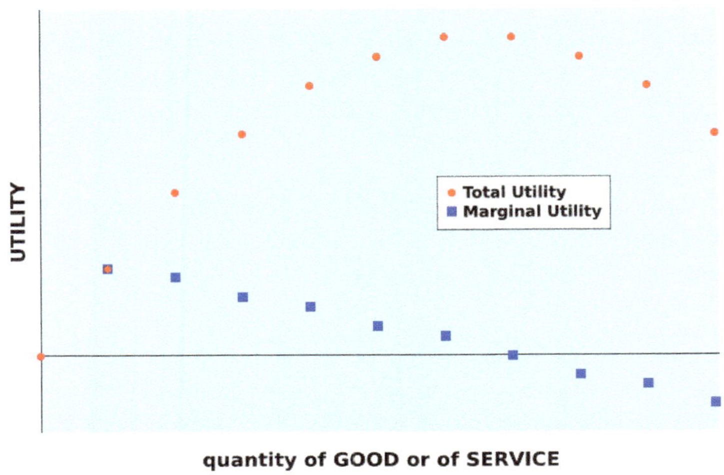

Diminishing marginal utility, given quantification

$$\left.\frac{\Delta U}{\Delta g}\right|_{c.p.}$$

(where "c.p." indicates that the *only* independent variable to change is g).

Mainstream neoclassical economics will typically assume that the limit

$$\lim_{\Delta g \to 0} \left.\frac{\Delta U}{\Delta g}\right|_{c.p.}$$

exists, and use "marginal utility" to refer to the partial derivative

$$\frac{\partial U}{\partial g} = \lim_{\Delta g \to 0} \left.\frac{\Delta U}{\Delta g}\right|_{c.p.}.$$

Accordingly, diminishing marginal utility corresponds to the condition

$$\frac{\partial^2 U}{\partial g^2} < 0.$$

History

The concept of marginal utility grew out of attempts by economists to explain the determination of price. The term "marginal utility", credited to the Austrian economist Friedrich von Wieser by Alfred Marshall, was a translation of Wieser's term "Grenznutzen" (*border-use*).

Proto-marginalist Approaches

Perhaps the essence of a notion of diminishing marginal utility can be found in Aristotle's *Politics*, wherein he writes

external goods have a limit, like any other instrument, and all things useful are of such a nature that where there is too much of them they must either do harm, or at any rate be of no use

(There has been marked disagreement about the development and role of marginal considerations in Aristotle's value theory.)

A great variety of economists have concluded that there is *some* sort of interrelationship between utility and rarity that affects economic decisions, and in turn informs the determination of prices. Diamonds are priced higher than water because their marginal utility is higher than water .

Eighteenth-century Italian mercantilists, such as Antonio Genovesi, Giammaria Ortes, Pietro Verri, Marchese Cesare di Beccaria, and Count Giovanni Rinaldo Carli, held that value was explained in terms of the general utility and of scarcity, though they did not typically work-out a theory of how these interacted. In *Della moneta* (1751), Abbé Ferdinando Galiani, a pupil of Genovesi, attempted to explain value as a ratio of two ratios, *utility* and *scarcity*, with the latter component ratio being the ratio of quantity to use.

Richard Whately

Anne Robert Jacques Turgot, in *Réflexions sur la formation et la distribution de richesse* (1769), held that value derived from the general utility of the class to which a good belonged, from comparison of present and future wants, and from anticipated difficulties in procurement.

Like the Italian mercantists, Étienne Bonnot, Abbé de Condillac, saw value as determined by utility associated with the class to which the good belong, and by estimated scarcity. In *De commerce et le gouvernement* (1776), Condillac emphasized that value is not based upon cost but that costs were paid because of value.

This last point was famously restated by the Nineteenth Century proto-marginalist, Richard Whately, who in *Introductory Lectures on Political Economy* (1832) wrote

It is not that pearls fetch a high price because men have dived for them; but on the contrary, men dive for them because they fetch a high price.

Marginalists before the Revolution

Gabriel Cramer

The first unambiguous published statement of any sort of theory of marginal utility was by Daniel Bernoulli, in "Specimen theoriae novae de mensura sortis". This paper appeared in 1738, but a draft had been written in 1731 or in 1732. In 1728, Gabriel Cramer had produced fundamentally the same theory in a private letter. Each had sought to resolve the St. Petersburg paradox, and had concluded that the marginal desirability of money decreased as it was accumulated, more specifically such that the desirability of a sum were the natural logarithm (Bernoulli) or square root (Cramer) thereof. However, the more general implications of this hypothesis were not explicated, and the work fell into obscurity.

In "A Lecture on the Notion of Value as Distinguished Not Only from Utility, but also from Value in Exchange", delivered in 1833 and included in *Lectures on Population, Value, Poor Laws and Rent* (1837), William Forster Lloyd explicitly offered a general marginal utility theory, but did not offer its derivation nor elaborate its implications. The importance of his statement seems to have been lost on everyone (including Lloyd) until the early 20th century, by which time others had independently developed and popularized the same insight.

In *An Outline of the Science of Political Economy* (1836), Nassau William Senior asserted that marginal utilities were the ultimate determinant of demand, yet apparently did not pursue implications, though some interpret his work as indeed doing just that.

In "De la mesure de l'utilité des travaux publics" (1844), Jules Dupuit applied a conception of marginal utility to the problem of determining bridge tolls.

In 1854, Hermann Heinrich Gossen published *Die Entwicklung der Gesetze des menschlichen Verkehrs und der daraus fließenden Regeln für menschliches Handeln*, which presented a marginal utility theory and to a very large extent worked-out its implications for the behavior of a market economy. However, Gossen's work was not well received in the Germany of his time, most copies were destroyed unsold, and he was virtually forgotten until rediscovered after the so-called Marginal Revolution.

The Marginal Revolution

Marginalism eventually found a foothold by way of the work of three economists, Jevons in England, Menger in Austria, and Walras in Switzerland.

William Stanley Jevons

William Stanley Jevons first proposed the theory in "A General Mathematical Theory of Political Economy" (PDF), a paper presented in 1862 and published in 1863, followed by a series of works culminating in his book *The Theory of Political Economy* in 1871 that established his reputation as a leading political economist and logician of the time. Jevons' conception of utility was in the utilitarian tradition of Jeremy Bentham and of John Stuart Mill, but he differed from his classical predecessors in emphasizing that "value depends entirely upon utility", in particular, on "final utility upon which the theory of Economics will be found to turn." He later qualified this in deriving the result that in a model of exchange equilibrium, price ratios would be proportional not only to ratios of "final degrees of utility," but also to costs of production.

Carl Menger presented the theory in *Grundsätze der Volkswirtschaftslehre* (translated as *Principles of Economics*) in 1871. Menger's presentation is peculiarly notable on two points. First, he took special pains to explain *why* individuals should be expected to rank possible uses and then to use marginal utility to decide amongst trade-offs. (For this reason, Menger and his followers are sometimes called "the Psychological School", though they are more frequently known as "the Austrian School" or as "the Vienna School".) Second, while his illustrative examples present utility as quantified, his essential assumptions do not. (Menger in fact crossed-out the numerical tables in his own copy of the published *Grundsätze*.) Menger also developed the law of diminishing marginal utility. Menger's work found a significant and appreciative audience.

Marie-Esprit-Léon Walras introduced the theory in *Éléments d›économie politique pure*, the first part of which was published in 1874 in a relatively mathematical exposition. Walras's work found relatively few readers at the time but was recognized and incorporated two decades later in the work of Pareto and Barone.

An American, John Bates Clark, is sometimes also mentioned. But, while Clark independently arrived at a marginal utility theory, he did little to advance it until it was clear that the followers of Jevons, Menger, and Walras were revolutionizing economics. Nonetheless, his contributions thereafter were profound.

The Second Generation

Vilfredo Pareto

Although the Marginal Revolution flowed from the work of Jevons, Menger, and Walras, their work might have failed to enter the mainstream were it not for a second generation of economists. In England, the second generation were exemplified by Philip Henry Wicksteed, by William Smart, and by Alfred Marshall; in Austria by Eugen von Böhm-Bawerk and by Friedrich von Wieser; in Switzerland by Vilfredo Pareto; and in America by Herbert Joseph Davenport and by Frank A. Fetter.

There were significant, distinguishing features amongst the approaches of Jevons, Menger, and Walras, but the second generation did not maintain distinctions along national or linguistic lines. The work of von Wieser was heavily influenced by that of Walras. Wicksteed was heavily influenced by Menger. Fetter referred to himself and Davenport as part of "the American Psychological School", named in imitation of the Austrian "Psychological School". (And Clark's work from this period onward similarly shows heavy influence by Menger.) William Smart began as a conveyor of Austrian School theory to English-language readers, though he fell increasingly under the influence of Marshall.

Böhm-Bawerk was perhaps the most able expositor of Menger's conception. He was further noted for producing a theory of interest and of profit in equilibrium based upon the interaction of diminishing marginal utility with diminishing marginal productivity of time and with time preference. (This theory was adopted in full and then further developed by Knut Wicksell and, with modifications including formal disregard for time-preference, by Wicksell's American rival Irving Fisher.)

Marshall was the second-generation marginalist whose work on marginal utility came most to inform the mainstream of neoclassical economics, especially by way of his *Principles of Economics*, the first volume of which was published in 1890. Marshall constructed the demand curve with the aid of assumptions that utility was quantified, and that the marginal utility of money was constant (or nearly so). Like Jevons, Marshall did not see an explanation for supply in the theory of marginal utility, so he synthesized an explanation of demand thus explained with supply explained in a more classical manner, determined by costs which were taken to be objectively determined. (Marshall later actively mischaracterized the criticism that these costs were themselves ultimately determined by marginal utilities.)

The Marginal Revolution and Marxism

Karl Marx acknowledged that "nothing can have value, without being an object of utility", but, in his analysis, "use-value as such lies outside the sphere of investigation of political economy", with labor being the principal measure of value under capitalism.

The doctrines of marginalism and the Marginal Revolution are often interpreted as somehow a response to Marxist economics. However the first volume of *Das Kapital* was not published until July 1867, after the works of Jevons, Menger, and Walras were written or well under way (In 1874 Walras published Éléments d'économie politique pure and Carl Menger published Principles of Economics in 1871) ; and Marx was still a relatively minor figure when these works were completed. It is unlikely that any of them knew anything of him. (On the other hand, Hayek or Bartley has suggested that Marx, voraciously reading at the British Museum, may have come across the works of one or more of these figures, and that his inability to formulate a viable critique may account for his failure to complete any further volumes of *Kapital* before his death.)

Nonetheless, it is not unreasonable to suggest that the generation who followed the preceptors of the Revolution succeeded partly because they could formulate straightforward responses to Marxist economic theory. The most famous of these was that of Böhm-Bawerk, *Zum Abschluss des Marxschen Systems* (1896), but the first was Wicksteed's "The Marxian Theory of Value. *Das Kapital*: a criticism" (1884, followed by "The Jevonian criticism of Marx: a rejoinder" in 1885). Initially there were only a few Marxist responses to marginalism, of which the most famous were Rudolf Hilferding's *Böhm-Bawerks Marx-Kritik* (1904) and *Politicheskoy ekonomni rante* (1914) by (Nikolai Bukharin). However, over the course of the 20th century a considerable literature developed on the conflict between marginalism and the labour theory of value, with the work of the neo-Ricardian economist Piero Sraffa providing an important critique of marginalism.

It might also be noted that some followers of Henry George similarly consider marginalism and neoclassical economics a reaction to *Progress and Poverty*, which was published in 1879.

In the 1980s John Roemer and other analytical Marxists have worked to rebuild Marxian theses on a marginalist foundation.

Reformulation

In his 1881 work *Mathematical Psychics*, Francis Ysidro Edgeworth presented the indifference curve, deriving its properties from marginalist theory which assumed utility to be a differentiable function of quantified goods and services. Later work attempted to generalize to the indifference curve formulations of utility and marginal utility in avoiding unobservable measures of utility.

In 1915, Eugen Slutsky derived a theory of consumer choice solely from properties of indifference curves. Because of the World War, the Bolshevik Revolution, and his own subsequent loss of interest, Slutsky's work drew almost no notice, but similar work in 1934 by John Richard Hicks and R. G. D. Allen derived much the same results and found a significant audience. (Allen subsequently drew attention to Slutsky's earlier accomplishment.)

Although some of the third generation of Austrian School economists had by 1911 rejected the quantification of utility while continuing to think in terms of marginal utility, most economists presumed that utility must be a sort of quantity. Indifference curve analysis seemed to represent a way to dispense with presumptions of quantification, albeit that a seemingly arbitrary assumption (admitted by Hicks to be a "rabbit out of a hat") about decreasing marginal rates of substitution would then have to be introduced to have convexity of indifference curves.

For those who accepted that indifference curve analysis superseded earlier marginal utility analysis, the latter became at best perhaps pedagogically useful, but "old fashioned" and observationally unnecessary.

Revival

John von Neumann

When Cramer and Bernoulli introduced the notion of diminishing marginal utility, it had been to address a paradox of gambling, rather than the paradox of value. The marginalists of the revolution, however, had been formally concerned with problems in which there was neither risk nor uncertainty. So too with the indifference curve analysis of Slutsky, Hicks, and Allen.

The expected utility hypothesis of Bernoulli and others was revived by various 20th century thinkers, with early contributions by Ramsey (1926), von Neumann and Morgenstern (1944), and Savage (1954). Although this hypothesis remains controversial, it brings not only utility, but a quantified conception of utility (cardinal utility), back into the mainstream of economic thought.

A major reason why quantified models of utility are influential today is that risk and uncertainty have been recognized as central topics in contemporary economic theory. Quantified utility models simplify the analysis of risky decisions because, under quantified utility, diminishing marginal utility implies risk aversion. In fact, many contemporary analyses of saving and portfolio choice require stronger assumptions than diminishing marginal utility, such as the assumption of prudence, which means convex marginal utility.

Meanwhile, the Austrian School continued to develop its ordinalist notions of marginal utility analysis, formally demonstrating that from them proceed the decreasing marginal rates of substitution of indifference curves.

Marginal Rate of Substitution

In economics, the marginal rate of substitution (MRS) is the rate at which a consumer is ready to give up one good in exchange for another good while maintaining the same level of utility. At equilibrium consumption levels (assuming no externalities), marginal rates of substitution are identical.

As the Slope of Indifference Curve

Under the standard assumption of neoclassical economics that goods and services are continuously divisible, the marginal rates of substitution will be the same regardless of the direction of exchange, and will correspond to the slope of an indifference curve (more precisely, to the slope multiplied by −1) passing through the consumption bundle in question, at that point: mathematically, it is the implicit derivative. MRS of X for Y is the amount of Y for which a consumer is willing to exchange X locally. The MRS is different at each point along the indifference curve thus it is important to keep locus in the definition. Further on this assumption, or otherwise on the assumption that utility is quantified, the marginal rate of substitution of good or service Y for good or service X (MRS_{xy}) is also equivalent to the marginal utility of X over the marginal utility of Y. Formally,

$$MRS_{xy} = -m_{\text{indif}} = -(dy / dx)$$

$$MRS_{xy} = MU_x / MU_y$$

It is important to note that when comparing bundles of goods X and Y that give a constant utility (points along an indifference curve), the marginal utility of X is measured in terms of units of Y that is being given up.

For example, if the $MRS_{xy} = 2$, the consumer will give up 2 units of Y to obtain 1 additional unit of X.

As one moves down a (standardly convex) indifference curve, the marginal rate of substitution decreases (as measured by the absolute value of the slope of the indifference curve, which decreases). This is known as the law of diminishing marginal rate of substitution.

Since the indifference curve is convex with respect to the origin and we have defined the MRS as the negative slope of the indifference curve,

$$MRS_{xy} \geq 0$$

Simple Mathematical Analysis

Assume the consumer utility function is defined by $U(x, y)$, where U is consumer utility, x and y are goods. Then the marginal rate of substitution can be computed via partial differentiation, as follows.

Also, note that:

$$MU_x = \partial U / \partial x$$

$$MU_y = \partial U / \partial y$$

where MU_x is the marginal utility with respect to good x and MU_y is the marginal utility with respect to good y.

By taking the total differential of the utility function equation, we obtain the following results:

$dU = (\partial U / \partial x)dx + (\partial U / \partial y)dy$, or substituting from above,

$dU = MU_x dx + MU_y dy$, or, without loss of generality, the total derivative of the utility function with respect to good x,

$$\frac{dU}{dx} = MU_x \frac{dx}{dx} + MU_y \frac{dy}{dx}, \text{ that is,}$$

$$\frac{dU}{dx} = MU_x + MU_y \frac{dy}{dx}.$$

Through any point on the indifference curve, $dU/dx = 0$, because $U = c$, where c is a constant. It follows from the above equation that:

$$0 = MU_x + MU_y \frac{dy}{dx}, \text{ or rearranging}$$

$$-\frac{dy}{dx} = \frac{MU_x}{MU_y}$$

The marginal rate of substitution is defined as the absolute value of the slope of the indifference curve at whichever commodity bundle quantities are of interest. That turns out to equal the ratio of the marginal utilities:

$$MRS_{yx} = MU_x / MU_y.$$

When consumers maximize utility with respect to a budget constraint, the indifference curve is tangent to the budget line, therefore, with m representing slope:

$$m_{\text{indif}} = m_{\text{budget}}$$

$$-(MRS_{xy}) = -(P_x / P_y)$$

$$MRS_{xy} = P_x / P_y$$

Therefore, when the consumer is choosing his utility maximized market basket on his budget line,

$$MU_x / MU_y = P_x / P_y$$

$$MU_x / P_x = MU_y / P_y$$

This important result tells us that utility is maximized when the consumer's budget is allocated so that the marginal utility per unit of money spent is equal for each good. If this equality did not hold, the consumer could increase his/her utility by cutting spending on the good with lower marginal utility per unit of money and increase spending on the other good. To decrease the marginal rate of substitution, the consumer must buy more of the good for which he/she wishes the marginal utility to fall for (due to the law of diminishing marginal utility).

Marginal Rates of Substitution

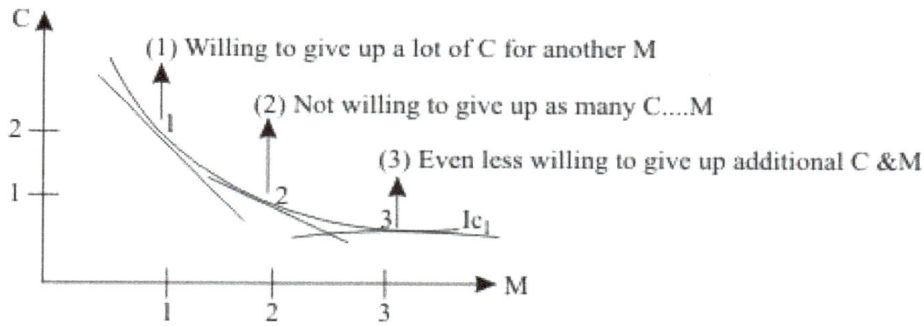

The individual is willing to give up fewer C to get more M when she has more M than less.

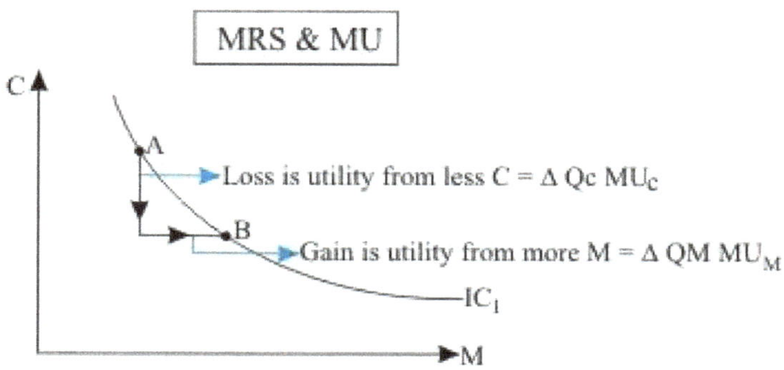

MRS & MU

Moving from point A to point B along indifference curve we have:

Loss in utility from less $C = \Delta Q_C MU_C$

Gain in utility from more $M = \Delta Q_M MU_M$

Since he is on the same Indifference Curve (IC), loss = gain, so that total utility is constant

$$\Rightarrow \Delta Q_M \; MU_M = -\Delta Q_C MU_C$$

$$\frac{dC}{dM} = \frac{-MU_M}{MU_C}$$

$\Rightarrow \frac{-MU_M}{MU_C} = +\frac{\Delta Q_C}{\Delta Q_M} \Rightarrow$ How much C she is willing to give up for an additional unit of M. This is defined as the marginal rate of substitution (MRS).

- Relationship between MRS and marginal utility is given by:
- $MRS_{M,C} = -\frac{MU_M}{MU_C}$ i.e. the MRS shows how relative Marginal utilities evolve over the IC.

  Moving from left to right

$$=> MU_M \downarrow and \; MU_C \uparrow$$

Slope of the indifference curve is called the Marginal rate of substitution and is the rate at which consumer is willing to trade off the two goods.

Is MRS constant along the IC?

MRS is diminishing (in absolute terms) as we move along an indifference curve.

This means that an individual is willing to give up fewer units of C to get more M when she has more M than when she has less M.

Budget Constraint

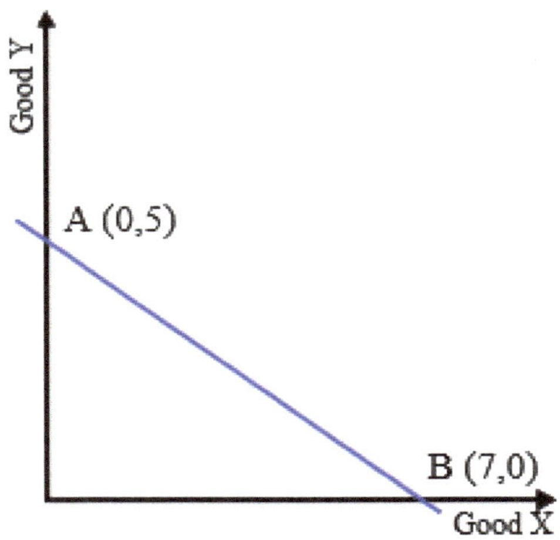

Budget constraint, where $A = \frac{m}{P_y}$ and $B = \frac{m}{P_x}$

A budget constraint represents all the combinations of goods and services that a consumer may purchase given current prices within his or her given income. Consumer theory uses the concepts of a budget constraint and a preference map to analyze consumer choices. Both concepts have a ready graphical representation in the two-good case.

Uses

Individual Choice

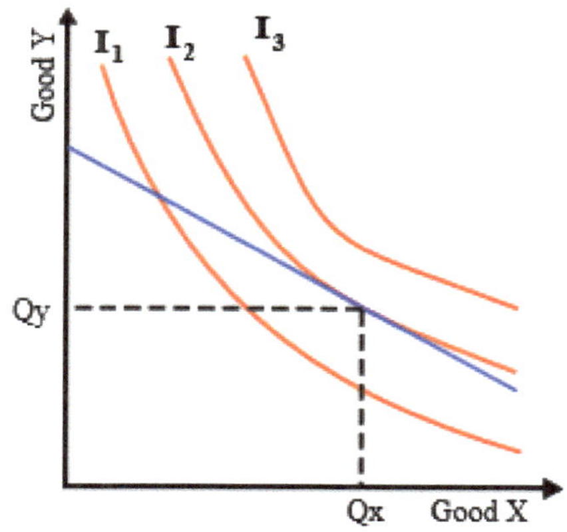

An individual should consume at (Qx, Qy).

Consumer behaviour is a maximisation problem. It means making the most of our limited resources to maximise our utility. As consumers are insatiable, and utility functions grow with quantity, the only thing that limits our consumption is our own budget.

An individual consumer should choose to consume goods at the point where the most preferred available indifference curve on his preference map is tangent to his budget constraint. That is, the indifference curve tangent to the budget constraint represents the maximum utility obtained utilizing the entire budget of the consumer. The tangent point (the xy coordinate) represents the amount of goods x and y the consumer should purchase to fully utilize their budget to obtain maximum utility. A line connecting all points of tangency between the indifference curve and the budget constraint is called the expansion path.

All two dimensional budget constraints are generalized into the equation:

$$P_x x + P_y y = m$$

Where:

- $m =$ money income allocated to consumption (after saving and borrowing)
- $P_x =$ the price of a specific good
- $P_y =$ the price of all other goods
- $x =$ amount purchased of a specific good
- $y =$ amount purchased of all other goods

The equation can be rearranged to represent the shape of the curve on a graph:

$y = (m / P_y) - (P_x / P_y)x$, where (m / P_y) is the y-intercept and $(-P_x / P_y)$ is the slope, representing a downward sloping budget line.

The factors that can shift the budget line are a change in income (m), a change in the price of a specific good (P_x), or a change in the price of all other goods (P_y).

International Economics

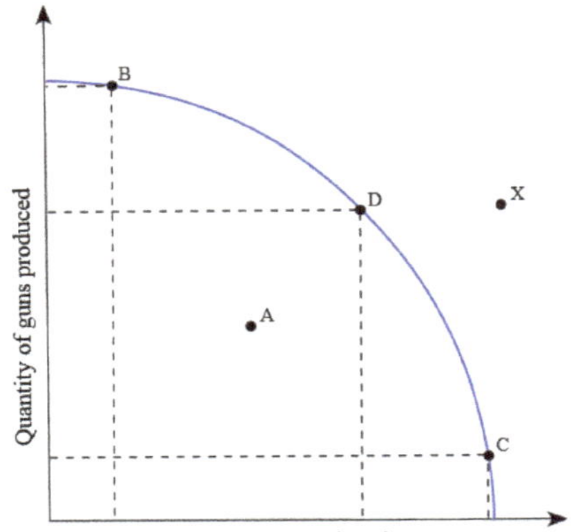

Point X is unobtainable given the current "budget" constraints on production.

A production-possibility frontier is a constraint in some ways analogous to a budget constraint, showing limitations on a country's production of multiple goods based on the limitation of available factors of production. Under autarky this is also the limitation of consumption by individuals in the country. However, the benefits of international trade are generally demonstrated through allowance of a shift in the consumption-possibility frontiers of each trade partner which allows access to a more appealing indifference curve. In the "toolbox" Hecksher-Ohlin and Krugman models of international trade, the budget constraint of the economy (its CPF) is determined by the terms-of-trade (TOT) as a downward-sloped line with slope equal to those TOTs of the economy. (The TOTs are given by the price ratio Px/Py, where x is the exportable commodity and y is the importable).

Many Goods

While low-level demonstrations of budget constraints are often limited to less than two good situations which provide easy graphical representation, it is possible to demonstrate the relationship between multiple goods through a budget constraint.

In such a case, assuming there are n goods, called x_i for $i = 1, \ldots, n,$, that the price of good x_i is denoted by p_i, and if W is the total amount that may be spent, then the budget constraint is:

$$\sum_{i=1}^{n} p_i x_i \leq W.$$

Further, if the consumer spends his income entirely, the budget constraint binds:

$$\sum_{i=1}^{n} p_i x_i = W.$$

In this case, the consumer cannot obtain an additional unit of good x_i without giving up some other good. For example, he could purchase an additional unit of good x_i by giving up P_i / P_j units of good x_j.

Constrained Utility Maximization

Budget constraint: The *budget constraint* is a representation of the combination of goods the consumer can afford to buy with a given income.

$$Y = P_M Q_M + P_C Q_c$$

- Where,
  - Y = Income level
  - P_M = Price of movie
  - P_C = Price of CD

Thus, the total amount spent must equal income, assuming no saving or borrowing.

- The slope of the budget constraint is:

$$-\frac{P_M}{P_C}$$

Optimization Problem :

- What is the highest IC that an individual can reach given a budget constraint?
- The individual chooses the bundle of goods that gives the highest utility, subject to the budget constraint.
- At the optimum: slope of the indifference curve equals the slope of the budget constraint.

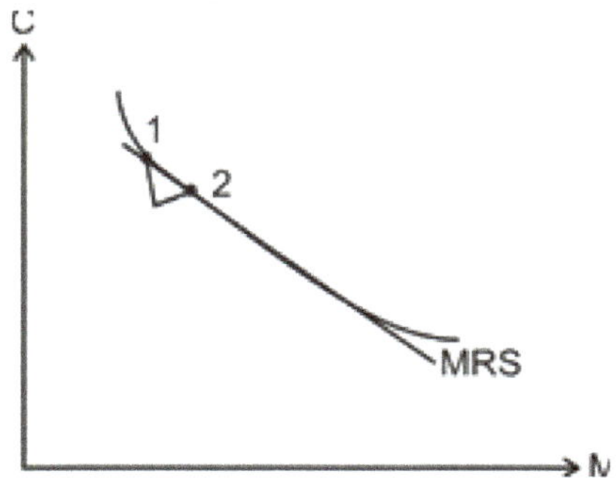

The benefit of her consuming another M is the MRS, the rate at which she is willing to trade C for M. The cost to her of making this trade is the price ratio, the rate at which the market allows her to trade C for M. Thus the optimal choice is one at which

- Thus, the marginal rate of substitution equals the ratio of prices:

$$MRS = -\frac{MU_M}{MU_C} = -\frac{P_M}{P_C}$$

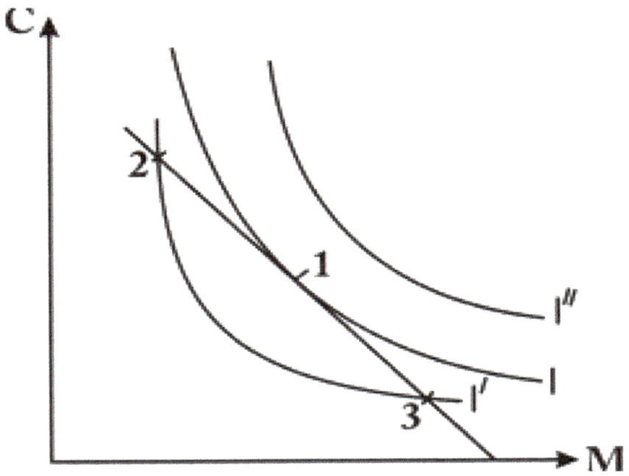

One way to demonstrate that 1 is optimal choice is to show that she is worse off with any others choice.

At 2, $MRS\Big|_{IC_{slope}} > \frac{P_M}{P_C}\Big|_{BC_{slope}}$

$\Rightarrow \frac{MU_M}{MU_C} > \frac{P_M}{P_C} \Rightarrow$ She is willing to give up more C for 1 unit of M than what the market is charging for an additional unit of M (the rel. price of M).

She can make herself better off by ↓ C & ↑ M & move from 2 to 1. Key result so far $\frac{MU_M}{MU_C} = \frac{P_M}{P_C}$.

- She is worse off at any other point on the indifference curve.

Substitution Effect

In economics and particularly in consumer choice theory, the substitution effect is one component of the effect of a change in the price of a good upon the amount of that good demanded by a consumer, the other being the income effect.

When a good's price decreases, if hypothetically the same consumption bundle were to be retained, income would be freed up which could be spent on a combination of more of each of the goods. Thus the new total consumption bundle chosen, compared to the old one, reflects both the effect of the changed relative prices of the two goods (one unit of one good can now be traded for a different quantity of the other good than before as the ratio of their prices has changed) *and* the effect of the freed-up income. The effect of the relative price change is called the *substitution effect*, while the effect due to income having been freed up is called the *income effect*.

If income is altered in response to the price change such that a new budget line is drawn passing through the old consumption bundle but with the slope determined by the new prices and the consumer's optimal choice is on this budget line, the resulting change in consumption is called the

Slutsky substitution effect. The idea is that the consumer is given enough money to purchase her old bundle at the new prices, and her choice changes are seen.

If instead, a new budget line is found with the slope determined by the new prices but tangent to the indifference curve going through the old bundle, the difference between the new point of tangency and the old bundle is the Hicks substitution effect. The idea now is that the consumer is given just enough income to achieve her old utility at the new prices, and how her choice changes is seen.

Some authors refer to one of these two concepts as simply the substitution effect. The popular textbook by Varian describes the Slutsky variant as the primary one, but also gives a good explanation of the distinction.

The same concepts also apply if the price of one good goes up instead of down, with the substitution effect reflecting the change in relative prices and the income effect reflecting the fact the income has been soaked up into additional spending on the retained units of the now-pricier good.

Graphical Analysis

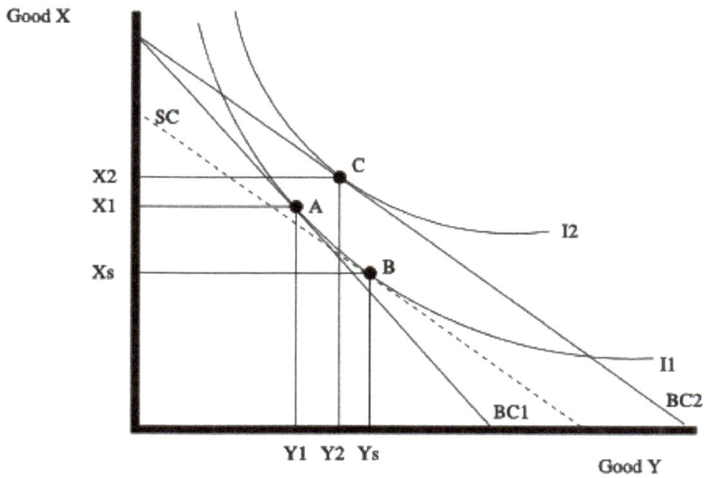

Suppose the initial situation is given by the graph (with good Y plotted horizontally) with the indicated (and never-changing) indifference curves shown and with budget constraint BC1 and with the consumer choosing point A because it puts him on the highest possible indifference curve consistent with BC1. The position and slope of the budget constraint are based on the consumer's income and on the prices of the two goods X and Y. If the price of Y falls, the budget constraint pivots to BC2, with a greater intercept of good Y because if all income were spent on Y more of it could be purchased at the now-lower price. The overall effect of the price change is that the consumer now chooses the consumption bundle at point C.

But the move from A to C can be decomposed into two parts. The substitution effect is the change that would occur if the consumer were required to remain on the original indifference curve; this is the move from A to B. The income effect is the simultaneous move from B to C that occurs because the lower price of one good in fact allows movement to a higher indifference curve.(In this graph Y is an inferior good)

Income–consumption Curve

In economics and particularly in consumer choice theory, the income-consumption curve is a curve in a graph in which the quantities of two goods are plotted on the two axes; the curve is the locus of points showing the consumption bundles chosen at each of various levels of income.

The income effect in economics can be defined as the change in consumption resulting from a change in real income. This income change can come from one of two sources: from external sources, or from income being freed up (or soaked up) by a decrease (or increase) in the price of a good that money is being spent on. The effect of the former type of change in available income is depicted by the income-consumption curve discussed in the remainder of this article, while the effect of the freeing-up of existing income by a price drop is discussed along with its companion effect, the substitution effect.

The consumer's preferences, monetary income and prices play an important role in solving the consumer's optimization problem (choosing how much of various goods to consume so as to maximize their utility subject to a budget constraint). The comparative statics of consumer behavior investigates the effects of changes in the exogenous or independent variables (especially prices and money incomes of the consumers) on the chosen values of the endogenous or dependent variables (the consumer's demands for the goods). When the income of the consumer rises with the prices held constant, the optimal bundle chosen by the consumer changes as the feasible set available to him changes. The income–consumption curve is the set of tangency points of indifference curves with the various budget constraint lines, with prices held constant, as income increases shifting the budget constraint out.

Consumer Theory

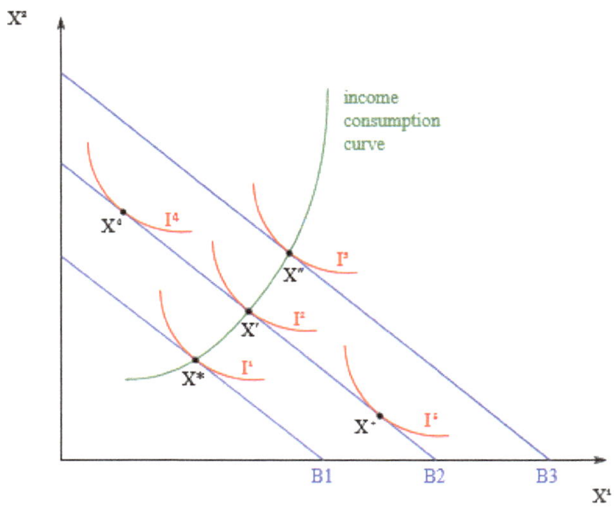

An increase in the income, with the prices of all goods fixed, causes consumers to alter their choice of market basket. The extreme left and right indifference curves belong to different individuals with different preferences, while the three central indifference curves belong to one individual for whom the income-consumption curve is shown. Each blue line represents one level of total consumption expenditure common to all its points; its slope depends on the two goods' relative prices.

The income effect is a phenomenon observed through changes in purchasing power. It reveals the change in quantity demanded brought by a change in real income. The figure on the left shows the consumption patterns of the consumer of two goods X^1 and X^2, the prices of which are p_1 and p_2 respectively. The initial bundle X^*, is the bundle which is chosen by the consumer on the budget line B_1. An increase in the money income of the consumer, with p_1 and p_2 constant, will shift the budget line outward parallel to itself.

In the figure, this means that the change in the money income of the consumer will shift the budget line B1 outward parallel to itself to B2 where the bundle X' bundle will be chosen. Again, an increase in the money income of the consumer will push the budget line B2 outward parallel to itself to B3 where the bundle X'' will be the bundle which will be chosen. Thus, it can be said that, with variations in income of the consumers and with the prices held constant the income–consumption curve can be traced out as the set of optimal points.

Income–Consumption Curve for Different Types of Goods

In the case illustrated with the help of Figure both X^1 and X^2 are normal goods in which case, the demand for the good increases as money income rises. However, if the consumer has different preferences, he has the option to choose X^o or X^+ on budget line B2. As the income of the consumer rises,and the consumer chooses X^o instead of X' i.e. if the consumer's indifference curve is I^4 and not I^2, then the demand for X^1 would fall . In that case, X^1 would be called an inferior good i.e. demand for good X^1 decreases with a rise in income of the consumer. Thus, a rise in income of the consumer may lead his demand for a good to rise, fall or not change at all. It is important to note here that, the knowledge of preferences of the consumer is essential to predict whether a particular good is inferior or normal.

Normal Goods

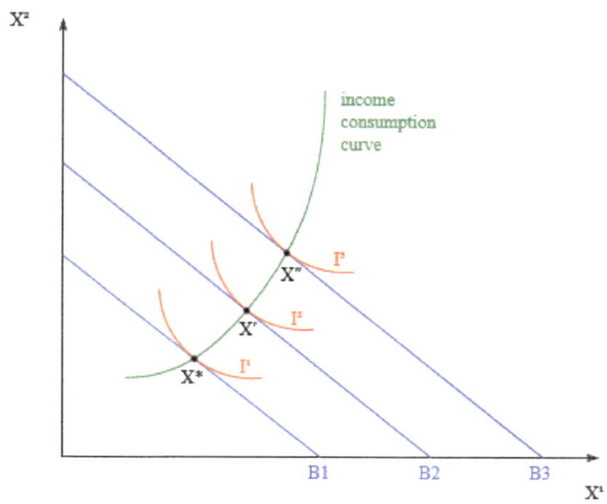

Income-consumption curve for Normal goods

In the figure to the left, B1, B2 and B3 are the different budget lines and I^1, I^2 and I^3 are the indifference curves that are available to the consumer. As shown earlier, as the income of the consumer rises, the budget line moves outwards parallel to itself. In this case, from initial bundle X^*, with an increase in the income of the consumer the budget line moves from B1 to B2 and the consumer would choose X' bundle and subsequently, with a further rise in consumer's income the budget line moves from B2 to B3 and the consumer would choose X" bundle and so on. The consumer would thus maximize his utility at the points X*, X' and X", and by joining these points, the income-consumption curve can be obtained.

The upward sloping income-consumption curve implies that there will be an increase in the demand for both X^1 and X^2 as the income of the consumer rises and will cause the demand curves of the goods to shift to the right. When the income-consumption curve has a positive slope then the income elasticity of demand will be positive. The greater the shifts of the demand curve to the right, the greater the income-elasticity of demand. In such a case, the goods will be normal goods.

Inferior Goods

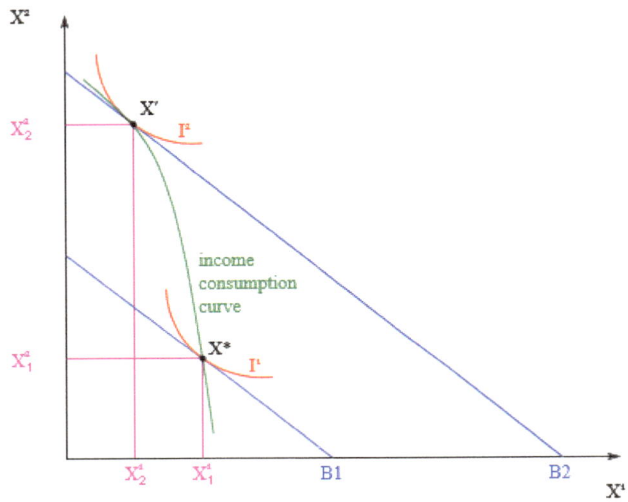

with an increase of income, demand for normal good X^2 rises while, demand for inferior good X^1 falls.

The figure on the right, shows the consumption patterns of the consumer of two goods X^1 and X^2, the prices of which are p_1 and p_2 respectively, where B1 and B2 are the budget lines and I^1 and I^2 are the indifference curves. Figure clearly shows that, with a rise in the income of the consumer, the initial budget line B1 moves outward parallel to itself to B2 and the consumer now chooses X' bundle to the initial bundle X*. The figure shows that, the demand for X^2 has risen from X^2_1 to X^2_2 with an outward shift of the budget line from B1 to B2 (caused due to rise in the income of the consumer). This essentially means that, good X^2 is a normal good as the demand for X^2 rose with an increase in the income of the consumer.

In contrast, it is to be noted from the figure, that the demand for X^1 has fallen from X^1_1 to X^1_2 with an outward shift of the budget line from B1 to B2 (caused due to rise in the income of the consumer). This implies that, good X^1 is an inferior good as the demand for X^1 fell with an increase in the income of the consumer.

The consumer maximizes his utility at points X* and X' and by joining these points, the income–consumption curve can be obtained. In figure, the income–consumption curve bends back on itself as with an increase income, the consumer demands more of X^2 and less of X^1. The income–consumption curve in this case is negatively sloped and the income elasticity of demand will be negative. Also the price effect for X^2 is positive, while it is negative for X^1.

ΔX_n^1 is the change in the demand for good 1 when we change income from m' to m, holding the price of good 1 fixed at p_1 :

$$\Delta X_n^1 = X^1(p_1, m) - X^1(p_1, m').$$

Perfect Substitutes

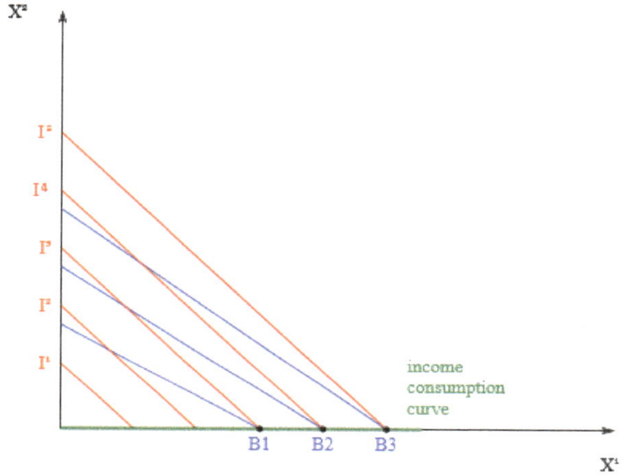

Income–consumption curve for perfect substitutes

The figure on the right depicts the case of two goods X^1 and X^2 which are perfect substitutes, prices of which are p_1 and p_2 respectively. Here, I^1, I^2, I^3, I^4 and I^5 are the straight line indifference curves, B1, B2 and B3 are the budget constraints and X^*, X' and X'' are the bundles chosen by the consumer. If it is assumed that $p_1 < p_2$ then the consumer would consume only X^1 as this would maximize his utility.

In the figure on the right, B1 is the initial budget line and the consumer chooses X^* as his optimal bundle and as the money income of the consumer rises, his budget line will shift outward and parallel to itself to B2. At the budget line B2 and the indifference curve I^4, the consumer will choose X'. Subsequently, as the income rises further, the budget line will again shift outward and parallel to itself to B3, where, the consumer will choose the optimal bundle X''.

Thus, it can be said that, the amount of good X^1 that the consumer consumes will increase, with an increase in the income of the consumer. Thus, the income–consumption curve for the perfect substitutes X^1 and X^2 will be the horizontal axis.

Perfect Complements

In case of perfect complements, the same amount of goods will be consumed by the consumer irrespective of say income, prices etc. As the level of consumption remains the same, the income–consumption curve for perfect complements is the diagonal line passing through the origin as shown in Figure.

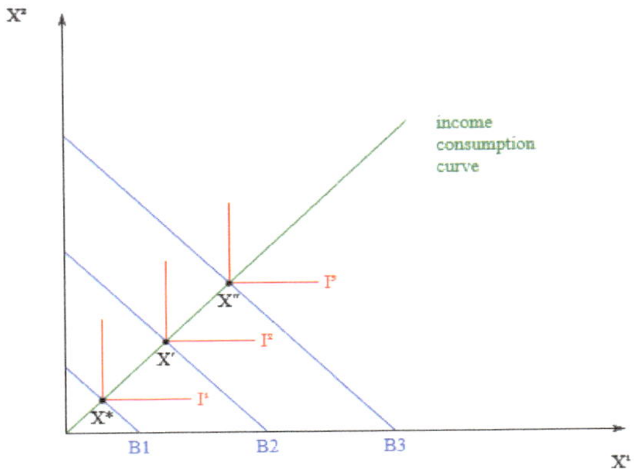

Income–consumption curve for perfect complements

In the figure on the left, X*, X' and X" are the utility maximization points where the budget constraint lines B1, B2 and B3 touch the kinks of the *L*-shaped indifference curves I^1, I^2 and I^3 respectively. By joining these points of utility maximization, the income–consumption curve for perfect complements is obtained.

Cobb–Douglas Preferences

The demand functions for both good 1 with quantity demanded X_1 and good 2 with quantity demanded X_2 under Cobb-Douglas preferences are linear functions of income *m*, and thus the income-consumption curve will be a straight line through the origin. If

$$u(X_1, X_2) = X_1^a X_2^{(1-a)}$$

then the demand for good 1 will have the form $X_1 = am / p_1$

If p_1 is kept at a fixed value, then this will be a linear function of *m*. By doubling *m*, the demand will double. In fact, if *m* is multiplied by any positive number, say *t*, the demand will be multiplied with the same amount.

For good 2, the demand is given by $X_2 = (1-a)m / p_1$. This too is clearly linear and homogeneous in *m*, thus making the income-consumption curves for both the goods 1 and 2 straight lines passing through the origin.

Income–consumption Curve and Engel Curves

At each level of income level, say *m*, there would be an optimal choice for each of the goods. If only the case of a good say, good X^1 is taken, the optimal choice at each set of prices and income or in other words, the demand function for good X^1 can be written as:

$$X^1 = X^1(p_1, p_2, m)$$

Here, p_1 is the price of good X^1, p_2 is the price of good X^2 and *m* is the income of the consumer.

If the prices of the goods X^1 and X^2 are held constant and the changes in demand are observed in relation to changes in income, the Engel curve can be generated. With all prices held constant, the Engel curve can be defined as a graph depicting the demand for one good as a function of income.

Substitution and Income Effects

- Consider an, Increase in the price of M, P_M
- A change in price consists of two effects:
  - *Substitution effect*–change in consumption due to change in relative prices, *holding utility constant.*
  - *Income effect*–change in consumption due to feeling "poorer" after price increase.

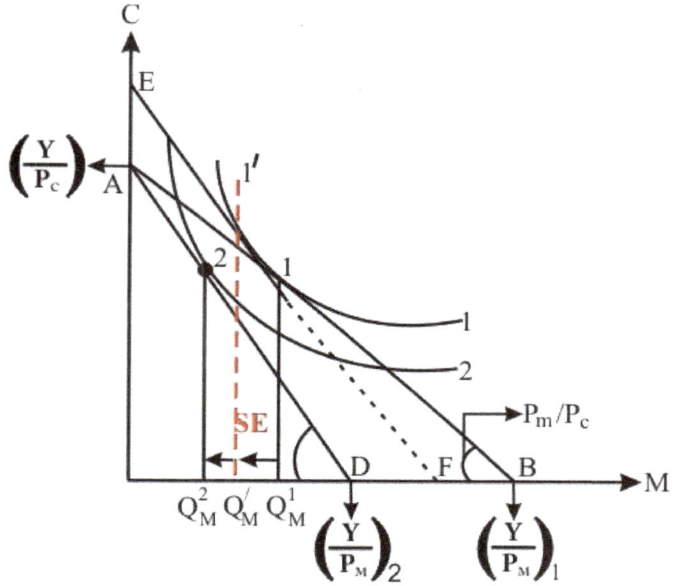

- In Figure as $P_M \uparrow, \frac{P_M}{P_C} \uparrow \Rightarrow$ Budget constraint becomes steeper. Let the budget constraint shift from AB to AD.
- $P_M \uparrow \Rightarrow$ Relative price of $M \uparrow \Rightarrow M$ is more expensive now.
  Moreover $P_M \uparrow \Rightarrow$ real income falls.
- Suppose government provides subsidy to compensate for the $\uparrow$ in P_M
- If we keep utility level constant $\Rightarrow$ the individual is on the same level of indifference curve. Only the slope of the budget constraint changes. Decline in Q_M is due to Substitution effect.
- As you move along indifference curve (1-1'), for same level of utilities, M is relatively more expensive. Hence $Q_M \downarrow, C$ is relatively cheaper. Hence $Q_c \uparrow$. You substitute more expensive M by cheaper C.
- This effect of a price change is called a Substitution Effect.

- $1' \to 2$ is going to another indifference curve with new slope of Budget constraint
  $\Rightarrow$ relative price is same as EF but income falls .

  $\Rightarrow Q_M \downarrow$ further as we move from $1'$ *to* 2. This change is purely due to a change in real income and hence constitutes the income effect.

Movement along indifference curve =Substitution Effect Movement from indifference curve = Income Effect.

Assistance Programs on the Budget Constraint

- Let's consider Temporary Assistance programs common in many countries.
- It generally distributes money from tax payers to low-income families.
- Example: Progresa (Mexico), TANF (US), NREGA (INDIA).
- Optimal Choice: Labor vs. Consumption.

Budget Constraint

- Assume 2 goods in the utility max problem: leisure & food consumption.
- Whatever time is not devoted to leisure is spent working & earning money.
- There is a tradeoff so far we considered two goods, both normal. Now 1 good & 1 bad.
- The tride is to model leisure instead of labor.
- Assume the person can work up to 2000 hours per year, at a wage rate of 10 per hour, and that temporary assistance is not yet in place.
- By working more hours, she can earn more money for food. But there is cost to work. More work makes her worse off and more food better. Now consider the utility maximization problem of an individual facing a laborleisure choice.
- The budget constraint faced by the individual can be described using the following concepts: – Price of food (Assume that this is 1 per unit).

  – "price" of leisure

  – tradeoff between leisure and food

  – Slope of Budget Constraint
- By working 1 less hour in a year she will lower her consumption by 10 rupees and increase her leisure time by 1 hour. Thus the price or opportunity cost of 1 hour of leisure is the wage rate 10. Thus the price of 1 hr of leisure is 10, the foregone wage she could have earned working.

- Slope of Budget Constraint: -W/PF .

Figure: Illustrates this

- Total hours =2000/yr
- Wage rate = 10/hr
- Price of food = 1/unit
- Price of leisure = opportunity cost of leisure.
- More leisure ⇒ less labor ⇒ less income ⇒ less food.
- Slope of budget constraint = $-P_L/P_F = -W/P_F = -10$
- All work, no leisure ⇒ 2000 hrs of work ⇒ 2000 * 10 (wage) = 20,000 rupees income.
- If leisure = 1000 = labor = income = 10,000

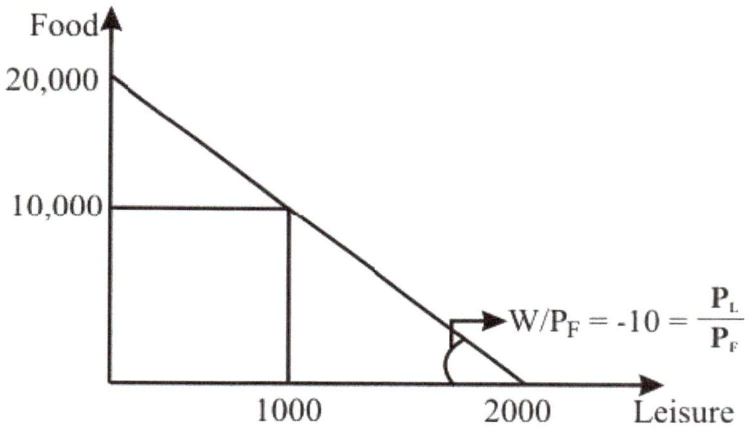

The Effect of Temporary Assistance Programs on the Budget Constraint

- Let's consider Temporary Assistance programs, a typical welfare program.
- TANF was created in 1996 in the US by restructuring the cash welfare system.
- Distributes cash from taxpayers to low income families
- A typical TANF program generally has the following features, has two key features.
  - Benefit guarantee, G – baseline amount that a recipient gets for enrolling in the program.
  - Benefit reduction rate – rate at which baseline benefit amount is reduced if recipients have other income; an implicit tax rate.
  - 100% vs. 50% benefit reduction rates.
    - ◇ 100% benefit reduction rate implies that TANF recipients are entitled to the benefit

guarantee if they have no other income or below a specific income, but they lose a rupee of benefit guarantee for each unit of extra income earned.

- ◇ 50% benefit reduction rate implies that TANF recipients are entitled to the benefit guarantee if they have no other income, but they lose 0.50 rupee of benefit guarantee for each unit of other income earned.
- ◇ Thus, Benefit guarantee falls as earnings increases.

- A poor single mother spends all the income on food. By working more hrs she can earn more money but has less time at home.
- She faces a labor-food choice.
- Convert this to a leisure-food choice & then analyze her trade oft. Assume that
  - Benefit Guarantee is 5,000 per year.
  - Benefit Reduction rate is 50%.

The following figure illustrates the effect of TANF on the budget constraint we saw in the previous graph.

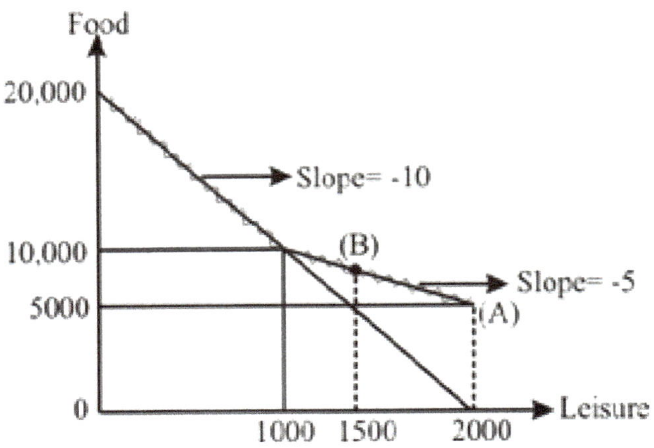

slope =

$$\frac{-P_L}{P_F} = \frac{wage}{P_F} = \frac{-10}{P_F} \text{ without TANF} =$$

$$\frac{-5}{P_F} \text{ with TANF}$$

- Benefit Guarantee (BG) = 5000
- Benefit Reduction (BR) = 50%
- For each additional rupee earned, BR = 50% of 1=0.5 Rupee
- Leisure = 2000 hrs ⇒ guaranteed benefit = 5000 rupees, ∵ no other income.
- $\frac{5000}{P_F(=1)}$ = 5000 units of food (A). Can be purchased with no work.
- If he works 1000 hrs, income = 10,000

$BG = 5000, BR = \frac{10000}{2} = 5000$

Net Benefit = 0

Remain on initial Budget constraint for income greater than 10,000.

(leisure < 1000)

- For leisure > 1000, 1 Additional hours of work involve an income of 10.
- Wage = 10 /hr. $BR = \frac{10}{2} = 5$ per hour of additional work → price of leisure ↓.
- Net wage = 10 - 5 = 5. (cost/price of leisure has fallen).
- When leisure = 1500, labor = 500 ⇒ income = 5000
- $BG = 5000, BR = \frac{5000}{2} = 2500.$

  ⇒ Net income = 5000+2500 = 7500.

The Effect of Various Policy Changes

- One possible "policy experiment" is reducing the benefit guarantee level *G*.
- What happens when *G* falls from 5,000 to 3,000, holding all other parameters constant?

Figure: Illustrates this.

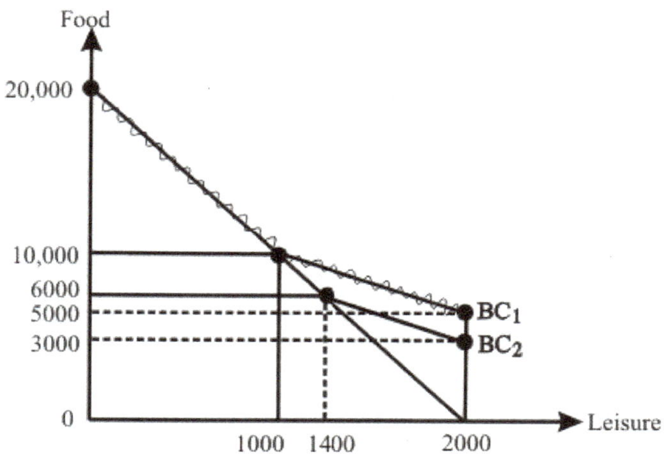

- BG = 5000

  BR = 50%
- BG = 3000

  BR = 50%
- Now at 1000 hrs of Work

income =10,000

BG = 3000

$$BR = \frac{10000}{2} = 5000$$

- Net benefit = BG – BR < 0
- Where will net benefit be zero?

BG - BR=0

- $3000 = \frac{income}{2} = 0 \Rightarrow income = 6000.$
- Labor = 600 hrs, leisure = 1400 hrs.

At, 1400 Leisure hrs, income = 6000, BR = 3000

- No net benefit ⇒ for all income > 6000, BR>BG => the individual is better off without enrolling into the TANF program. Thus she will face the same old Budget Constraint.
- Below 6000 rupees of income, wage = 10/hr

BR = 10/2 = 5 ⇒Net wage = 5 ⇒ slope = - 5

How will individuals respond to this policy change, Recall the concepts of income effect (IE) & substitution effect (SE). Suppose she earned < 6000 before the policy change.⇒no SE associated with the↓ in BG from 5000 to3000 ∵ there is no change in the relative price of leisure $\frac{-P_L}{P_F} = -5$ before & after.

But there is IE ∵ income↓ s with ↓ in BG = leisure↓ .

If income is between 6000-10000 before ↓ in BG, then the relative price changes as well.

⇒Leisure is more expensive ⇒ SE+IE. (Price of leisure charges from 5 to 10 as BG↓ form 5000 to 3000)

⇒Leisure↓ more than before.

$$\text{Now } \frac{P_L}{P_F} = -10$$

$$\text{Earlier } \frac{P_L}{P_F} = -5$$

What Happens to Labor Supply in Response to Such a Policy Change?

- How large would the labor supply response be?
- How sizable this response would be is not answered by the model above.
- It depends on where the individual initially was on the budget constraint.

- To explain the different possible magnitudes of response consider 2 different preference functions.

Figure: Illustrates this.

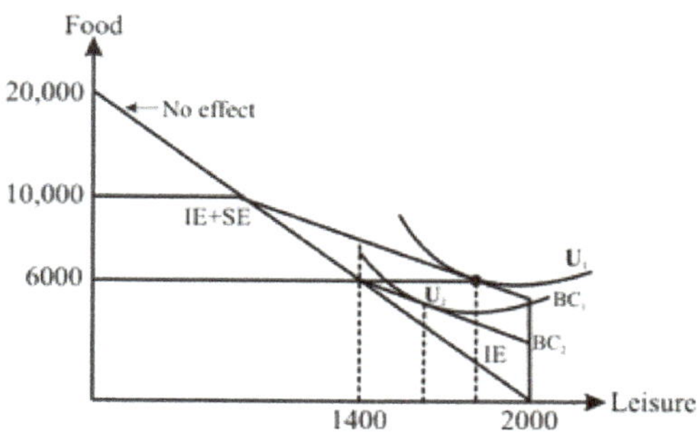

Income < 6000 = IE

10000> Income > 6000 = IE + SE

Income > 10000 = no effect

Expected change in labor supply.

- BG = 5000, BR = 50%
- BG = 3000, BR = 50%
- Suppose initial income is less than 6000 per yr.

  The policy change involves no change in relative price of leisure / food.

  Relative price of leisure to food is – 5 at policy 1

  Relative price of leisure to food is – 5 at policy 2

- Only income effect, since net income ↓ at every level of leisure over 1400.
- Income effects ⇒ food consumption ↓, leisure ↓
- Suppose the individual has the following utility function:

$$U = 100 \log (C) + 175 \log (L)$$

- She values leisure somewhat more.

Figure: Illustrates this

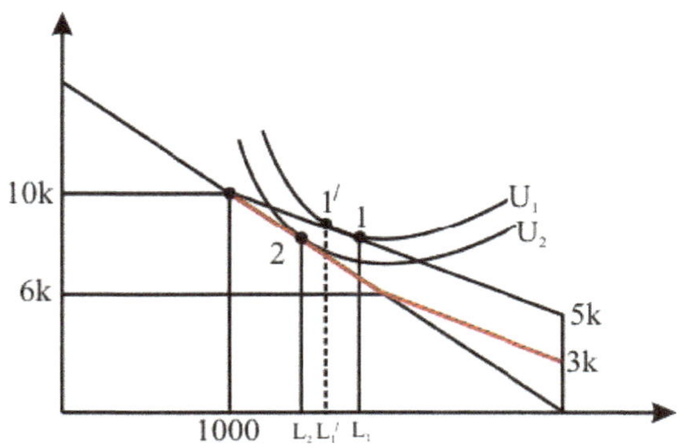

- BG = 5000, BR = 50%
- BG = 3000 , BR = 50%

- Initial Income > 6000 but < 10000
- $1 \rightarrow 1' \Rightarrow$ Substitution Effect : Earlier relative price of leisure (slope of BC_1) =5

  Now relative price of leisure (slove of BC_2) = 10
- Price of leisure ↑ ⇒ Substitution Effect.
- Real Income falls : Earlier at 5000 BG she was eligible for TANF at income levels between 6000 & 10,000

  But now as BG ↓ to 3000, she is not eligible for TANF for income between 6000 & 10000
- Income also ↓ s ⇒ Income effect amounts to a movements from u'_1 to u_2
- What happens if BG ↓ when income is greater than 10000? No

  Substitution Effect or Income Effects, not eligible for TANF either ways.

A Different Preference Function

- Economic theory clearly suggests that a benefit reduction will increase labor supply, but does not speak about the *magnitude* of the response.
- For example, some welfare recipients who were not initially working might continue not to work.
- Consider a specific preference function to illustrate the above point.

  Suppose the utility function is given by

  U = 75 log (C) + 300 log (L) → A very strong preference for leisure.

Figure: Illustrates this

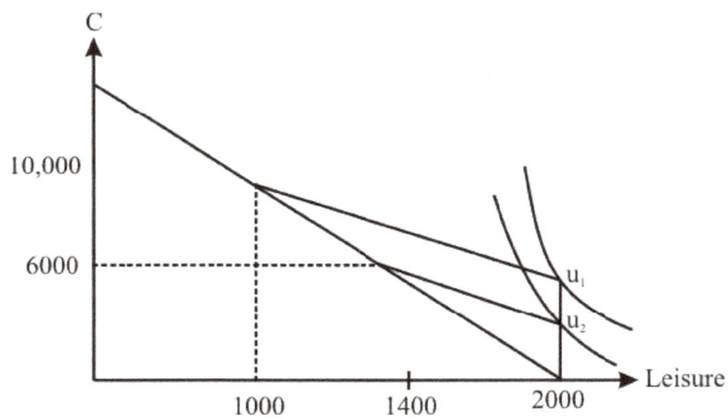

- BG ↓
- When BG was 5000, the optimal choice was not to work at all.

- The person was initially out of the labor force.
- She puts a significant weight on leisure.

$\Rightarrow$ Steep indifference curve

- A large ↑ in consumption is required to compensate for a unit ↓ in leisure.
- Optimal choice ⇒ No labor, all leisure for BG = 5000, BR = 50%.

  Corresponding to point u_1 (2000,5000)
- Suppose there is a policy change and BG ↓ to 3000. → the individual

  Continues not to work & just lets consumption ↓ to 3000.
- Thus the individual, in this case continues to stay out of the lab force even after benefit reduction.

Summary of Labor Supply Effects

- The actual magnitude of the labor supply response therefore depends on the preferences of various welfare recipients.
  - To the extent the preference is more like the former case, labor supply increases.
- Theory alone cannot say whether this policy change will increase labor supply, or by how much.
  - Must analyze available data using empirical methods to figure out the magnitude of labor supply response.

Welfare Economics

Welfare economics is a branch of economics that uses microeconomic techniques to evaluate well-being (welfare) at the aggregate (economy-wide) level. A typical methodology begins with the derivation (or assumption) of a social welfare function, which can then be used to rank economically feasible allocations of resources in terms of the social welfare they entail. Such functions typically include measures of economic efficiency and equity, though more recent attempts to quantify social welfare have included a broader range of measures including economic freedom (as in the capability approach).

The field of welfare economics is associated with two fundamental theorems. The first states that given certain assumptions, competitive markets produce (Pareto) efficient outcomes; it captures the logic of Adam Smith's invisible hand. The second states that given further restrictions, any Pareto efficient outcome can be supported as a competitive market equilibrium. Thus a social planner could use a social welfare function to pick the most equitable efficient outcome, then use lump sum transfers followed by competitive trade to bring it about. Because of welfare economics' close ties to social choice theory, Arrow's impossibility theorem is sometimes listed as a third fundamental theorem.

Attempting to apply the principles of welfare economics gives rise to the field of public economics, the study of how government might intervene to improve social welfare. Welfare economics also provides the theoretical foundations for particular instruments of public economics, including cost–benefit analysis, while the combination of welfare economics and insights from behavioural economics has led to the creation of a new subfield, behavioural welfare economics.

Measuring Social Welfare

Cardinal Utility

The early *Neoclassical approach* was developed by Edgeworth, Sidgwick, Marshall, and Pigou. It assumes the following:

- Utility is cardinal, that is, scale-measurable by observation or judgment.
- Preferences are exogenously given and stable.
- Additional consumption provides smaller and smaller increases in utility (diminishing marginal utility).
- All individuals have interpersonally commensurable utility functions (an assumption that Edgeworth avoided in his *Mathematical Psychics*).

With these assumptions, it is possible to construct a social welfare function simply by summing all the individual utility functions. Note that such a measure would still be concerned with the distribution of income (distributive efficiency) but not the distribution of final utilities. In normative terms, such authors were writing in the Benthamite tradition.

Ordinal Utility

The *New Welfare Economics* approach is based on the work of Pareto, Hicks, and Kaldor. It explicitly recognizes the differences between the efficiency aspect of the discipline and the distribution aspect and treats them differently. Questions of efficiency are assessed with criteria such as Pareto efficiency and the Kaldor-Hicks compensation tests, while questions of income distribution are covered in social welfare function specification. Further, efficiency dispenses with cardinal measures of utility, replacing it with ordinal utility, which merely ranks commodity bundles (with an indifference-curve map, for example).

Criteria

Efficiency

Situations are considered to have distributive efficiency when goods are distributed to the people who can gain the most utility from them.

Many economists use Pareto efficiency as their efficiency goal. According to this measure of social welfare, a situation is optimal only if no individuals can be made better off without making someone else worse off.

This ideal state of affairs can only come about if four criteria are met:

- The marginal rates of substitution in consumption are identical for all consumers. This occurs when no consumer can be made better off without making others worse off.
- The marginal rate of transformation in production is identical for all products. This occurs when it is impossible to increase the production of any good without reducing the production of other goods.
- The marginal resource cost is equal to the marginal revenue product for all production processes. This takes place when marginal physical product of a factor must be the same for all firms producing a good.
- The marginal rates of substitution in consumption are equal to the marginal rates of transformation in production, such as where production processes must match consumer wants.

There are a number of conditions that, most economists agree, may lead to inefficiency. They include:

- Imperfect market structures, such as a monopoly, monopsony, oligopoly, oligopsony, and monopolistic competition.
- Factor allocation inefficiencies in production theory basics.
- Market failures and externalities; there is also social cost.
- Price discrimination and price skimming.
- Asymmetric information, principal–agent problems.
- Long run declining average costs in a natural monopoly.
- Certain types of taxes and tariffs.

To determine whether an activity is moving the economy towards Pareto efficiency, two compensation tests have been developed. Any change usually makes some people better off while making others worse off, so these tests ask what would happen if the winners were to compensate the losers. Using the *Kaldor criterion*, an activity will contribute to Pareto optimality if the maximum amount the gainers are prepared to pay is greater than the minimum amount that the losers are prepared to accept. Under the *Hicks criterion*, an activity will contribute to Pareto optimality if the maximum amount the losers are prepared to offer to the gainers in order to prevent the change is less than the minimum amount the gainers are prepared to accept as a bribe to forgo the change. The Hicks compensation test is from the losers' point of view, while the Kaldor compensation test is from the gainers' point of view. If both conditions are satisfied, both gainers and losers will agree that the proposed activity will move the economy toward Pareto optimality. This is referred to as Kaldor–Hicks efficiency or the Scitovsky criterion.

Equity

There are many combinations of consumer utility, production mixes, and factor input combinations consistent with efficiency. In fact, there are an infinity of consumption and production equilibria that yield Pareto optimal results. There are as many optima as there are points on the aggregate production–possibility frontier. Hence, Pareto efficiency is a necessary, but not a sufficient condition for social welfare. Each Pareto optimum corresponds to a different income distribution in the economy. Some may involve great inequalities of income. So how do we decide which Pareto optimum is most desirable? This decision is made, either tacitly or overtly, when we specify the social welfare function. This function embodies value judgements about interpersonal utility. The social welfare function shows the relative importance of the individuals that comprise society.

A utilitarian welfare function (also called a Benthamite welfare function) sums the utility of each individual in order to obtain society's overall welfare. All people are treated the same, regardless of their initial level of utility. One extra unit of utility for a starving person is not seen to be of any greater value than an extra unit of utility for a millionaire. At the other extreme is the Max-Min, or Rawlsian utility function (Stiglitz, 2000, p102). According to the Max-Min criterion, welfare is maximized when the utility of those society members that have the least is the greatest. No economic activity will increase social welfare unless it improves the position of the society member that is the worst off. Most economists specify social welfare functions that are intermediate between these two extremes.

The social welfare function is typically translated into social indifference curves so that they can be used in the same graphic space as the other functions that they interact with. A utilitarian social indifference curve is linear and downward sloping to the right. The Max-Min social indifference curve takes the shape of two straight lines joined so as they form a 90-degree angle. A social indifference curve drawn from an intermediate social welfare function is a curve that slopes downward to the right.

The intermediate form of social indifference curve can be interpreted as showing that as inequality increases, a larger improvement in the utility of relatively rich individuals is needed to compensate for the loss in utility of relatively poor individuals.

A crude social welfare function can be constructed by measuring the subjective dollar value of goods and services distributed to participants in the economy.

Fundamental Theorems

The field of welfare economics is associated with two fundamental theorems. The first states that given certain assumptions, competitive markets (price equilibria with transfers, e.g. Walrasian equilibria) produce Pareto efficient outcomes. The assumptions required are generally characterised as "very weak". More specifically, the existence of competitive equilibrium implies both price-taking behaviour and complete markets, but the only additional assumption is the local non-satiation of agents' preferences – that consumers would like, at the margin, to have slightly more of any given good. The first fundamental theorem is said to capture the logic of Adam Smith's invisible hand, though in general there is no reason to suppose that the "best" Pareto efficient point (of which there are a set) will be selected by the market without intervention, only that some such point will be.

The second fundamental theorem states that given further restrictions, any Pareto efficient outcome can be supported as a competitive market equilibrium. These restrictions are stronger than for the first fundamental theorem, with convexity of preferences and production functions a sufficient but not necessary condition. A direct consequence of the second theorem is that a benevolent social planner could use a system of lump sum transfers to ensure that the "best" Pareto efficient allocation was supported as a competitive equilibrium for some set of prices. More generally, it suggests that redistribution should, if possible, be achieved without affecting prices (which should continue to reflect relative scarcity), thus ensuring that the final (post-trade) result is efficient. Put into practice, such a policy might resemble predistribution.

Because of welfare economics' close ties to social choice theory, Arrow's impossibility theorem is sometimes listed as a third fundamental theorem.

Social Welfare Maximization

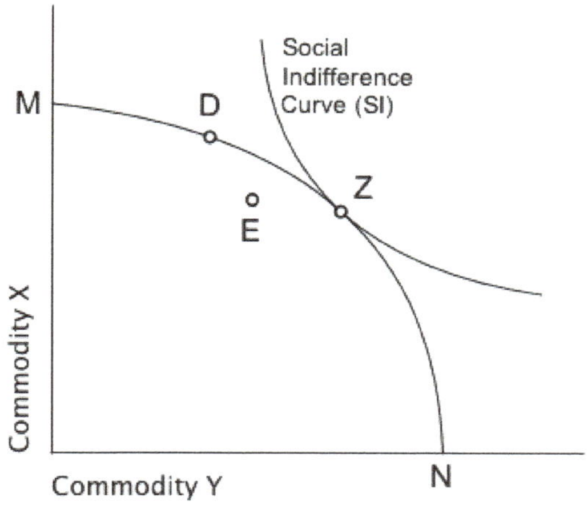

Although all the points on the grand social utility frontier are Pareto efficient, only one point identifies where social welfare is maximized. Such point is called "the point of bliss". This point is Z where the social utility frontier MN is tangent to the highest possible social indifference curve labelled SI.

Utility functions can be derived from the points on a contract curve. Numerous utility functions can be derived, one for each point on the production possibility frontier (PQ in the diagram above).

A social utility frontier (also called a grand utility frontier) can be obtained from the outer envelope of all these utility functions. Each point on a social utility frontier represents an efficient allocation of an economy's resources; that is, it is a Pareto optimum in factor allocation, in production, in consumption, and in the interaction of production and consumption (supply and demand). In the diagram below, the curve MN is a social utility frontier. Point D corresponds with point C from the earlier diagram. Point D is on the social utility frontier because the marginal rate of substitution at point C is equal to the marginal rate of transformation at point A. Point E corresponds with point B in the previous diagram, and lies inside the social utility frontier (indicating inefficiency) because the MRS at point C is not equal to the MRT at point A.

Criticisms

Some, such as economists in the tradition of the Austrian School, doubt whether a cardinal utility function, or cardinal social welfare function, is of any value. The reason given is that it is difficult to aggregate the utilities of various people that have differing marginal utility of money, such as the wealthy and the poor.

Also, the economists of the Austrian School question the relevance of pareto optimal allocation considering situations where the framework of means and ends is not perfectly known, since neo-classical theory always assumes that the ends-means framework is perfectly defined.

Some even question the value of ordinal utility functions. They have proposed other means of measuring well-being as an alternative to price indices, "willingness to pay" functions, and other price oriented measures. These price based measures are seen as promoting consumerism and productivism by many. It should be noted that it is possible to do welfare economics without the use of prices, however this is not always done.

Value assumptions explicit in the social welfare function used and implicit in the efficiency criterion chosen tend to make welfare economics a normative and perhaps subjective field. This can make it controversial.

However, perhaps most significant of all are concerns about the limits of a utilitarian approach to welfare economics. According to this line of argument utility is not the only thing that matters and so a comprehensive approach to welfare economics should include other factors. The capabilities approach is an attempt to construct a more comprehensive approach to welfare economics, one in which an individual's well-being and agency are evaluated in terms of their capabilities and functionings.

Production Function

In economics, a production function relates physical output of a production process to physical inputs or factors of production. The production function is one of the key concepts of mainstream neoclassical theories, used to define marginal product and to distinguish allocative efficiency, the defining focus of economics. The primary purpose of the production function is to address allocative efficiency in the use of factor inputs in production and the resulting distribution of income to those factors, while abstracting away from the technological problems of achieving technical efficiency, as an engineer or professional manager might understand it. Production function denotes an efficient combination of inputs and outputs.

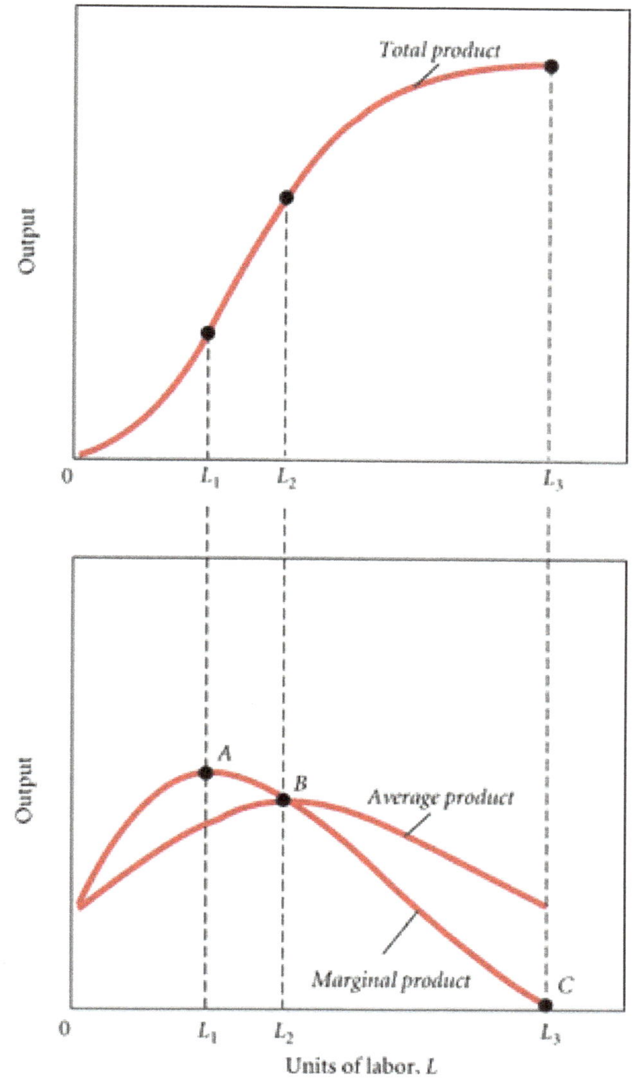

Graph of total, average, and marginal product

In macroeconomics, aggregate production functions are estimated to create a framework in which to distinguish how much of economic growth to attribute to changes in factor allocation (e.g. the accumulation of capital) and how much to attribute to advancing technology. Some non-mainstream economists, however, reject the very concept of an aggregate production function.

The Theory of Production Functions

In general, economic output is *not* a (mathematical) function of input, because any given set of inputs can be used to produce a range of outputs. To satisfy the mathematical definition of a function, a production function is customarily assumed to specify the *maximum* output obtainable from a given set of inputs. The production function, therefore, describes a boundary or frontier representing the limit of output obtainable from each feasible combination of input. (Alternatively, a production function can be defined as the specification of the minimum input requirements needed to produce designated quantities of output.) Assuming that maximum output is obtained from given inputs allows economists to abstract away from technological and managerial problems associated with realizing such a technical maximum, and to focus exclusively on the problem of allocative efficiency, associated with the *economic* choice of how much of a factor input to use, or the degree to which one factor may be substituted for another. In the production function itself, the relationship of output to inputs is non-monetary; that is, a production function relates physical inputs to physical outputs, and prices and costs are not reflected in the function.

In the decision frame of a firm making economic choices regarding production—how much of each factor input to use to produce how much output—and facing market prices for output and inputs, the production function represents the possibilities afforded by an exogenous technology. Under certain assumptions, the production function can be used to derive a marginal product for each factor. The profit-maximizing firm in perfect competition (taking output and input prices as given) will choose to add input right up to the point where the marginal cost of additional input matches the marginal product in additional output. This implies an ideal division of the income generated from output into an income due to each input factor of production, equal to the marginal product of each input.

The inputs to the production function are commonly termed factors of production and may represent primary factors, which are stocks. Classically, the primary factors of production were Land, Labor and Capital. Primary factors do not become part of the output product, nor are the primary factors, themselves, transformed in the production process. The production function, as a theoretical construct, may be abstracting away from the secondary factors and intermediate products consumed in a production process. The production function is not a full model of the production process: it deliberately abstracts from inherent aspects of physical production processes that some would argue are essential, including error, entropy or waste, and the consumption of energy or the co-production of pollution. Moreover, production functions do not ordinarily model the business processes, either, ignoring the role of strategic and operational business management. (For a primer on the fundamental elements of microeconomic production theory).

The production function is central to the marginalist focus of neoclassical economics, its definition of efficiency as allocative efficiency, its analysis of how market prices can govern the achievement of allocative efficiency in a decentralized economy, and an analysis of the distribution of income, which attributes factor income to the marginal product of factor input.

Specifying the Production Function

A production function can be expressed in a functional form as the right side of

$$Q = f(X_1, X_2, X_3, \dots, X_n)$$

where Q is the quantity of output and $X_1, X_2, X_3, \dots, X_n$ are the quantities of factor inputs (such as capital, labour, land or raw materials).

If Q is not a matrix (i.e., a scalar, a vector, or even a diagonal matrix), then this form does not encompass joint production, which is a production process that has multiple co-products. On the other hand, if f maps from R^{n^k} then it is a joint production function expressing the determination of k different types of output based on the joint usage of the specified quantities of the n inputs.

One formulation, unlikely to be relevant in practice, is as a linear function:

$$Q = a + bX_1 + cX_2 + dX_3 + \cdots$$

where a, b, c, d are parameters that are determined empirically. Another is as a Cobb-Douglas production function:

$$Q = aX_1^b X_2^c \cdots.$$

The Leontief production function applies to situations in which inputs must be used in fixed proportions; starting from those proportions, if usage of one input is increased without another being increased, output will not change. This production function is given by

$$Q = \min(aX_1, bX_2, \ldots).$$

Other forms include the constant elasticity of substitution production function (CES), which is a generalized form of the Cobb-Douglas function, and the quadratic production function. The best form of the equation to use and the values of the parameters ($a, b, c, \ldots$) vary from company to company and industry to industry. In a short run production function at least one of the X ‘s (inputs) is fixed. In the long run all factor inputs are variable at the discretion of management.

Production Function as a Graph

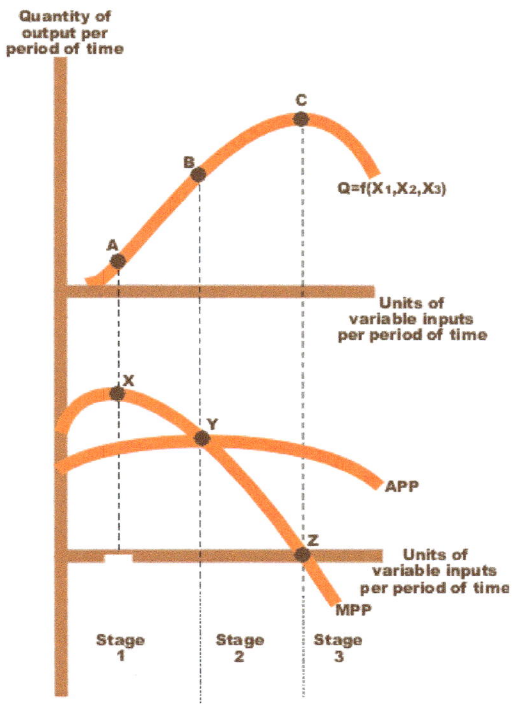

Quadratic production function

Any of these equations can be plotted on a graph. A typical (quadratic) production function is shown in the following diagram under the assumption of a single variable input (or fixed ratios of inputs so they can be treated as a single variable). All points above the production function are unobtainable with current technology, all points below are technically feasible, and all points on the function show the maximum quantity of output obtainable at the specified level of usage of the input. From point A to point C, the firm is experiencing positive but decreasing marginal returns to the variable input. As additional units of the input are employed, output increases but at a decreasing rate. Point B is the point beyond which there are diminishing average returns, as shown by the declining slope of the average physical product curve (APP) beyond point Y. Point B is just tangent to the steepest ray from the origin hence the average physical product is at a maximum. Beyond point B, mathematical necessity requires that the marginal curve must be below the average curve.

Stages of Production

To simplify the interpretation of a production function, it is common to divide its range into 3 stages. In Stage 1 (from the origin to point B) the variable input is being used with increasing output per unit, the latter reaching a maximum at point B (since the average physical product is at its maximum at that point). Because the output per unit of the variable input is improving throughout stage 1, a price-taking firm will always operate beyond this stage.

In Stage 2, output increases at a decreasing rate, and the average and marginal physical product are declining. However, the average product of fixed inputs (not shown) is still rising, because output is rising while fixed input usage is constant. In this stage, the employment of additional variable inputs increases the output per unit of fixed input but decreases the output per unit of the variable input. The optimum input/output combination for the price-taking firm will be in stage 2, although a firm facing a downward-sloped demand curve might find it most profitable to operate in Stage 1. In Stage 3, too much variable input is being used relative to the available fixed inputs: variable inputs are over-utilized in the sense that their presence on the margin obstructs the production process rather than enhancing it. The output per unit of both the fixed and the variable input declines throughout this stage. At the boundary between stage 2 and stage 3, the highest possible output is being obtained from the fixed input.

Shifting a Production Function

By definition, in the long run the firm can change its scale of operations by adjusting the level of inputs that are fixed in the short run, thereby shifting the production function upward as plotted against the variable input. If fixed inputs are lumpy, adjustments to the scale of operations may be more significant than what is required to merely balance production capacity with demand. For example, you may only need to increase production by million units per year to keep up with demand, but the production equipment upgrades that are available may involve increasing productive capacity by 2 million units per year.

If a firm is operating at a profit-maximizing level in stage one, it might, in the long run, choose to reduce its scale of operations (by selling capital equipment). By reducing the amount of fixed capital inputs, the production function will shift down. The beginning of stage 2 shifts from B1 to B2. The (unchanged) profit-maximizing output level will now be in stage 2.

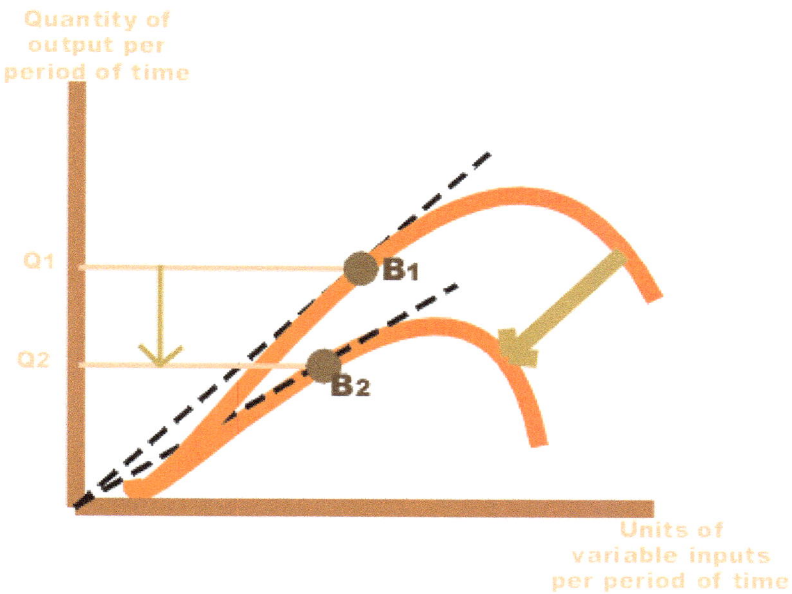

Shifting a production function

Homogeneous and Homothetic Production Functions

There are two special classes of production functions that are often analyzed. The production function $Q = f(X_1, X_2)$ is said to be homogeneous of degree n, if given any positive constant k, $f(kX_1, kX_2) = k^n f(X_1, X_2)$. If $n > 1$, the function exhibits increasing returns to scale, and it exhibits decreasing returns to scale if $n < 1$. If it is homogeneous of degree 1, it exhibits constant returns to scale. The presence of increasing returns means that a one percent increase in the usage levels of all inputs would result in a greater than one percent increase in output; the presence of decreasing returns means that it would result in a less than one percent increase in output. Constant returns to scale is the in-between case. In the Cobb-Douglas production function referred to above, returns to scale are increasing if $b + c + \cdots > 1$, decreasing if $b + c + \cdots < 1$, and constant if $b + c + \cdots = 1$..

If a production function is homogeneous of degree one, it is sometimes called "linearly homogeneous". A linearly homogeneous production function with inputs capital and labour has the properties that the marginal and average physical products of both capital and labour can be expressed as functions of the capital-labour ratio alone. Moreover, in this case if each input is paid at a rate equal to its marginal product, the firm's revenues will be exactly exhausted and there will be no excess economic profit.

Homothetic functions are functions whose marginal technical rate of substitution (the slope of the isoquant, a curve drawn through the set of points in say labour-capital space at which the same quantity of output is produced for varying combinations of the inputs) is homogeneous of degree zero. Due to this, along rays coming from the origin, the slopes of the isoquants will be the same. Homothetic functions are of the form $F(h(X_1, X_2))$ where $F(y)$ is a monotonically increasing function (the derivative of $F(y)$ is positive ($dF / dy > 0$)), and the function $h(X_1, X_2)$ is a homogeneous function of any degree.

Aggregate Production Functions

In macroeconomics, aggregate production functions for whole nations are sometimes constructed. In theory they are the summation of all the production functions of individual producers; however there are methodological problems associated with aggregate production functions, and economists have debated extensively whether the concept is valid.

Criticisms of the Production Function Theory

There are two major criticisms of the standard form of the production function.

On the Concept of Capital

During the 1950s, '60s, and '70s there was a lively debate about the theoretical soundness of production functions. Although the criticism was directed primarily at aggregate production functions, microeconomic production functions were also put under scrutiny. The debate began in 1953 when Joan Robinson criticized the way the factor input capital was measured and how the notion of factor proportions had distracted economists. She wrote:

"The production function has been a powerful instrument of miseducation. The student of economic theory is taught to write $Q = f(L, K)$ where L is a quantity of labor, K a quantity of capital and Q a rate of output of commodities. He is instructed to assume all workers alike, and to measure L in man-hours of labor; he is told something about the index-number problem in choosing a unit of output; and then he is hurried on to the next question, in the hope that he will forget to ask in what units K is measured. Before he ever does ask, he has become a professor, and so sloppy habits of thought are handed on from one generation to the next".

According to the argument, it is impossible to conceive of capital in such a way that its quantity is independent of the rates of interest and wages. The problem is that this independence is a precondition of constructing an isoquant. Further, the slope of the isoquant helps determine relative factor prices, but the curve cannot be constructed (and its slope measured) unless the prices are known beforehand.

On the Empirical Relevance

As a result of the criticism on their weak theoretical grounds, it has been claimed that empirical results firmly support the use of neoclassical *well behaved* aggregate production functions. Nevertheless, Anwar Shaikh has demonstrated that they also have no empirical relevance, as long as alleged good fit outcomes from an accounting identity, not from any underlying laws of production/distribution.

Natural Resources

Natural resources are usually absent in production functions. When Robert Solow and Joseph Stiglitz attempted to develop a more realistic production function by including natural resources, they did it in a manner economist Nicholas Georgescu-Roegen criticized as a "conjuring trick": Solow and Stiglitz had failed to take into account the laws of thermodynamics, since their variant allowed man-made capital to be a complete substitute for natural resources. Neither Solow nor Stiglitz reacted to Georgescu-Roegen's criticism, despite an invitation to do so in the September 1997 issue of the journal *Ecological Economics*.

The Practice of Production Functions

The theory of production function depicts the relation between physical outputs of a production process and physical inputs, i.e. factors of production. The practical application of production function is obtained by valuing the physical outputs and inputs by their prices. The economic value of physical outputs minus the economic value of physical inputs is the income generated by the production process. By keeping the prices fixed between two periods under review we get the income change generated by the change of production function. This is the principle how the production function is made a practical concept, i.e. measureable and understandable in practical situations.

About Production

Economic well-being is created in a production process, meaning all economic activities that aim directly or indirectly to satisfy human needs. The degree to which the needs are satisfied is often accepted as a measure of economic well-being. In production there are two features which explain increasing economic well-being. They are improving quality-price-ratio of commodities and increasing incomes from growing and more efficient market production. The most important forms of production are

- market production
- public production
- household production

In order to understand the origin of the economic well-being we must understand these three production processes. All of them produce commodities which have value and contribute to well-being of individuals.

The satisfaction of needs originates from the use of the commodities which are produced. The need satisfaction increases when the quality-price-ratio of the commodities improves and more satisfaction is achieved at less cost. Improving the quality-price-ratio of commodities is to a producer an essential way to improve the competitiveness of products but this kind of gains distributed to customers cannot be measured with production data. Improving the competitiveness of products means often to the producer lower product prices and therefore losses in incomes which are to compensated with the growth of sales volume.

Economic well-being also increases due to the growth of incomes that are gained from the growing and more efficient market production. Market production is the only one production form which creates and distributes incomes to stakeholders. Public production and household production are financed by the incomes generated in market production. Thus market production has a double role in creating well-being, i.e. the role of producing developing commodities and the role to creating income. Because of this double role market production is the "primus motor" of economic well-being and therefore here under review.

Main Processes of a Producing Company

A producing company can be divided into sub-processes in different ways; yet, the following five are identified as main processes, each with a logic, objectives, theory and key figures of its own. It is important to examine each of them individually, yet, as a part of the whole, in order to be able to measure and understand them. The main processes of a company are as follows:

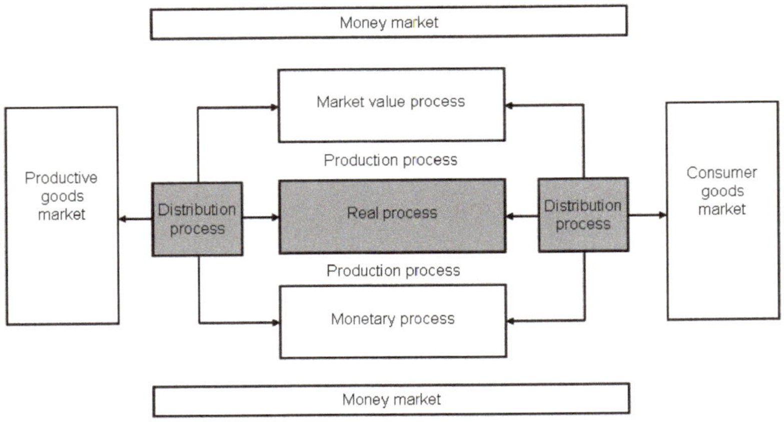

Main processes of a producing company (Saari 2006,3)

- real process.
- income distribution process
- production process.
- monetary process.
- market value process.

Production output is created in the real process, gains of production are distributed in the income distribution process and these two processes constitute the production process. The production process and its sub-processes, the real process and income distribution process occur simultaneously, and only the production process is identifiable and measurable by the traditional accounting practices. The real process and income distribution process can be identified and measured by extra calculation, and this is why they need to be analysed separately in order to understand the logic of production and its performance.

Real process generates the production output from input, and it can be described by means of the production function. It refers to a series of events in production in which production inputs of different quality and quantity are combined into products of different quality and quantity. Products can be physical goods, immaterial services and most often combinations of both. The characteristics created into the product by the producer imply surplus value to the consumer, and on the basis of the market price this value is shared by the consumer and the producer in the marketplace. This is the mechanism through which surplus value originates to the consumer and the producer likewise. It is worth noting that surplus values to customers cannot be measured from any production data. Instead the surplus value to a producer can be measured. It can be expressed both in terms of nominal and real values. The real surplus value to the producer is an outcome of the real process, real income, and measured proportionally it means productivity.

The concept "real process" in the meaning quantitative structure of production process was introduced in Finnish management accounting in 1960´s. Since then it has been a cornerstone in the Finnish management accounting theory. (Riistama et al. 1971)

Income distribution process of the production refers to a series of events in which the unit prices of constant-quality products and inputs alter causing a change in income distribution among those participating in the exchange. The magnitude of the change in income distribution is directly proportionate to the change in prices of the output and inputs and to their quantities. Productivity gains are distributed, for example, to customers as lower product sales prices or to staff as higher income pay.

The production process consists of the real process and the income distribution process. A result and a criterion of success of the owner is profitability. The profitability of production is the share of the real process result the owner has been able to keep to himself in the income distribution process. Factors describing the production process are the components of profitability, i.e., returns and costs. They differ from the factors of the real process in that the components of profitability are given at nominal prices whereas in the real process the factors are at periodically fixed prices.

Monetary process refers to events related to financing the business. Market value process refers to a series of events in which investors determine the market value of the company in the investment markets.

Production Growth and Performance

Production growth is often defined as a production increase of an output of a production process. It is usually expressed as a growth percentage depicting growth of the real production output. The real output is the real value of products produced in a production process and when we subtract the real input from the real output we get the real income. The real output and the real income are generated by the real process of production from the real inputs.

The real process can be described by means of the production function. The production function is a graphical or mathematical expression showing the relationship between the inputs used in production and the output achieved. Both graphical and mathematical expressions are presented and demonstrated. The production function is a simple description of the mechanism of income generation in production process. It consists of two components. These components are a change in production input and a change in productivity.

The figure illustrates an income generation process(exaggerated for clarity). The Value T2 (value at time 2) represents the growth in output from Value T1 (value at time 1). Each time of measurement has its own graph of the production function for that time (the straight lines). The output measured at time 2 is greater than the output measured at time one for both of the components of growth: an increase of inputs and an increase of productivity. The portion of growth caused by the increase in inputs is shown on line 1 and does not change the relation between inputs and outputs. The portion of growth caused by an increase in productivity is shown on line 2 with a steeper slope. So increased productivity represents greater output per unit of input.

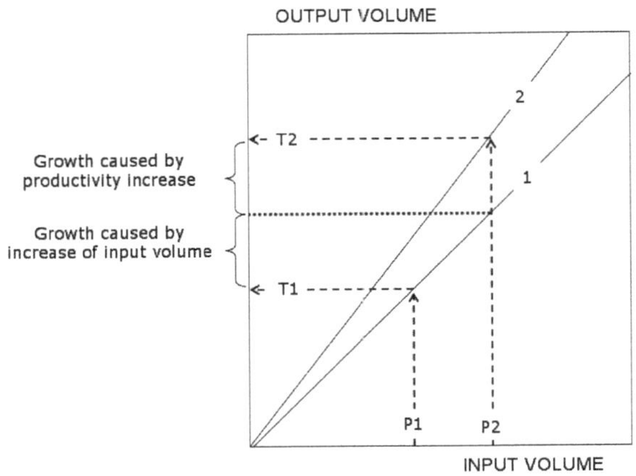

Components of production growth (Saari 2006,2)

The growth of production output does not reveal anything about the performance of the production process. The performance of production measures production's ability to generate income. Because the income from production is generated in the real process, we call it the real income. Similarly, as the production function is an expression of the real process, we could also call it "income generated by the production function".

The real income generation follows the logic of the production function. Two components can also be distinguished in the income change: the income growth caused by an increase in production input (production volume) and the income growth caused by an increase in productivity. The income growth caused by increased production volume is determined by moving along the production function graph. The income growth corresponding to a shift of the production function is generated by the increase in productivity. The change of real income so signifies a move from the point 1 to the point 2 on the production function (above). When we want to maximize the production performance we have to maximize the income generated by the production function.

The sources of productivity growth and production volume growth are explained as follows. Productivity growth is seen as the key economic indicator of innovation. The successful introduction of new products and new or altered processes, organization structures, systems, and business models generates growth of output that exceeds the growth of inputs. This results in growth in productivity or output per unit of input. Income growth can also take place without innovation through replication of established technologies. With only replication and without innovation, output will increase in proportion to inputs. (Jorgenson et al. 2014,2) This is the case of income growth through production volume growth.

Jorgenson et al. (2014,2) give an empiric example. They show that the great preponderance of economic growth in the US since 1947 involves the replication of existing technologies through investment in equipment, structures, and software and expansion of the labor force. Further they show that innovation accounts for only about twenty percent of US economic growth.

In the case of a single production process (described above) the output is defined as an economic value of products and services produced in the process. When we want to examine an entity of many production processes we have to sum up the value-added created in the single processes. This is done in order to avoid the double accounting of intermediate inputs. Value-added is obtained by subtracting the intermediate inputs from the outputs. The most well-known and used measure of value-added is the GDP (Gross Domestic Product). It is widely used as a measure of the economic growth of nations and industries.

Absolute (Total) and Average Income

The production performance can be measured as an average or an absolute income. Expressing performance both in average (avg.) and absolute (abs.) quantities is helpful for understanding the welfare effects of production. For measurement of the average production performance, we use the known productivity ratio

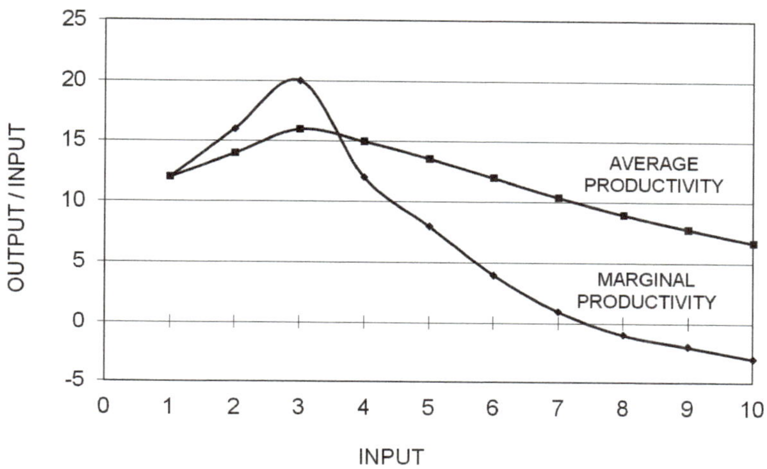

Average and marginal productivity (Saari 2011,8)

- Real output / Real input.

The absolute income of performance is obtained by subtracting the real input from the real output as follows:

- Real income (abs.) = Real output – Real input

The growth of the real income is the increase of the economic value which can be distributed between the production stakeholders. With the aid of the production model we can perform the average and absolute accounting in one calculation. Maximizing production performance requires using the absolute measure, i.e. the real income and its derivatives as a criterion of production performance.

The differences between the absolute and average performance measures can be illustrated by the following graph showing marginal and average productivity. The figure is a traditional expression of average productivity and marginal productivity. The maximum for production performance is achieved at the volume where marginal productivity is zero. The maximum for production performance is the maximum of the real incomes. In this illustrative example the maximum real income is achieved, when the production volume is 7.5 units. The maximum average productivity is reached when the production volume is 3.0 units. It is worth noting that the maximum average productivity is not the same as the maximum of real income.

Figure above is a somewhat exaggerated depiction because the whole production function is shown. In practice, decisions are made in a limited range of the production functions, but the principle is still the same; the maximum real income is aimed for. An important conclusion can be drawn. When we try to maximize the welfare effects of production we have to maximize real income formation. Maximizing productivity leads to a suboptimum, i.e. to losses of incomes.

A practical example illustrates the case. When a jobless person obtains a job in market production we may assume it is a low productivity job. As a result, average productivity decreases but the real income per capita increases. Furthermore, the well-being of the society also grows. This example reveals the difficulty to interpret the total productivity change correctly. The combination of volume increase and total productivity decrease leads in this case to the improved performance because we are on the "diminishing returns" area of the production function. If we are on the part of "increasing returns" on the production function, the combination of production volume increase and total productivity increase leads to improved production performance. Unfortunately we do not know in practice on which part of the production function we are. Therefore, a correct interpretation of a performance change is obtained only by measuring the real income change.

Production Models

A production model is a numerical description of the production process and is based on the prices and the quantities of inputs and outputs. There are two main approaches to operationalize the concept of production function. We can use mathematical formulae, which are typically used in macroeconomics (in growth accounting) or arithmetical models, which are typically used in microeconomics and management accounting.

We use here arithmetical models because they are like the models of management accounting, illustrative and easily understood and applied in practice. Furthermore, they are integrated to management accounting, which is a practical advantage. A major advantage of the arithmetical model is its capability to depict production function as a part of production process. Consequently, production function can be understood, measured, and examined as a part of production process.

There are different production models according to different interests. Here we use a production income model and a production analysis model in order to demonstrate production function as a phenomenon and a measureable quantity. Malakooti (2013) provides an overview and problems of production models such as Aggregate planning, Push-and-Pull Systems, Inventory Planning and Control, and so on.

Production Income Model

The scale of success run by a going concern is manifold, and there are no criteria that might be universally applicable to success. Nevertheless, there is one criterion by which we can generalise the rate of success in production. This criterion is the ability to produce surplus value. As a criterion of profitability, surplus value refers to the difference between returns and costs, taking into consideration the costs of equity in addition to the costs included in the profit and loss statement as usual. Surplus value indicates that the output has more value than the sacrifice made for it, in other words, the output value is higher than the value (production costs) of the used inputs. If the surplus value is positive, the owner's profit expectation has been surpassed.

	Period 1			Period 2		
	Quantity	Price	Value	Quantity	Price	Value
Product 1	210.00	7.20	1512	247.25	7.10	1755
Product 2	200.00	7.00	1400	195.03	7.15	1394
Output			2912			3150
Labour	100.00	7.50	750	115.00	7.70	886
Materials	80.00	8.60	688	79.20	8.50	673
Energy	400.00	1.50	600	428.00	1.55	663
Capital	160.00	3.80	608	164.80	3.90	643
Input			2646			2865
Surplus value (abs.)			266.00			285.12
Surplus value (rel.)			*1.101*			*1.100*

Profitability of production measured by surplus value (Saari 2006,3)

The table presents a surplus value calculation. We call this set of production data a basic example and we use the data through the article in illustrative production models. The basic example is a simplified profitability calculation used for illustration and modelling. Even as reduced, it comprises all phenomena of a real measuring situation and most importantly the change in the output-input mix between two periods. Hence, the basic example works as an illustrative "scale model" of production without any features of a real measuring situation being lost. In practice, there may be hundreds of products and inputs but the logic of measuring does not differ from that presented in the basic example.

In this context we define the quality requirements for the production data used in productivity accounting. The most important criterion of good measurement is the homogenous quality of the measurement object. If the object is not homogenous, then the measurement result may include changes in both quantity and quality but their respective shares will remain unclear. In productivity accounting this criterion requires that every item of output and input must appear in accounting as being homogenous. In other words, the inputs and the outputs are not allowed to be aggregated in measuring and accounting. If they are aggregated, they are no longer homogenous and hence the measurement results may be biased.

Both the absolute and relative surplus value have been calculated in the example. Absolute value is the difference of the output and input values and the relative value is their relation, respectively. The surplus value calculation in the example is at a nominal price, calculated at the market price of each period.

Production Analysis Model

A model used here is a typical production analysis model by help of which it is possible to calculate the outcome of the real process, income distribution process and production process. The starting point is a profitability calculation using surplus value as a criterion of profitability. The surplus value calculation is the only valid measure for understanding the connection between profitability and productivity or understanding the connection between real process and production process. A valid analysis of production necessitates considering all production inputs, and the surplus value calculation is the only calculation to conform to the requirement. If we omit an input in productivity or income accounting, this means that the omitted input can be used unlimitedly in production without any cost impact on accounting results.

		Period 1			$Q_1 \times P_2$	Period 2		
		1	2	3	4	5	6	7
		Quantity	Price	Value		Quantity	Price	Value
a	Product 1	210.00	7.20	1512.00	1491.00	247.25	7.10	1755.48
b	Product 2	200.00	7.00	1400.00	1430.00	195.03	7.15	1394.46
c	Output			2912.00	2921.00			3149.94
d	Labour	100.00	7.50	750.00	770.00	115.00	7.70	885.50
e	Materials	80.00	8.60	688.00	680.00	79.20	8.50	673.20
f	Energy	400.00	1.50	600.00	620.00	428.00	1.55	663.40
g	Capital	160.00	3.80	608.00	624.00	164.80	3.90	642.72
h	Input			2646.00	2694.00			2864.82
i	Surplus value (abs.)			266.00	227.00			285.12
j	*Surplus value (rel.)*			*1.101*				*1.100*
k	Change of distribution (abs.); i4-i3				-39.00			
l	Distribution index of output; c4/c3				1.003			
m	Distribution index of input; h4/h3				1.018			
n	Distribution index; l4/m4				0.985			
	Distribution process							
p	Productivity; c4/h4, c7/h7				1.084			1.100
q	Productivity index; p7/p4							1.014
r	Change of productivity (abs.); (q7-1)×c4							41.12
s	Volume index of output; c7/c4							1.078
t	Volume index of input; h7/h4							1.063
u	Change of input volume (abs); (t7-1)×(i4+r7)							17.00
					Real process			
v	Change of profitability; j7/j3							0.999
x	Change of returns; c7/c3							1.082
z	Change of costs; h7/h3							1.083
	Production process							

Production Model Saari 2004(Saari 2006,4)

Accounting and Interpreting

The process of calculating is best understood by applying the term *ceteris paribus*, i.e. "all other things being the same," stating that at a time only the impact of one changing factor be introduced to the phenomenon being examined. Therefore, the calculation can be presented as a process advancing step by step. First, the impacts of the income distribution process are calculated, and then, the impacts of the real process on the profitability of the production.

The first step of the calculation is to separate the impacts of the real process and the income distribution process, respectively, from the change in profitability (285.12 – 266.00 = 19.12). This takes place by simply creating one auxiliary column (4) in which a surplus value calculation is compiled using the quantities of Period 1 and the prices of Period 2. In the resulting profitability calculation, Columns 3 and 4 depict the impact of a change in income distribution process on the profitability and in Columns 4 and 7 the impact of a change in real process on the profitability.

The accounting results are easily interpreted and understood. We see that the real income has increased by 58.12 units from which 41.12 units come from the increase of productivity growth and the rest 17.00 units come from the production volume growth. The total increase of real income (58.12) is distributed to the stakeholders of production, in this case 39.00 units to the customers and to the suppliers of inputs and the rest 19.12 units to the owners.

Here we can make an important conclusion. Income formation of production is always a balance between income generation and income distribution. The income change created in a real process (i.e. by production function) is always distributed to the stakeholders as economic values within the review period. Accordingly, the changes in real income and income distribution are always equal in terms of economic value.

Based on the accounted changes of productivity and production volume values we can explicitly conclude on which part of the production function the production is. The rules of interpretations are the following:

The production is on the part of "increasing returns" on the production function, when

- productivity and production volume increase or
- productivity and production volume decrease

The production is on the part of "diminishing returns" on the production function, when

- productivity decreases and volume increases or
- productivity increases and volume decreases.

In the basic example the combination of volume growth (+17.00) and productivity growth (+41.12) reports explicitly that the production is on the part of "increasing returns" on the production function.

Another productivity model also gives details of the income distribution. Because the accounting techniques of the two models are different, they give differing, although complementary, analytical information. The accounting results are, however, identical. We do not present the model here in detail but we only use its detailed data on income distribution.

Objective Functions

An efficient way to improve the understanding of production performance is to formulate different objective functions according to the objectives of the different interest groups. Formulating the objective function necessitates defining the variable to be maximized (or minimized). After that other variables are considered as constraints or free variables. The most familiar objective function is profit maximization which is also included in this case. Profit maximization is an objective function that stems from the owner's interest and all other variables are constraints in relation to maximizing of profits.

INCOME FORMATION - changes between two periods			
Income generation		Income distribution	
		= Real income	+58.12
		+/- Customers	+9.00
		+/- Suppliers	-28.00
+/- Productivity	+41.12	= Producer income	39.12
+/- Volume	+17.00	- Labour compensation	-20.00
		- Taxes	N/a
= Real income	+58.12	= Owner income	+19.12
TOTAL GENERATION	58.12	TOTAL DISTRIBUTION	58.12

Summary of objective function formulations (Saari 2011,17)

The Procedure for Formulating Objective Functions

The procedure for formulating different objective functions, in terms of the production model, is introduced next. In the income formation from production the following objective functions can be identified:

- Maximizing the real income
- Maximizing the producer income
- Maximizing the owner income.

These cases are illustrated using the numbers from the basic example. The following symbols are used in the presentation: The equal sign (=) signifies the starting point of the computation or the result of computing and the plus or minus sign (+ / –) signifies a variable that is to be added or subtracted from the function. A producer means here the producer community, i.e. labour force, society and owners.

Objective function formulations can be expressed in a single calculation which concisely illustrates the logic of the income generation, the income distribution and the variables to be maximized.

The calculation resembles an income statement starting with the income generation and ending with the income distribution. The income generation and the distribution are always in balance so that their amounts are equal. In this case it is 58.12 units. The income which has been generated in the real process is distributed to the stakeholders during the same period. There are three variables which can be maximized. They are the real income, the producer income and the owner income. Producer income and owner income are practical quantities because they are addable quantities and they can be computed quite easily. Real income is normally not an addable quantity and in many cases it is difficult to calculate.

The Dual Approach for the Formulation

Here we have to add that the change of real income can also be computed from the changes in income distribution. We have to identify the unit price changes of outputs and inputs and calculate their profit impacts (i.e. unit price change x quantity). The change of real income is the sum of these profit impacts and the change of owner income. This approach is called the dual approach because the framework is seen in terms of prices instead of quantities (ONS 3, 23).

The dual approach has been recognized in growth accounting for long but its interpretation has remained unclear. The following question has remained unanswered: "Quantity based estimates of the residual are interpreted as a shift in the production function, but what is the interpretation of the price-based growth estimates?" We have demonstrated above that the real income change is achieved by quantitative changes in production and the income distribution change to the stakeholders is its dual. In this case the duality means that the same accounting result is obtained by accounting the change of the total income generation (real income) and by accounting the change of the total income distribution.

Cost Curve

In economics, a cost curve is a graph of the costs of production as a function of total quantity produced. In a free market economy, productively efficient firms use these curves to find the optimal point of production (minimizing cost), and profit maximizing firms can use them to decide output quantities to achieve those aims. There are various types of cost curves, all related to each other, including total and average cost curves, and marginal ("for each additional unit") cost curves, which are equal to the differential of the total cost curves. Some are applicable to the short run, others to the long run.

Short-run Average Variable Cost Curve (SRAVC)

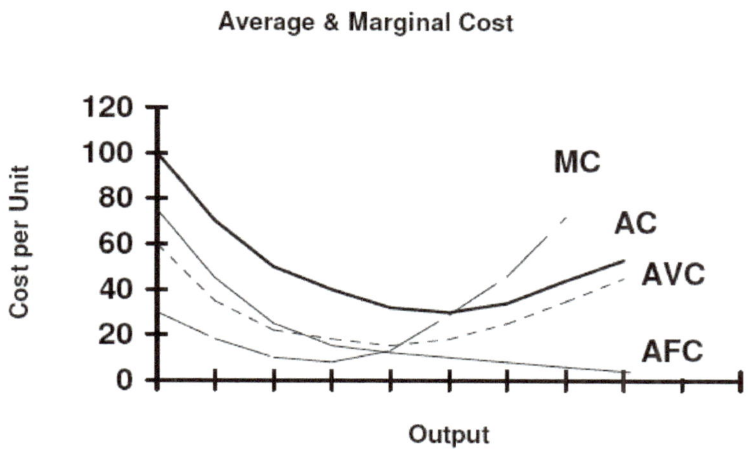

A U shaped short run Average Cost(AC) curve. AVC is the Average Variable Cost, AFC the Average Fixed Cost, MC the marginal cost crossing the minimum of the Average Cost curve.

Average variable cost (which is a short-run concept) is the variable cost (typically labor cost) per unit of output: SRAVC = wL / Q where w is the wage rate, L is the quantity of labor used, and Q is the quantity of output produced. The SRAVC curve plots the short-run average variable cost against the level of output and is typically drawn as U-shaped.

Short-run Average Total Cost Curve (SRATC or SRAC)

The average total cost curve is constructed to capture the relation between cost per unit of output and the level of output, *ceteris paribus*. A perfectly competitive and productively efficient firm organizes its factors of production in such a way that the factors of production is at the lowest point. In the short run, when at least one factor of production is fixed, this occurs at the output level where it has enjoyed all possible average cost gains from increasing production. This is at the minimum point in the diagram on the right.

Short-run total cost is given by:

$$STC = P_K.K + P_L.L,$$

where P_K is the unit price of using physical capital per unit time, P_L is the unit price of labor per unit time (the wage rate), K is the quantity of physical capital used, and L is the quantity of labor used. From this we obtain short-run average cost, denoted either SATC or SAC, as STC / Q:

$$\text{SRATC or SRAC} = P_K K/Q + P_L L/Q = P_K / AP_K + P_L / AP_L,$$

where $AP_K = Q/K$ is the average product of capital and $AP_L = Q/L$ is the average product of labor.

Within the graph shown in the figure, The Marginal cost curve, Average Fixed Cost curve and Average Variable cost curve can not start with zero as at quantity zero, these values are not defined.

Short run average cost equals average fixed costs plus average variable costs. Average fixed cost continuously falls as production increases in the short run, because K is fixed in the short run. The shape of the average variable cost curve is directly determined by increasing and then diminishing marginal returns to the variable input (conventionally labor).

Short-run Marginal Cost Curve (SRMC)

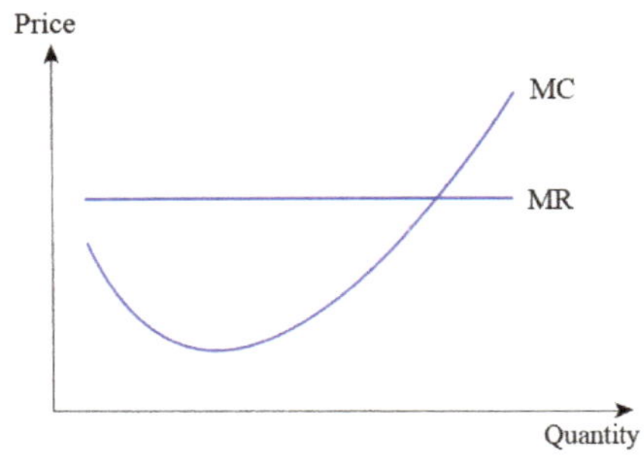

Typical marginal cost curve

A short-run marginal cost curve graphically represents the relation between marginal (i.e., incremental) cost incurred by a firm in the short-run production of a good or service and the quantity of output produced. This curve is constructed to capture the relation between marginal cost and the level of output, holding other variables, like technology and resource prices, constant. The marginal cost curve is usually U-shaped. Marginal cost is relatively high at small quantities of output; then as production increases, marginal cost declines, reaches a minimum value, then rises. The marginal cost is shown in relation to marginal revenue (MR), the incremental amount of sales revenue that an additional unit of the product or service will bring to the firm. This shape of the marginal cost curve is directly attributable to increasing, then decreasing marginal returns (and the law of diminishing marginal returns). Marginal cost equals w/MP_L. For most production processes the marginal product of labor initially rises, reaches a maximum value and then continuously falls as production increases. Thus marginal cost initially falls, reaches a minimum value and then increases. The marginal cost curve intersects both the average variable cost curve and (short-run) average total cost curve at their minimum points. When the marginal cost curve is above an average cost curve the average curve is rising. When the marginal costs curve is below an average curve the average curve is falling. This relation holds regardless of whether the marginal curve is rising or falling.

Long-run Marginal Cost Curve (LRMC)

The long-run marginal cost curve shows for each unit of output the added total cost incurred in the long run, that is, the conceptual period when all factors of production are variable so as minimize long-run average total cost. Stated otherwise, LRMC is the minimum increase in total cost associated with an increase of one unit of output when all inputs are variable.

The long-run marginal cost curve is shaped by returns to scale, a long-run concept, rather than the law of diminishing marginal returns, which is a short-run concept. The long-run marginal cost curve tends to be flatter than its short-run counterpart due to increased input flexibility as to cost minimization. The long-run marginal cost curve intersects the long-run average cost curve at the minimum point of the latter. When long-run marginal costs are below long-run average costs, long-run average costs are falling (as to additional units of output). When long-run marginal costs are above long run average costs, average costs are rising. Long-run marginal cost equals short run marginal-cost at the least-long-run-average-cost level of production. LRMC is the slope of the LR total-cost function.

Graphing Cost Curves Together

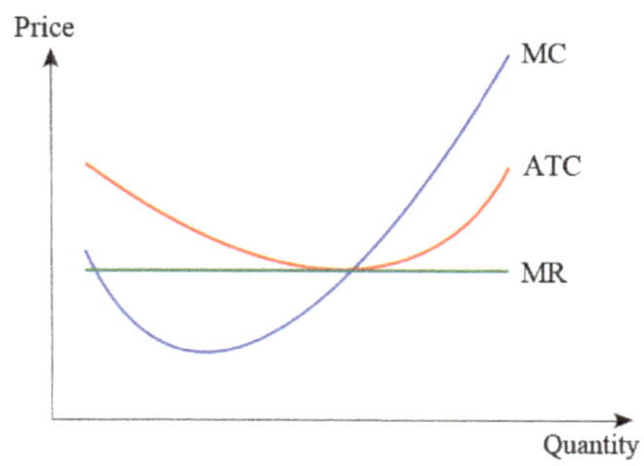

Cost curves in perfect competition compared to marginal revenue

Cost curves can be combined to provide information about firms. In this diagram for example, firms are assumed to be in a perfectly competitive market. In a perfectly competitive market the price that firms are faced with would be the price at which the marginal cost curve cuts the average cost curve.

Cost Curves and Production Functions

Assuming that factor prices are constant, the production function determines all cost functions. The variable cost curve is the inverted short-run production function or total product curve and its behavior and properties are determined by the production function. Because the production function determines the variable cost function it necessarily determines the shape and properties of marginal cost curve and the average cost curves.

If the firm is a perfect competitor in all input markets, and thus the per-unit prices of all its inputs are unaffected by how much of the inputs the firm purchases, then it can be shown that at a particular level of output, the firm has economies of scale (i.e., is operating in a downward sloping region of the long-run average cost curve) if and only if it has increasing returns to scale. Likewise, it has diseconomies of scale (is operating in an upward sloping region of the long-run average cost curve) if and only if it has decreasing returns to scale, and has neither economies nor diseconomies of scale if it has constant returns to scale. In this case, with perfect competition in the output market the long-run market equilibrium will involve all firms operating at the minimum point of their long-run average cost curves (i.e., at the borderline between economies and diseconomies of scale).

If, however, the firm is not a perfect competitor in the input markets, then the above conclusions are modified. For example, if there are increasing returns to scale in some range of output levels, but the firm is so big in one or more input markets that increasing its purchases of an input drives up the input's per-unit cost, then the firm could have diseconomies of scale in that range of output levels. Conversely, if the firm is able to get bulk discounts of an input, then it could have economies of scale in some range of output levels even if it has decreasing returns in production in that output range.

Relationship between Different Curves

- Total Cost = Fixed Costs (FC) + Variable Costs (VC)
- Marginal Cost (MC) = dC/dQ; MC equals the slope of the total cost function and of the variable cost function
- Average Total Cost (ATC) = Total Cost/Q
- Average Fixed Cost (AFC) = FC/Q
- Average Variable Cost (AVC) = VC/Q.
- ATC = AFC + AVC
- The MC curve is related to the shape of the ATC and AVC curves:
    - At a level of Q at which the MC curve is above the average total cost or average variable cost curve, the latter curve is rising.
    - If MC is below average total cost or average variable cost, then the latter curve is falling.
    - If MC equals average total cost, then average total cost is at its minimum value.
    - If MC equals average variable cost, then average variable cost is at its minimum value.

Relationship between Short Run and Long Run Cost Curves

Basic: For each quantity of output there is one cost minimizing level of capital and a unique short run average cost curve associated with producing the given quantity.

- Each STC curve can be tangent to the LRTC curve at only one point. The STC curve cannot cross (intersect) the LRTC curve. The STC curve can lie wholly "above" the LRTC curve with no tangency point.
- One STC curve is tangent to LRTC at the long-run cost minimizing level of production. At the point of tangency LRTC = STC. At all other levels of production STC will exceed LRTC.
- Average cost functions are the total cost function divided by the level of output. Therefore, the SATC curveis also tangent to the LRATC curve at the cost-minimizing level of output. At the point of tangency LRATC = SATC. At all other levels of production SATC > LRATC To the left of the point of tangency the firm is using too much capital and fixed costs are too high. To the right of the point of tangency the firm is using too little capital and diminishing returns to labor are causing costs to increase.
- The slope of the total cost curves equals marginal cost. Therefore, when STC is tangent to LTC, SMC = LRMC.
- At the long run cost minimizing level of output LRTC = STC; LRATC = SATC and LRMC = SMC.
- The long run cost minimizing level of output may be different from minimum SATC,.
- With fixed unit costs of inputs, if the production function has constant returns to scale, then at the minimal level of the SATC curve we have SATC = LRATC = SMC = LRMC.
- With fixed unit costs of inputs, if the production function has increasing returns to scale, the minimum of the SATC curve is to the right of the point of tangency between the LRAC and the SATC curves. Where LRTC = STC, LRATC = SATC and LRMC = SMC.
- With fixed unit costs of inputs and decreasing returns the minimum of the SATC curve is to the left of the point of tangency between LRAC and SATC. Where LRTC = STC, LRATC = SATC and LRMC = SMC.
- With fixed unit input costs, a firm that is experiencing increasing (decreasing) returns to scale and is producing at its minimum SAC can always reduce average cost in the long run by expanding (reducing) the use of the fixed input.
- LRATC will always equal to or be less than SATC.
- If production process is exhibiting constant returns to scale then minimum SRAC equals minimum long run average cost. The LRAC and SRAC intersect at their common minimum values. Thus under constant returns to scale SRMC = LRMC = LRAC = SRAC .
- If the production process is experiencing decreasing or increasing, minimum short run average cost does not equal minimum long run average cost. If increasing returns to scale exist long run minimum will occur at a lower level of output than SRAC. This is because there are economies of scale that have not been exploited so in the long run a firm could always produce a quantity at a price lower than minimum short run average cost simply by using a larger plant.

- With decreasing returns, minimum SRAC occurs at a lower production level than minimum LRAC because a firm could reduce average costs by simply decreasing the size or its operations.
- The minimum of a SRAC occurs when the slope is zero. Thus the points of tangency between the U-shaped LRAC curve and the minimum of the SRAC curve would coincide only with that portion of the LRAC curve exhibiting constant economies of scale. For increasing returns to scale the point of tangency between the LRAC and the SRAC would have to occur at a level of output below level associated with the minimum of the SRAC curve.

These statements assume that the firm is using the optimal level of capital for the quantity produced. If not, then the SRAC curve would lie "wholly above" the LRAC and would not be tangent at any point.

U-shaped curves

Both the SRAC and LRAC curves are typically expressed as U-shaped. However, the shapes of the curves are not due to the same factors. For the short run curve the initial downward slope is largely due to declining average fixed costs. Increasing returns to the variable input at low levels of production also play a role, while the upward slope is due to diminishing marginal returns to the variable input. With the long run curve the shape by definition reflects economies and diseconomies of scale. At low levels of production long run production functions generally exhibit increasing returns to scale, which, for firms that are perfect competitors in input markets, means that the long run average cost is falling; the upward slope of the long run average cost function at higher levels of output is due to decreasing returns to scale at those output levels.

Cost Curves in reality

Evidence shows that cost curves are not typically U-shaped. In a survey by Wilford J. Eiteman and Glenn E. Guthrie in 1952 managers of 334 companies were shown a number of different cost curves, and asked to specify which one best represented the company's cost curve. 95% of managers responding to the survey reported cost curves with constant or falling costs.

Alan Blinder, former vice president of the American Economics Association, conducted the same type of survey in 1998, which involved 200 US firms in a sample that should be representative of the US economy at large. He found that about 40% of firms reported falling variable or marginal cost, and 48.4% reported constant marginal/variable cost.

Social Welfare and Demand Curves

Social Welfare

- Welfare economics is the study of the determinates of well- being, or welfare, in society.

- o Determinants of social efficiency, or size of the economic —pie.‖
- o Redistribution.

Demand Curves

- *Demand curve* is the relationship between the price of a good and the quantity demanded.
- Demand curve is derived from utility maximization problem.

Utility maximization gives various (P_M, Q_M) combinations that can be mapped into price/quantity space.

Figures: Illustrate this

Consider the product space of two goods C and M.

Utility maximization at various prices provide optimal combinations of (P_M, Q_M) and (P^C, Q^C)

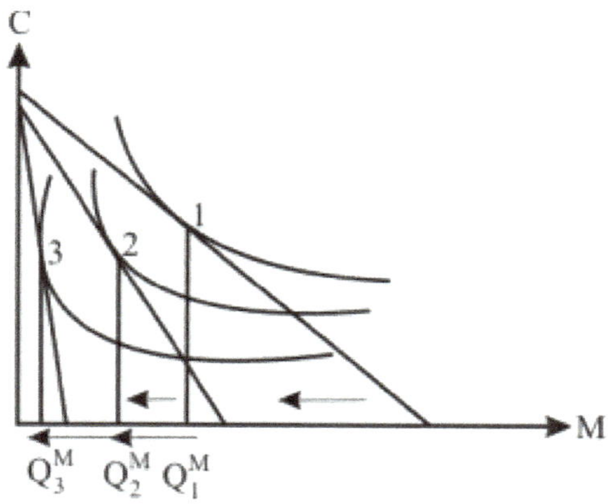

Deriving demand curves

$$P_M \uparrow (\text{or} P_c \downarrow)$$

$$= \frac{P_M}{P_C} \uparrow$$

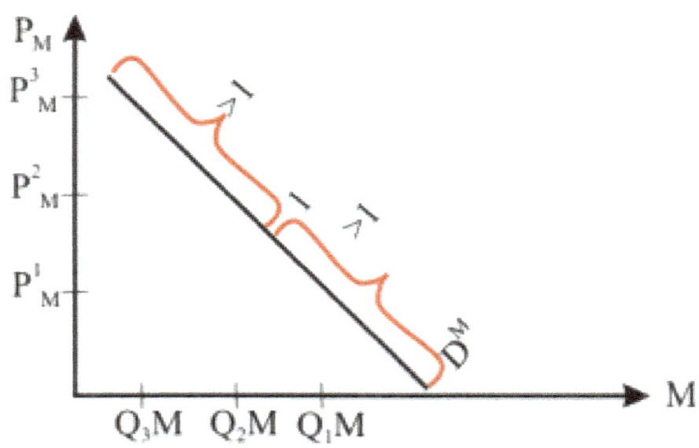

Elasticity of Demand

$$\varepsilon_D = \frac{\Delta Q_D / Q_D}{\Delta P / P}$$

- Percent change in quantity demanded for a percent change in price.
- Does Elasticity vary along the demand curve?
  - Depends, normally yes.

Perfectly Inelastic

For a vertical demand curve elasticity of demand is zero—quantity does not change as price goes up or down.

Perfectly Elastic

For a horizontal demand curve elasticity of demand is negative infinity—quantity changes infinitely for even a small change in price.

$\mathcal{E}$ =Price of demand Elasticity $= \frac{dQ}{dP} \cdot \frac{P}{Q}$

$$\varepsilon \uparrow \Rightarrow \frac{dQ}{dP} \uparrow \Rightarrow \frac{dP}{dQ} \downarrow \Rightarrow \text{flatter demand curve.}$$

$$\varepsilon \downarrow \Rightarrow \frac{dQ}{dP} \downarrow \Rightarrow \frac{dP}{dQ} \uparrow \text{steeper demand curve.}$$

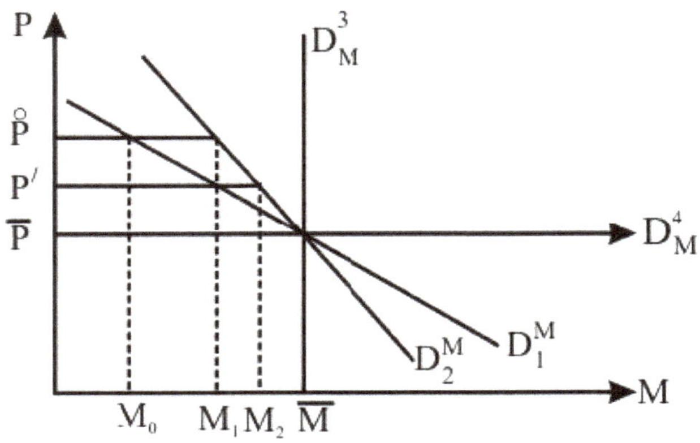

M_0M_1: $\uparrow$ in M for price of M falling from P° to P' on D_1^M

M_1M_2: $\uparrow$ in M for price of M falling form P° to P' on D_2^M

$M_0 - M_1 > M_1 - M_2 = D_1^M$ is more elastic than D_2^M

Vertical D_3^M $\rightarrow$ perfectly in elastic demand curve (no change in Q, for change in P)

$$\varepsilon \rightarrow 0$$

Horizontal D_{M^4} $\rightarrow$ perfectly elastic demand curve, choose any Q at $\bar{P} \varepsilon \rightarrow 0$

Understanding Production and Cost Function

Now consider the production side for the good M

- Production function, where $Q_M = f(L_M, K_M)$, L = labor used in the production of M , K = Capital used in the production of M
- Let the specific functional form be

  $Q_M = \sqrt{L_M K_M}$
- Marginal Productivity $\dfrac{\partial Q_M}{\partial L_M} = \dfrac{1}{2}\sqrt{\dfrac{K_M}{L_M}} > 0$
- Diminishing Marginal Productivity $\dfrac{\partial^2 Q_M}{\partial L_M} = -\dfrac{1}{4}\sqrt{\dfrac{K_M}{L_M^3}} < 0$
- Total costs of production TC =rk +wL, where r = rental on capital

  w = wage rate for labor.
- Marginal Cost: Diminishing Marginal Productivity implies rising Marginal Cost.

  Since each additional unit of Q means calling forth less & less productive labor at the same wage, cost of product ↑ at the margin.

Profit Maximization

Firms producing M will maximize profits to determine the optimal supply of M for a given price level P_M.

- Supply curve: Derived from profit maximization problem.
- Profit maximization ⇒ Marginal Revenue (MR)=Marginal Cost (MC)
  - At any price, quantity supplied is such that MC = Price
  - MC curve implies supply curve
  - A perfect competitive market implies P = MR = MC = AR

Equilibrium: Aggregate Demand

- Aggregate Demand: horizontal sum of individual demand curves.

- Consumer surplus is the benefit that consumers derive from a good, beyond what they paid for it.
- Each point on the demand curve represents —willingness-to-pay‖ for that quantity. The difference between what they actually pay and their willingness to pay is the surplus enjoyed. Consumer surplus is determined by market price and the elasticity of demand.
- With more inelastic demand, demand curve is more vertical: so surplus is higher. For instance basic food in poor countries. Inelasticity arises from lack of good substitutes; hence there is enormous surplus from consuming that particular good.

Equilibrium: Aggregate Supply

- Aggregate Supply: horizontal sum of individual supply curves.
- Producer surplus is the benefit derived by producers from the sale of a unit above and beyond their cost of producing it.
- Each point on the supply curve represents the marginal cost of producing it. Similar to consumer surplus, producer surplus is determined by market price and the elasticity of supply.
- With more inelastic supply curve, producer surplus is higher.
- Social Efficiency or total social surplus is the sum of the consumer's and producer's surplus, potential size of the pie.

Competitive Equilibrium

- Competitive equilibrium represents the point at which both consumers and suppliers are satisfied with the price/quantity combination.
- Social efficiency represents the net gain from trade between consumers and producers. Total surplus received by consumers and producers in the market sums up to social efficiency

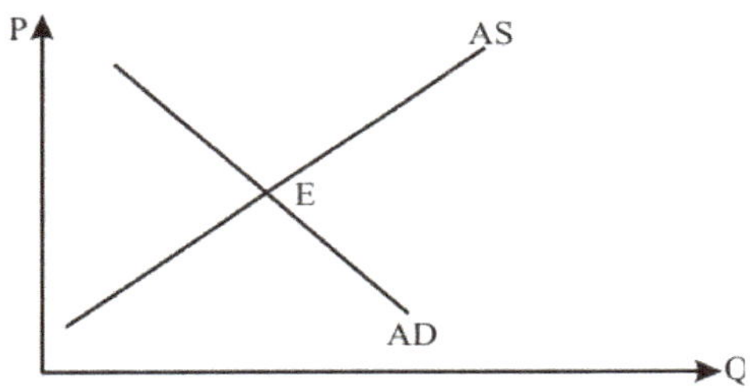

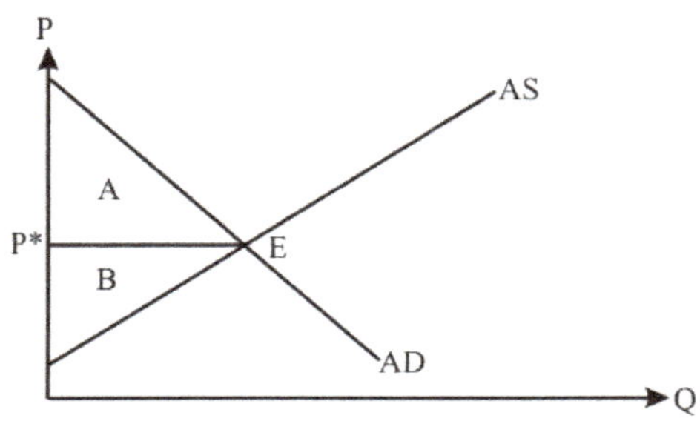

A= Consumer surplus. B= Producer surplus.

More inelastic Aggregate demand, AD implies more consumer surplus, CS.

More inelastic Aggregate supply implies Producer Surplus.

Equilibrium

- First Fundamental Theorem of Welfare Economics: competitive equilibrium, Q^*,maximizes social efficiency.
- Any quantity other than Q^* reduces social efficiency, or the size of the "economic pie."
- Suppose, quantity is regulated at Q_R

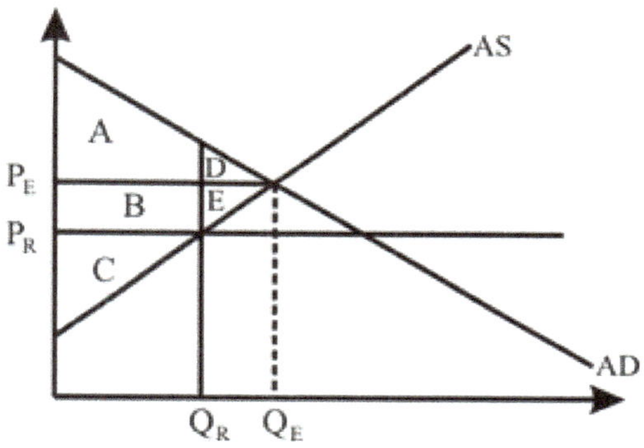

At P_R

CS = A + B

PS = C

At P_E

CS = A + D
PS = C + B + E } MB > MC =
Total surples

⇒ loss of surplus = D + E
Dead weight loss (MB > MC but still no production

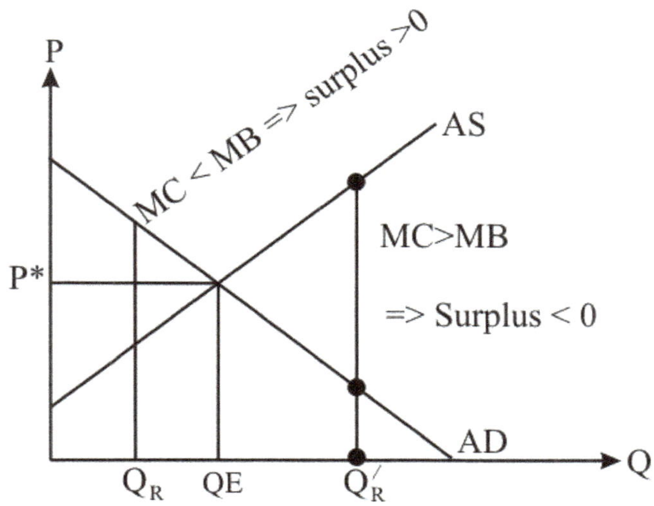

- A policy like price or quantity controls creates *deadweight loss*, the reduction in social efficiency by restricting price quantity below the competitive equilibrium.

The Role of Equity

- *Social welfare* is determined by both efficiency and equity.
- The *Second Fundamental Theorem of Welfare Economics* states that society can attain any efficient outcome by a suitable redistribution of resources and free trade.
- In reality, society often faces an equity-efficiency tradeoff.
- Resolving this tradeoff is harder than devising efficiency maximizing policies. It raises the tricky issue of making interpersonal comparisons- who should have more & who should have less.
- *Social Welfare Function*: Maps individual utilities into an overall social utility function.
- This function incorporates the equity-efficiency tradeoff in to decision making
- Loss of efficiency.
    - All worse off.
    - Redistribution might compensatefor the loss of efficiency.
- The *utilitarian* social welfare function is: $SWF = \Sigma_i U_i$.
- The utilities of all individuals are given equal weight.
- Utilitarian SWF is defined in terms of utility, not rupees.
    - Society not indifferent between Re1 to rich and poor; rather indifferent between 1 utility to rich & 1 utility to poor.

Welfare Maximization

- Utilitarian SWF is maximized when

$$MU_1 = MU_2 = \ldots = MU_i$$

- Thus, society should redistribute from rich to poor if the marginal utility of the next dollar is higher to the poor person than to the rich person.

The Role of Equity

- The *Rawlsian* social welfare function is:

$$SWF = \min\left(U_1, U_2, \ldots, U_N\right)$$

- Societal welfare is maximized by maximizing the well-being of the worst-off person in society.
- Generally suggests more redistribution than the Utilitarian SWF.

Implications of Cutting Welfare Benefit

- Efficiency and equity considerations in introducing or cutting TANF benefits.
- In a typical labor supply/labor demand framework, these changes shift the labor supply curve for the welfare recipients.

Figure: Illustrates this.

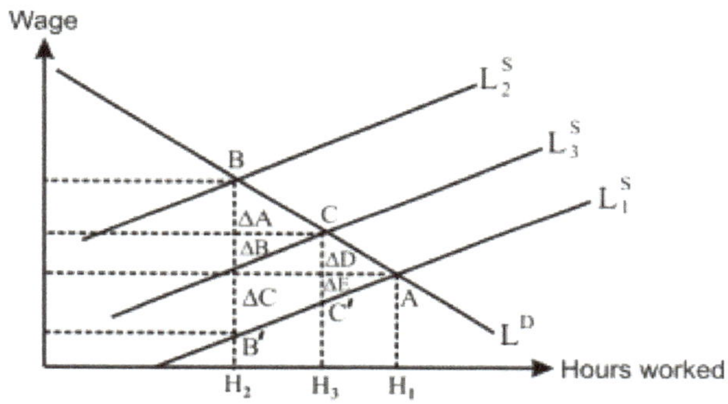

Benefits or costs to society of changing TANF

- Apply tools of welfare analysis to determine the welfare implications of cutting TANF benefits.
- Lab supply is obtained from utility maximization. Labor demand is obtained from profit maximization by firms $\rightarrow$ opposite of the regular goods market.
- Market for labor by low income people.
- A $\rightarrow$ equilibrium with no government intervention; Max social efficiency
- TANF Benefit $\uparrow \Rightarrow L^S \downarrow \Rightarrow$ new equilibrium at B $\Rightarrow$ Deadweight loss = ABB' $\Rightarrow$ Efficiency $\downarrow$.
- TANF Benefit $\downarrow \Rightarrow L^S \uparrow \Rightarrow$ new equilibrium at B $\Rightarrow$ Deadweight loss = ACC'
- At each point between B & A, MP of L (Demand) > MC of L (Supply)

$\Rightarrow$ Must produce more & employ more labor.

$\Rightarrow$ Deadweight Loss = ABB'.

- If we know the slopes of Labor Supply & Labor Demand then we can compute the magnitude of the Deadweight Loss. Slopes can be estimated using data $\rightarrow$ determined by preferences & production function.

- If efficiency is max at TANF benefit = 0, then why TANF?
- The competitive equilibrium might be the social efficiency maximizing point but may not be social - welfare maxing point.
- Cutting TANF benefits would worsen out comes for the worst off in the society.

  → May have dramatic equity costs that offset efficiency gains.

- What generally happens when TANF ↓
  - Total income in the economy will ↑ ⇒ efficiency ↑
  - But the total utility is likely ↓
  - This is because we are adding only a small fraction of income to high income individuals and taking away a large fraction of income from low income individuals.

So the utility of the high income individual might ↑ only a little but utility of low income might ↓ by a large margin.

- Different policies involve different deadweight loss triangles, but also different levels of redistribution for the poor.
- SWF helps determine the right policy for society.

References

- Grechuk, B., Zabarankin, M. (2016). Inverse portfolio problem with coherent risk measures, European Journal of Operational Research 249(2), 740-750
- Feldman, Allan M. (2008), "Welfare Economics", The New Palgrave: A Dictionary of Economics (online ed.), 4, pp. 889–95, retrieved 9 June 2014
- Ingersoll, Jonathan E., Jr. (1987). Theory of Financial Decision Making. Totowa: Rowman and Littlefield. p. 21. ISBN 0-8476-7359-6
- Sexton, Robert L., Philip E. Graves, and Dwight R. Lee, 1993. "The Short- and Long-Run Marginal Cost Curve: A Pedagogical Note", Journal of Economic Education, 24(1), p. 34. [Pp. 34-37 (press +)]
- Bernheim, B. Douglas (December 2008), Behavioral Welfare Economics, NBER, doi:10.3386/w14622, retrieved 8 June 2014
- Berger, J. O. (1985). "Utility and Loss". Statistical Decision Theory and Bayesian Analysis (2nd ed.). Berlin: Springer-Verlag. ISBN 3-540-96098-8
- Gelles, Gregory M., and Mitchell, Douglas W., "Returns to scale and economies of scale: Further observations," Journal of Economic Education 27, Summer 1996, 259-261
- Deardorff, Alan V. (2014), "Welfare economics", Deardorffs' Glossary of International Economics, retrieved 9 June 2014
- Varian, Hal R. (2006). Intermediate Microeconomics: A modern approach. W.W. Norton & Co. p. 754. ISBN 0-393-92702-4
- Bordley, R.; Pollock, S. (2009). "A Decision-Analytic Approach to Reliability-Based Design Optimization". Operations Research. 57 (5): 1262–1270. doi:10.1287/opre.1080.0661

3

Externality: An Integrated Study

The cost or benefit an individual incurs whose causality is indirectly related to the individual is known as externality. It can be divided into negative externality or positive externality. The major components of externality are discussed in this chapter.

Externality

In economics, an externality is the cost or benefit that affects a party who did not choose to incur that cost or benefit. Economists often urge governments to adopt policies that "internalize" an externality, so that costs and benefits will affect mainly parties who choose to incur them.

Air pollution from motor vehicles is an example of a negative externality. The costs of the air pollution for the rest of society is not compensated for by either the producers or users of motorized transport.

For example, manufacturing activities that cause air pollution impose health and clean-up costs on the whole society, whereas the neighbors of an individual who chooses to fire-proof his home may benefit from a reduced risk of a fire spreading to their own houses. If external costs exist, such as pollution, the producer may choose to produce more of the product than would be produced if the producer were required to pay all associated environmental costs. Because responsibility or consequence for self-directed action lies partly outside the self, an element of externalization is involved. If there are external benefits, such as in public safety, less of the good may be produced than would be the case if the producer were to receive payment for the external benefits to others. For the purpose of these statements, overall cost and benefit to society is defined as the sum of the imputed monetary value of benefits and costs to all parties involved. Thus, unregulated markets in goods or services with significant externalities generate prices that do not reflect the full social cost or benefit of their transactions; such markets are therefore inefficient.

History of the Concept

Two British economists are credited with having initiated the formal study of externalities, or "spillover effects": Henry Sidgwick (1838-1900) is credited with first articulating, and Arthur C. Pigou (1877-1959) is credited with formalizing the concept of externalities.

Definition

Suppose that there are K different possible allocations and N different agents, where $K, N < \infty$ and $N \geq 2$. Suppose that each agent has a type $\theta_i \sim F_i[0,1]$ and that each agent gets payoff $v_i(\theta_i, k) + t_i$, where t_i is the transfer paid by the i-th agent. A map $f = (\kappa, t_1, \ldots, t_N)$ is a *social choice function* if

$$\sum_{i=1}^{N} t_i(\theta) \leq 0$$

for all $\theta \in [0,1]^N$. An allocation $\kappa : [0,1]^N \to K$ is *ex-post efficient* if

$$\sum_{i=1}^{N} v_i(\theta_i, \kappa(\theta)) \geq \sum_{i=1}^{N} v_i(\theta_i, k)$$

for all $\theta = (\theta_1, \ldots, \theta_N) \in [0,1]^N$ and all $k \in K$..

Let κ^* denote an ex-post efficient allocation and let $\widetilde{\kappa_i}$ denote an ex-post efficient allocation without agent i. Then the *externality* imposed by agent i on the other agents is

$$\sum_{j \neq i} v_j(\theta_j, \widetilde{\kappa_i}(\theta_{-i})) - \sum_{j \neq i} v_j(\theta_j, \kappa^*(\theta)),$$

where θ_{-i} is the type vector θ without its i-th component. Intuitively, the first term is the hypothetical total payoff for all agents $j \neq i$ given that agent i does not exist, and the second (subtracted) term is the actual total payoff for all agents $j \neq i$ given that agent i does exist.

Implications

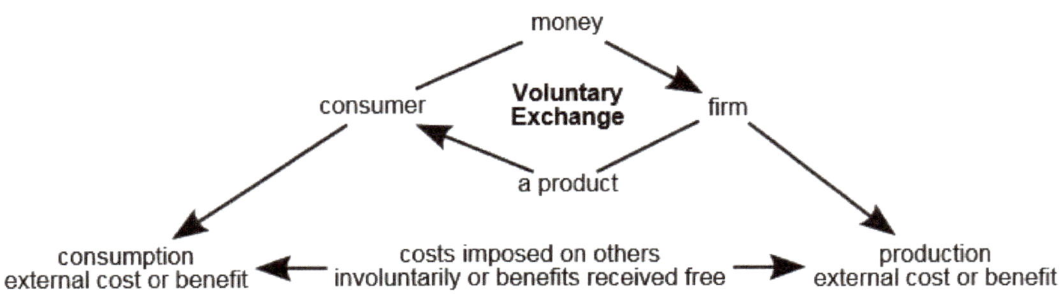

External costs and benefits

Voluntary exchange is considered mutually beneficial to both parties involved, because buyers or sellers would not trade if either thought it detrimental to themselves. However, a transaction can cause additional effects on third parties. From the perspective of those affected, these effects may be negative (pollution from a factory), or positive (honey bees kept for honey that also pollinate neighboring crops). Neoclassical welfare economics asserts that, under plausible conditions, the existence of externalities will result in outcomes that are not socially optimal. Those who suffer from external costs do so involuntarily, whereas those who enjoy external benefits do so at no cost.

A voluntary exchange may reduce societal welfare if external costs exist. The person who is affected by the negative externalities in the case of air pollution will see it as lowered utility: either subjective displeasure or potentially explicit costs, such as higher medical expenses. The externality may even be seen as a trespass on their lungs, violating their property rights. Thus, an external cost may pose an ethical or political problem. Alternatively, it might be seen as a case of poorly defined property rights, as with, for example, pollution of bodies of water that may belong to no one (either figuratively, in the case of publicly owned, or literally, in some countries and/or legal traditions).

On the other hand, a positive externality would increase the utility of third parties at no cost to them. Since collective societal welfare is improved, but the providers have no way of monetizing the benefit, less of the good will be produced than would be optimal for society as a whole. Goods with positive externalities include education (believed to increase societal productivity and well-being; but controversial, as these benefits are generally internalized, e.g., in the form of higher wages), public health initiatives (which may reduce the health risks and costs for third parties for such things as transmittable diseases) and law enforcement. Positive externalities are often associated with the free rider problem. For example, individuals who are vaccinated reduce the risk of contracting the relevant disease for all others around them, and at high levels of vaccination, society may receive large health and welfare benefits; but any one individual can refuse vaccination, still avoiding the disease by "free riding" on the costs borne by others.

There are a number of potential means of improving overall social utility when externalities are involved. The market-driven approach to correcting externalities is to "*internalize*" third party costs and benefits, for example, by requiring a polluter to repair any damage caused. But, in many cases internalizing costs or benefits is not feasible, especially if the true monetary values cannot be determined.

Laissez-faire economists such as Friedrich Hayek and Milton Friedman sometimes refer to externalities as "neighborhood effects" or "spillovers", although externalities are not necessarily minor or localized. Similarly, Ludwig von Mises argues that externalities arise from lack of "clear personal property definition."

Examples

A negative externality (also called "external cost" or "external diseconomy") is an economic activity that imposes a negative effect on an unrelated third party. It can arise either during the production or the consumption of a good or service. Pollution is termed an externality because it imposes costs on people who are "external" to the producer and consumer of the polluting product. Barry Commoner commented on the costs of externalities:

Clearly, we have compiled a record of serious failures in recent technological encounters with the environment. In each case, the new technology was brought into use before the ultimate hazards were known. We have been quick to reap the benefits and slow to comprehend the costs.

Light pollution is an example of an externality because the consumption of street lighting has an effect on bystanders that is not compensated for by the consumers of the lighting.

Many negative externalities are related to the environmental consequences of production and use. The article on environmental economics also addresses externalities and how they may be addressed in the context of environmental issues.

Examples for negative production externalities include:

- Air pollution from burning fossil fuels. This activity causes damages to crops, (historic) buildings and public health.
- Anthropogenic climate change as a consequence of greenhouse gas emissions from burning oil, gas, and coal. The *Stern Review on the Economics Of Climate Change* says "Climate change presents a unique challenge for economics: it is the greatest example of market failure we have ever seen."
- Water pollution by industries that adds effluent, which harms plants, animals, and humans.
- Noise pollution during the production process, which may be mentally and psychologically disruptive.
- Systemic risk: the risks to the overall economy arising from the risks that the banking system takes. A condition of moral hazard can occur in the absence of well-designed banking regulation, or in the presence of badly designed regulation.
- Negative effects of Industrial farm animal production, including "the increase in the pool of antibiotic-resistant bacteria because of the overuse of antibiotics; air quality problems; the contamination of rivers, streams, and coastal waters with concentrated animal waste; animal welfare problems, mainly as a result of the extremely close quarters in which the animals are housed."
- The depletion of the stock of fish in the ocean due to overfishing. This is an example of a common property resource, which is vulnerable to the *Tragedy of the commons* in the absence of appropriate environmental governance.

- In the United States, the cost of storing nuclear waste from nuclear plants for more than 1,000 years (over 100,000 for some types of nuclear waste) is, in principle, included in the cost of the electricity the plant produces in the form of a fee paid to the government and held in the nuclear waste superfund, although much of that fund was spent on Yucca Mountain without producing a solution. Conversely, the costs of managing the long term risks of disposal of chemicals, which may remain hazardous on similar time scales, is not commonly internalized in prices. The USEPA regulates chemicals for periods ranging from 100 years to a maximum of 10,000 years.

Examples of negative consumption externalities include:

- Noise pollution Sleep deprivation due to a neighbour listening to loud music late at night.
- Antibiotic resistance, caused by increased usage of antibiotics. Individuals do not consider this efficacy cost when making usage decisions. Government policies proposed to preserve future antibiotic effectiveness include educational campaigns, regulation, Pigouvian taxes, and patents.
- Passive smokingShared costs of declining health and vitality caused by smoking and/or alcohol abuse. Here, the "cost" is that of providing minimum social welfare. Economists more frequently attribute this problem to the category of moral hazards, the prospect that parties insulated from risk may behave differently from the way they would if they were fully exposed to the risk. For example, individuals with insurance against automobile theft may be less vigilant about locking their cars, because the negative consequences of automobile theft are (partially) borne by the insurance company.
- Traffic Congestion When more people use public roads, road users experience [(congestion costs)] such as more waiting in traffic and longer trip times. Increased road users also increase the likelihood of road accidents.
- Price Increases Consumption by one consumer of goods in addition to their existing supply causes prices to rise and therefore makes other consumers worse off, perhaps by preventing, reducing or delaying their consumption. These effects are sometimes called "pecuniary externalities" and are distinguished from "real externalities" or "technological externalities". Pecuniary externalities appear to be externalities, but occur within the market mechanism and are not considered to be a source of market failure or inefficiency, although they may still result in substantial harm to others.

Positive

A positive externality (also called "external benefit" or "external economy" or "beneficial externality") is the positive effect an activity imposes on an unrelated third party. Similar to a negative externality, it can arise either on the production side, or on the consumption side.

Examples of positive production externalities include:

- A beekeeper who keeps the bees for their honey. A side effect or externality associated with such activity is the pollination of surrounding crops by the bees. The value generated by the pollination may be more important than the value of the harvested honey.

- The construction and operation of an airport. This will benefit local businesses, because of the increased accessibility.
- An industrial company providing first aid classes for employees to increase on the job safety. This may also save lives outside the factory.
- A foreign firm that demonstrates up-to-date technologies to local firms and improves their productivity.

Examples of positive consumption externalities include:

- An individual who maintains an attractive house may confer benefits to neighbors in the form of increased market values for their properties.
- An individual receiving a vaccination for a communicable disease not only decreases the likelihood of the individual's own infection, but also decreases the likelihood of others becoming infected through contact with the individual.
- Driving an electric vehicle charged by electricity from a renewable source, reducing greenhouse gas emissions and improving local air quality and public health. Although this may increase emissions from power plants burning fossil fuels, this is usually more than offset by reduced vehicle emissions, especially where hydroelectric, nuclear and renewable sources are prevalent.
- Increased education of individuals, as this can lead to broader society benefits in the form of greater economic productivity, a lower unemployment rate, greater household mobility and higher rates of political participation.
- An individual buying a product that is interconnected in a network (e.g., a smartphone). This will increase the usefulness of such phones to other people who have a video cellphone. When each new user of a product increases the value of the same product owned by others, the phenomenon is called a network externality or a network effect. Network externalities often have "tipping points" where, suddenly, the product reaches general acceptance and near-universal usage.
- In an area that does not have a public fire department, homeowners who purchase private fire protection services provide a positive externality to neighboring properties, which are less at risk of the protected neighbor's fire spreading to their (unprotected) house.

The existence or management of externalities may give rise to political or legal conflicts.

Collective solutions or public policies are sometimes implemented to regulate activities with positive or negative externalities.

Positional

A position externality "occurs when new purchases alter the relevant context within which an existing positional good is evaluated." Robert H. Frank gives the following example:

> if some job candidates begin wearing expensive custom-tailored suits, a side effect of their action is that other candidates become less likely to make favorable impressions on

interviewers. From any individual job seeker's point of view, the best response might be to match the higher expenditures of others, lest her chance s of landing the job fall. But this outcome may be inefficient, since when all spend more, each candidate's probability of success remains unchanged. All may agree that some form of collective restraint on expenditure would be useful."

Frank notes that treating positional externalities like other externalities might lead to "intrusive economic and social regulation." He argues, however, that less intrusive and more efficient means of "limiting the costs of expenditure cascades"—i.e., the hypothesized increase in spending of middle-income families beyond their means "because of indirect effects associated with increased spending by top earners"—exist; one such method is the personal income tax.

Inframarginal

Inframarginal externalities are externalities in which there is no benefit or loss to the marginal consumer. In other words, people neither gain nor lose anything at the margin, but benefits and costs do exist for those consumers within the given inframarginal range.

Technological

Technological externalities directly affect a firm's production and therefore, indirectly influence an individual's consumption; and the overall impact of society.

Supply and Demand Diagram

The usual economic analysis of externalities can be illustrated using a standard supply and demand diagram if the externality can be valued in terms of money. An extra supply or demand curve is added, as in the diagrams below. One of the curves is the *private cost* that consumers pay as individuals for additional quantities of the good, which in competitive markets, is the marginal private cost. The other curve is the *true* cost that society as a whole pays for production and consumption of increased production the good, or the marginal social cost. Similarly there might be two curves for the demand or benefit of the good. The social demand curve would reflect the benefit to society as a whole, while the normal demand curve reflects the benefit to consumers as individuals and is reflected as effective demand in the market.

What curve is added depends on the type of externality that is described, but not whether it is positive or negative. Whenever an externality arises on the production side, there will be two supply curves (private and social cost). However, if the externality arises on the consumption side, there will be two demand curves instead (private and social benefit). This distinction is essential when it comes to resolving inefficiencies that are caused by externalities.

External Costs

The graph shows the effects of a negative externality. For example, the steel industry is assumed to be selling in a competitive market – before pollution-control laws were imposed and enforced (e.g. under laissez-faire). The marginal private cost is less than the marginal social or public cost by the amount of the external cost, i.e., the cost of air pollution and water pollution. This is represented by the vertical distance between the two supply curves. It is assumed that there are no external benefits, so that social benefit *equals* individual benefit.

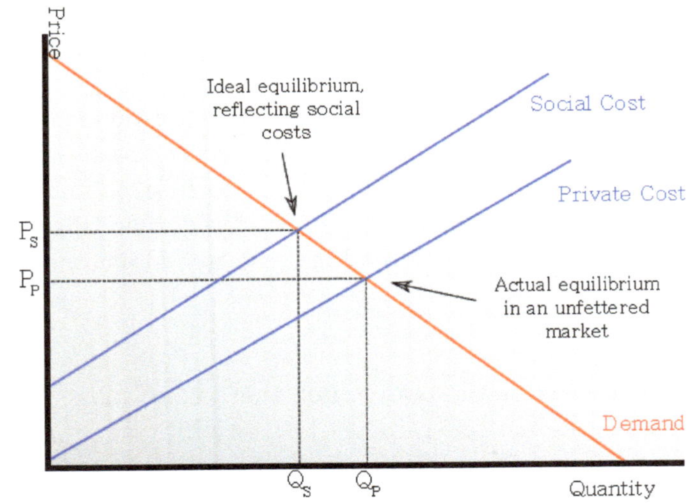

Demand curve with external costs; if social costs are not accounted for price is too low to cover all costs and hence quantity produced is unnecessarily high (because the producers of the good and their customers are essentially underpaying the total, real factors of production.)

If the consumers only take into account their own private cost, they will end up at price P_p and quantity Q_p, instead of the more efficient price P_s and quantity Q_s. These latter reflect the idea that the marginal social benefit should equal the marginal social cost, that is that production should be increased *only* as long as the marginal social benefit exceeds the marginal social cost. The result is that a free market is *inefficient* since at the quantity Q_p, the social benefit is less than the social cost, so society as a whole would be better off if the goods between Q_p and Q_s had not been produced. The problem is that people are buying and consuming *too much* steel.

This discussion implies that negative externalities (such as pollution) are *more than* merely an ethical problem. The problem is one of the disjuncture between marginal private and social costs that is not solved by the free market. It is a problem of societal communication and coordination to balance costs and benefits. This also implies that pollution is not something solved by competitive markets. Some *collective* solution is needed, such as a court system to allow parties affected by the pollution to be compensated, government intervention banning or discouraging pollution, or economic incentives such as green taxes.

External Benefits

The graph shows the effects of a positive or beneficial externality. For example, the industry supplying smallpox vaccinations is assumed to be selling in a competitive market. The marginal private benefit of getting the vaccination is less than the marginal social or public benefit by the amount of the external benefit (for example, society as a whole is increasingly protected from smallpox by each vaccination, including those who refuse to participate). This marginal external benefit of getting a smallpox shot is represented by the vertical distance between the two demand curves. Assume there are no external costs, so that social cost *equals* individual cost.

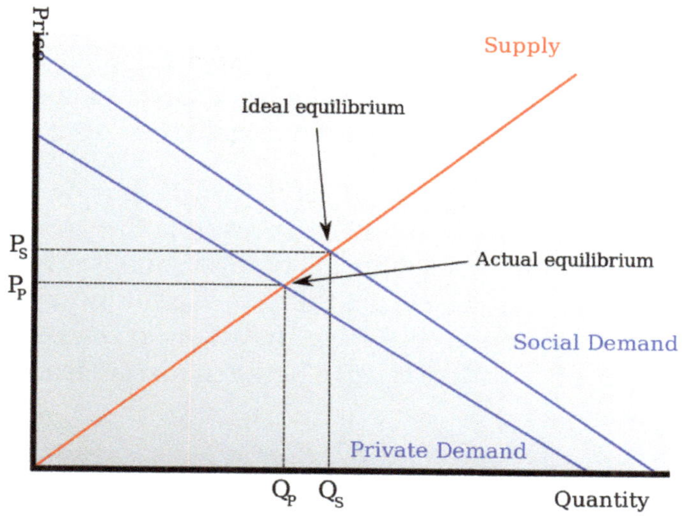

Supply curve with external benefits; when the market does not account for additional social benefits of a good both the price for the good and the quantity produced are lower than the market could bear.

If consumers only take into account their own private benefits from getting vaccinations, the market will end up at price P_p and quantity Q_p as before, instead of the more efficient price P_s and quantity Q_s. These latter again reflect the idea that the marginal social benefit should equal the marginal social cost, i.e., that production should be increased as long as the marginal social benefit exceeds the marginal social cost. The result in an unfettered market is *inefficient* since at the quantity Q_p, the social benefit is greater than the societal cost, so society as a whole would be better off if more goods had been produced. The problem is that people are buying *too few* vaccinations.

The issue of external benefits is related to that of public goods, which are goods where it is difficult if not impossible to exclude people from benefits. The production of a public good has beneficial externalities for all, or almost all, of the public. As with external costs, there is a problem here of societal communication and coordination to balance benefits and costs. This also implies that vaccination is not something solved by competitive markets. The government may have to step in with a collective solution, such as subsidizing or legally requiring vaccine use. If the government does this, the good is called a merit good. Examples include policies to accelerate the introducing of Electric vehicles or promote Bicycling which benefit Public health.

Possible Solutions

There are several general types of solutions to the problem of externalities:

- Pigovian taxes or subsidies intended to redress economic injustices or imbalances.
- Regulation to limit activity that might cause negative externalities
- Government provision of services with positive externalities
- Lawsuits to compensate affected parties for negative externalities

- Mediation or negotiation between those affected by externalities and those causing them
- Ecological economics, if more widely known and applied, would shift the economic paradigm from the current reductionist, strictly financial view to something more cognizant of externalities, and thus more extensible and sustainable over time.

A Pigovian tax (also called Pigouvian tax, after economist Arthur C. Pigou) is a tax imposed that is equal in value to the negative externality. The result is that the market outcome would be reduced to the efficient amount. A side effect is that revenue is raised for the government, reducing the amount of distortionary taxes that the government must impose elsewhere. Governments justify the use of Pigovian taxes saying that these taxes help the market reach an efficient outcome because this tax bridges the gap between marginal social costs and marginal private costs.

Some arguments against Pigovian taxes say that the tax does not account for all the transfers and regulations involved with an externality. In other words, the tax only considers the amount of externality produced. Another argument against the tax is that it does not take private property into consideration. Under the Pigovian system, one firm, for example, can be taxed more than another firm, even though the other firm is actually producing greater amounts of the negative externality.

However, the most common type of solution is a tacit agreement through the political process. Governments are elected to represent citizens and to strike political compromises between various interests. Normally governments pass laws and regulations to address pollution and other types of environmental harm. These laws and regulations can take the form of "command and control" regulation (such as setting standards, targets, or process requirements), or environmental pricing reform (such as ecotaxes or other Pigovian taxes, tradable pollution permits or the creation of markets for ecological services). The second type of resolution is a purely private agreement between the parties involved.

Government intervention might not always be needed. Traditional ways of life may have evolved as ways to deal with external costs and benefits. Alternatively, democratically run communities can agree to deal with these costs and benefits in an amicable way. Externalities can sometimes be resolved by agreement between the parties involved. This resolution may even come about because of the threat of government action.

Ronald Coase argued that if all parties involved can easily organize payments so as to pay each other for their actions, then an efficient outcome can be reached without government intervention. Some take this argument further, and make the political claim that government should restrict its role to facilitating bargaining among the affected groups or individuals and to enforcing any contracts that result. This result, often known as the Coase theorem, requires that

- Property rights be well defined
- People act rationally
- Transaction costs be minimal

If all of these conditions apply, the private parties can bargain to solve the problem of externalities.

This theorem would not apply to the steel industry case discussed above. For example, with a steel factory that trespasses on the lungs of a large number of individuals with pollution, it is difficult if not impossible for any one person to negotiate with the producer, and there are large transaction costs. Hence the most common approach may be to regulate the firm (by imposing limits on the amount of pollution considered "acceptable") while paying for the regulation and enforcement with taxes. The case of the vaccinations would also not satisfy the requirements of the Coase theorem. Since the potential external beneficiaries of vaccination are the people themselves, the people would have to self-organize to pay each other to be vaccinated. But such an organization that involves the entire populace would be indistinguishable from government action.

In some cases, the Coase theorem is relevant. For example, if a logger is planning to clear-cut a forest in a way that has a negative impact on a nearby resort, the resort-owner and the logger could, in theory, get together to agree to a deal. For example, the resort-owner could pay the logger not to clear-cut – or could buy the forest. The most problematic situation, from Coase's perspective, occurs when the forest literally does not belong to anyone; the question of "who" owns the forest is not important, as any specific owner will have an interest in coming to an agreement with the resort owner (if such an agreement is mutually beneficial).

However, the Coase theorem is difficult to implement because Coase does not offer a negotiation method. Additionally, firms could potentially bribe each other since there is little to no government interaction under the Coase theorem. For example, if one oil firm has a high pollution rate and its neighboring firm is bothered by the pollution, then the latter firm may move depending on incentives. Thus, if the oil firm were to bribe the second firm, the first oil firm would suffer no negative consequences because the government would not know about the bribing.

Criticism

Ecological economics criticizes the concept of externality because there is not enough system thinking and integration of different sciences in the concept. Ecological economics is founded upon the view that the neoclassical economics (NCE) assumption that environmental and community costs and benefits are mutually canceling "externalities" is not warranted. Joan Martinez Alier, for instance shows that the bulk of consumers are automatically excluded from having an impact upon the prices of commodities, as these consumers are future generations who have not been born yet. The assumptions behind future discounting, which assume that future goods will be cheaper than present goods, has been criticized by Fred Pearce and by the recent Stern Report (although the Stern report itself does employ discounting and has been criticized for this and other reasons by ecological economists such as Clive Spash).

Concerning these externalities, some like the eco-businessman Paul Hawken argue an orthodox economic line that the only reason why goods produced unsustainably are usually cheaper than goods produced sustainably is due to a hidden subsidy, paid by the non-monetized human environment, community or future generations. These arguments are developed further by Hawken, Amory and Hunter Lovins to promote their vision of an environmental capitalist utopia in *Natural Capitalism: Creating the Next Industrial Revolution.*

In contrast, ecological economists, like Joan Martinez-Alier, appeal to a different line of reasoning. Rather than assuming some (new) form of capitalism is the best way forward, an older ecological economic critique questions the very idea of internalizing externalities as providing some corrective to the current system. The work by Karl William Kapp explains why the concept of "externality" is a misnomer. In fact the modern business enterprise operates on the basis of shifting costs onto others as normal practice to make profits. Charles Einsentein has argued that this method of privatising profits while socialising the costs through externalities, passing the costs to the community, to the natural environment or to future generations is inherently destructive As social ecological economist Clive Spash has noted, externality theory fallaciously assumes environmental and social problems are minor aberrations in an otherwise perfectly functioning efficient economic system. Internalizing the odd externality does nothing to address the structural systemic problem and fails to recognize the all pervasive nature of these supposed 'externalities'.

Measurement of Externalities

The revealed preference approach attempts to determine the cost of an externality by determining how much damage reduces the price of a good.

Revealed preference can also be used to estimate the price people pay for various protection (defense/ abatement) measures and the effectiveness of those measures. For instance, insulation costs a certain amount of money and provides a certain amount of effectiveness in reducing noise. The extent to which individuals then purchase insulation or double-glazed windows may suggest how much they value quiet. However individuals may be willing to spend some money (but less than the cost of insulation) if they could ensure quiet by some other means which they do not control - but which may be technically feasible.

According to some economists, the valuation of benefits and costs used in Cost benefit analysis should reflect the preferences revealed by choices which have actually been made by individuals and businesses in different markets.

Example:

20 employees are given the chance of using a new car park close to work for Rs 5 per day or parking further away from work for free – but involving an extra 10 minutes walk. Their decisions reveal how much they value time. If they all choose to spend the Rs 5 per day on car parking, this reveals that time is more important to them than 50p per minute. If only half take up the car parking option, this reveals that average value of time to them was 50p per minute. Hard choices made in markets are the best guide to private benefit.

Information contained in the demand curve tells us much about how much people are willing and able to pay for something. This is important in revealed preference theory. When consumers make purchases at market prices they reveal that the things they buy are at least as beneficial to them as the money they relinquish. However, consider that there was another option of taking a bus from the parking that costs less. We would not know whether people would prefer that to walking.

To recap, cost benefit analysis is basically an appraisal technique that tries to place monetary values on all benefits arising from a project and then compares the total value with the project's total cost. It has numerous potential applications although there are inherent difficulties with the issue of valuation.

Negative Production Externalities

- Consider the following example:
  - A profit-maximizing steel firm, as a by-product of its production, dumps sludge into a river.
  - The fishermen downstream are harmed by this activity, as the fish die and their profits fall.
- This is a negative production externality because:
  - Fishermen downstream are adversely affected.
  - And they are not compensated for this harm.

Production Externality

"Damage from steel production on the consumers" could also have cost instead of damage.

Case I (-ve) externality:

Firms produce steel by using a numeraire good y.

Pollution from production of x is given by dx

Consumers maximize utility $u(x) - dx - px$

d = damage from pollution, p= price of good x

Firms maximize profits $\pi(x) = px - c(x)$

Social Welfare

W= net utility of consumers + net profit of producers = $\{u(x) - px - dx\} + \{px - c(x)\} = u(x) - dx - c(x)$

In a Competitive Equilibrium

Firms max profits: $\pi(x) = p.x - c(x); P$ =price of cars

Consumers max utility $V(x) = u(x) - px$

$$\left.\begin{array}{l} Dd\ satisfies: u'(X^D) = p \\ SS\ satisfies: c'(X^S) = p \end{array}\right\} Competitive\ Equilibrium \Rightarrow u'^{(X^D)} = c'^{(X^s)} = p$$

But is this Pareto efficient?

No! Could raise the social welfare, by ↓ production of x by Δx

Suppose x falls by Δx, then:

$$\Delta w = u'(x)\Delta x - c'\Delta x - d.\Delta x \begin{Bmatrix} \downarrow x \, from \; a \; pt. \, where \; u'(x) = c'(x) \\ \Rightarrow u'(x)\Delta x = c'(x)\Delta x \end{Bmatrix}$$

$\Rightarrow \Delta w = -d\Delta x > 0 \; if \; \Delta x < 0$

$\Rightarrow$ Welfare could $\uparrow$ *if* $x \downarrow$

$\Rightarrow$ First welfare theorem does not hold. Since you do not maximize social efficiency at the competitive equilibrium point.

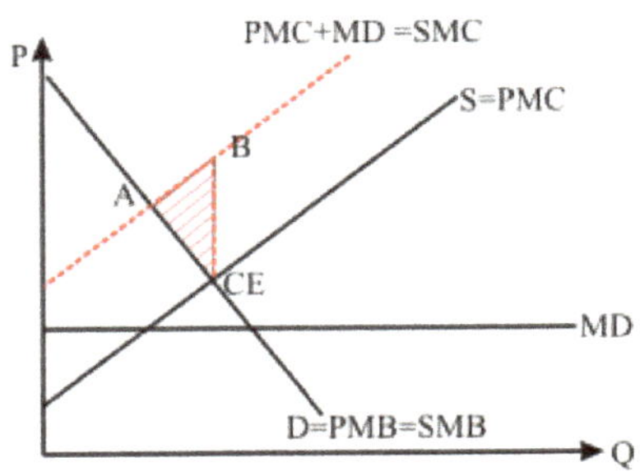

For private efficiency

MC=MB. This is satisfied privately at CE.

- Privately optimal production solves:

$$PMB = PMC$$

- This yields Competitive Equilibrium price and quantity.
- Firm A emits pollution causing damage to firm B. This is represented by the marginal damage curve. Ideally, B prefers:

$$MD = 0$$

- This would yield zero steel production, which is obviously *not* in firm A's best interests.
- The social marginal cost accounts for both the direct costs to firm A and the indirect harm to B:

$$SMC = PMC + MD$$

- We find the socially optimal quantity of Q_A by solving:

$$SMC = SMB$$

Negative Production Externalities

- Consider the following example:
  - A person at a restaurant smokes cigarettes.
  - That smoking has a negative effect on your enjoyment of the restaurant meal.
- In this case, the consumption of a good reduces the well-being of someone else.

Figure: Illustrates each party's incentives in the presence of a negative consumption externality.

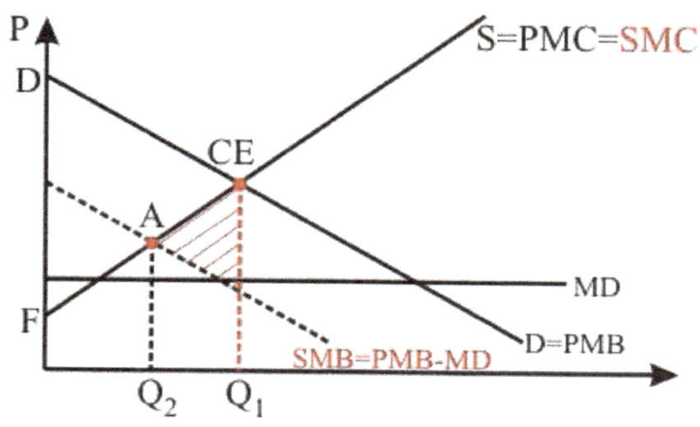

- The smoker sets PMB= PMC for Pvt. Optimal

  $CE \Delta DCE\ F\ is\ CS + PS =$ Total surplus at competitive equilibrium
- This does not capture the damage to nonsmokers.
- $MD \rightarrow$ nonsmoker's damage per cigarette.
  - MD is the difference between PMB and SMB.
  - At every pt between A & CE, $SMC > SMB$

    $\Delta x < 0 \Rightarrow welfare \uparrow$

SMB =PMB – costs associated with the consumption of that good, imposed on others.

- The socially optimal level of smoking is at A, SMB=SMC
- The smoker consumes too many cigarettes $(Q_1 - Q_2)$ from society's perspective

  $\Delta ACEB$ is DWL (the difference betwwen CE & B is SMC $-SMB \Rightarrow$ Net benefit <o
- $DWL = \Delta, width = extra\ production / consumption$
- Height=Marginal Damage
- The smoker's privately optimal quantity solves:

$$PMB = PMC$$

- Generates Competitive Equilibrium
- The smoker's consumption causes damage to the other restaurant patrons. They would prefer:

$$MD = 0$$

- This would yield zero cigarette smoking.
- The social marginal benefit accounts for both the direct benefit to the smoker and the indirect harm to the other patrons:

$$SMB = PMB - MD$$

- We find the socially optimal price and quantity of cigarettes by solving:

$$SMC = SMB$$

Positive Externalities

- The social marginal cost accounts for both the direct costs and the indirect benefit:
  - Production $SMC = PMC - EMB$
  - Consumption $SMB = PMB + EMB$
- Optimality Condition is same as before: $SMC = SMB$

Externalities and Dwl

- Negative externality implies that the private market will produce too much of the good, creating deadweight loss.
- Positive externality implies that the private market produces too little of the good, again creating deadweight loss.

Coase Theorem

In law and economics, the Coase theorem describes the economic efficiency of an economic allocation or outcome in the presence of externalities. The theorem states that if trade in an externality is possible and there are sufficiently low transaction costs, bargaining will lead to a Pareto efficient outcome regardless of the initial allocation of property. In practice, obstacles to bargaining or poorly defined property rights can prevent Coasian bargaining. This "theorem" is commonly attributed to Nobel Prize laureate Ronald Coase during his tenure at the London School of Economics, SUNY at Buffalo, University of Virginia, and University of Chicago. However, Coase himself stated that the theorem was based on perhaps four pages of his 1960 paper "The Problem of Social Cost", and that the "Coase theorem" is not about his work at all.

This 1960 paper, along with his 1937 paper on the nature of the firm (which also emphasizes the role of transaction costs), earned Ronald Coase the 1991 Nobel Memorial Prize in Economic Sciences. In this 1960 paper, Coase argued that real-world transaction costs are rarely low enough to allow for efficient bargaining and hence the theorem is almost always inapplicable to economic reality. Since then, others have demonstrated the importance of the perfect information assumption and shown using game theory that inefficient outcomes are to be expected when this assumption is not met.

Nevertheless, the Coase theorem is considered an important basis for most modern economic analyses of government regulation, especially in the case of externalities, and it has been used by jurists and legal scholars to analyse and resolve legal disputes. George Stigler summarized the resolution of the externality problem in the absence of transaction costs in a 1966 economics textbook in terms of private and social cost, and for the first time called it a "theorem." Since the 1960s, a voluminous amount of literature on the Coase theorem and its various interpretations, proofs, and criticism has developed and continues to grow.

The Theorem

Coase developed his theorem when considering the regulation of radio frequencies. Competing radio stations could use the same frequencies and would therefore interfere with each other's broadcasts. The problem faced by regulators was how to eliminate interference and allocate frequencies to radio stations efficiently. What Coase proposed in 1959 was that as long as property rights in these frequencies were well defined, it ultimately did not matter if adjacent radio stations interfered with each other by broadcasting in the same frequency band. Furthermore, it did not matter to whom the property rights were granted. His reasoning was that the station able to reap the higher economic gain from broadcasting would have an incentive to pay the other station not to interfere. In the absence of transaction costs, both stations would strike a mutually advantageous deal. It would not matter which station had the initial right to broadcast; eventually, the right to broadcast would end up with the party that was able to put it to the most highly valued use. Of course, the parties themselves would care who was granted the rights initially because this allocation would impact their wealth, but the end result of who broadcasts would not change because the parties would trade to the outcome that was overall most efficient. This counterintuitive insight—that the initial imposition of legal entitlement is irrelevant because the parties will eventually reach the same result—is Coase's invariance thesis.

Coase's main point, clarified in his article 'The Problem of Social Cost,' published in 1960 and cited when he was awarded the Nobel Prize in 1991, was that transaction costs, however, could not be neglected, and therefore, the initial allocation of property rights often mattered. As a result, one normative conclusion sometimes drawn from the Coase theorem is that liability should initially be assigned to the actors for whom avoiding the costs associated with the externality problem are the lowest. The problem in real life is that nobody knows ex ante the most valued use of a resource, and also that there exist costs involving the reallocation of resources by government. Another, more refined, normative conclusion also often discussed in law and economics is that government should create institutions that minimize transaction costs, so as to allow misallocations of resources to be corrected as cheaply as possible.

- Version 1: A clear delineation of private property rights is an essential prelude to market transactions.
- Version 2: As long as private property rights are well defined under zero transaction cost, exchange will eliminate divergence and lead to efficient use of resources or highest valued use of resources.
- Version 3: The allocation of resources is invariant to the assignment of private property rights under zero transaction cost and zero income effect.

Efficiency and Invariance

Because Ronald Coase himself did not originally intend to set forth any one particular theorem, it has largely been the effort of others who have developed the loose formulation of the Coase theorem. What Coase initially provided was fuel in the form of "counterintuitive insight" that externalities necessarily involved more than a single party engaged in conflicting activities and must be treated as a reciprocal problem. His work explored the relationship between the parties and their conflicting activities and the role of assigned rights/liabilities. While the exact definition of the Coase theorem remains unsettled, there are two issues or claims within the theorem: the results will be efficient and the results in terms of resource allocation will be the same regardless of initial assignments of rights/liabilities.

Efficiency Version: Aside from Transaction Costs, the Prevailing Outcome will be Efficient

The zero transaction cost condition is taken to mean that there are no impediments to bargaining. Since any inefficient allocation leaves unexploited contractual opportunities, the allocation cannot be a contractual equilibrium.

Invariance Version: Aside from Transaction Costs, the Same Efficient Outcome will Prevail

This version fits the legal cases cited by Coase. If it is more efficient to prevent cattle trampling a farmer's fields by fencing in the farm, rather than fencing in the cattle, the outcome of bargaining will be the fence around the farmer's fields, regardless of whether victim rights or unrestricted grazing-rights prevail. Subsequent authors have shown that this version of the theorem is not generally true, however. Changing liability placement changes wealth distribution, which in turn affects demand and prices. These wealth effects may be small, however.

Equivalence Version

In his UCLA dissertation and in subsequent work, Steven N. S. Cheung (1969) coined an extension of the Coase theorem: aside from transaction costs, all institutional forms are capable of achieving the same efficient allocation. Contracts, extended markets, and corrective taxation are equally capable of internalizing an externality. To be logically correct, some restrictive assumptions are needed. First, spillover effects must be bilateral. This applies to the cases that Coase investigated. Cattle trample a farmer's fields; a building blocks sunlight to a neighbor's swimming pool; a confectioner disturbs a dentist's patients etc. In each case the source of the externality is matched with a particular victim. It does not apply to pollution generally, since there are typically multiple victims. Equivalence also requires that each institution has equivalent property rights. Victim rights in contract law correspond to victim entitlements in extended markets and to the polluter pays principle in taxation.

Notwithstanding these restrictive assumptions, the equivalence version helps to underscore the Pigouvian fallacies that motivated Coase. Pigouvian taxation is revealed as not the only way to internalize an externality. Market and contractual institutions should also be considered, as well as corrective subsidies. The equivalence theorem also is a springboard for Coase's primary achievement—providing the pillars for the New Institutional Economics. First, the Coasean maximum-value solution becomes a benchmark by which institutions can be compared. And the institutional equivalence result establishes the motive for comparative institutional analysis and suggests the means by which institutions can be compared (according to their respective abilities to economize on transaction costs). The equivalency result also underlies Coase's (1937) proposition that the boundaries of the firm are chosen to minimize transaction costs. Aside from the "marketing costs" of using outside suppliers and the agency costs of central direction inside the firm, whether to put Fisher Body inside or outside of General Motors would have been a matter of indifference.

Application in United States Contract and Tort Law

The Coase Theorem has been used by jurists and legal scholars in the analysis and resolution of disputes involving both contract law and tort law.

In contract law, Coase is often used as a method to evaluate the relative power of the parties during the negotiation and acceptance of a traditional or classical bargained-for contract.

In modern tort law, application of economic analysis to assign liability for damages was popularized by Judge Learned Hand of the Second Circuit Court of Appeals in his decision, *United States v. Carroll Towing Co.* 159 F.2d 169 (2d. Cir. 1947). Judge Hand's holding resolved simply that liability could be determined by applying the formula of $B < PL$, where B = the burden (economic or otherwise) of adequate protection against foreseeable damages, P = the probability of damage (or loss) occurring and L = the gravity of the resulting injury (loss). This decision flung open the doors of economic analysis in tort cases, thanks in no small part to Judge Hand's popularity among legal scholars.

In resultant scholarship using economic models of analysis, prominently including the Coase theorem, theoretical models demonstrated that, when transaction costs are minimized or nonexistent, the legal appropriation of liability diminishes in importance or disappears completely. In other words, parties will arrive at an economically efficient solution that may ignore the legal framework in place.

Examples

Damage from Water Runoff

Two property owners own land on a mountainside. Property Owner A's land is upstream from Owner B and there is significant, damaging runoff from Owner A's land to Owner B's land. Four scenarios are considered:

1. If a cause of action exists (i.e. B could sue A for damages and win) and the property damage equals \$100 while the cost of building a wall to stop the runoff equals \$50, the wall will probably exist. Owner A will build the wall, or pay Owner B between \$1 and \$50 to tolerate the runoff.
2. If a cause of action exists and the damage equals \$50 while the cost of a wall is \$100, the wall will not exist. Owner B may sue, win the case and the court will order Owner A to pay B \$50. This is cheaper than actually building the wall. Courts rarely order persons to do or not do actions: they prefer monetary awards.
3. If a cause of action does not exist, and the damage equals \$100 while the cost of the wall equals \$50, the wall will exist. Even though B cannot win the lawsuit, he or she will still pay A some amount between \$51 and \$99 to build the wall.
4. If a cause of action does not exist, and the damage equals \$50 while the wall will cost \$100, the wall will not exist. B cannot win the lawsuit and the economic realities of trying to get the wall built are prohibitive.

The Coase theorem considers all four of these outcomes logical because the economic incentives will be stronger than legal incentives. Pure or traditional legal analysis will expect that the wall will exist in both scenarios where B has a cause of action and that the wall will never exist if B has no cause of action.

Planting Pear Trees

The Jones family plants pear trees on their property which is adjacent to the Smith family. The Smith family gets an external benefit from the Jones family's pear trees because they pick up whatever pears fall to the ground on their side of the property line. This is an externality because the Smith family does not pay the Jones family for utility received from gathering the fallen pears and, therefore, does not participate in the market transaction of pear production. It results in the pears being underproduced, which means too few pear trees are planted.

Let's assume the following:

Jones Family's demand	
Marginal Benefit	Quantity
$35	1
$30	2
$25	3
$20	4
$15	5
$10	6
$5	7
$0	8

Smith Family's demand	
Marginal Benefit	Quantity
$20	1
$15	2
$10	3
$5	4
$0	5

Societal demand for pear trees	
Marginal Benefit	Quantity
$55	1
$45	2
$35	3
$25	4
$15	5
$10	6
$5	7
$0	8

Possible solutions to internalize the externality:

By applying the Coase Theorem two possible solutions arise for internalizing this externality. These solutions can occur because the positive external benefits are clearly identified and we assume that 1) transaction costs are low; 2) property rights are clearly defined.

After realizing that the Smith family gets utility from the Jones family's pear trees, the Jones family thinks it is unfair that the Smiths get utility from picking up the pears that fall from their pear trees. The first option to eliminate the externality could be to put up a net fence that will prevent pears from falling to the ground of the Smith's side property line, which will automatically decrease the Smith family's marginal benefit to 0.

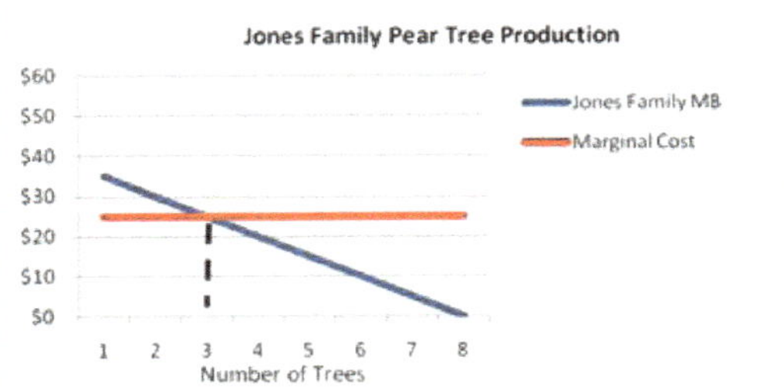

By graphing the Jones family's marginal benefit curve and the marginal cost curve for pear tree production, we can find the efficient number of trees to be produced for the Jones family alone (this occurs where $MB_{Jones} = MC$), which happens to be 3.

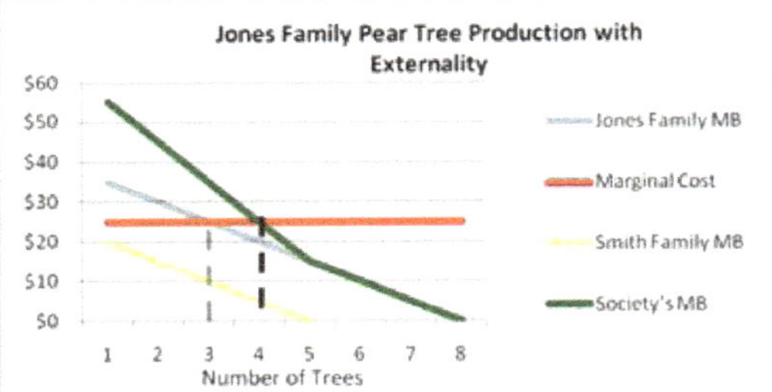

However, when we consider the positive externality we can see that the marginal benefit to society is greater than the marginal benefit to the Jones family alone. Using the new marginal benefit curve, $MB_{Society}$, we can see that the efficient number of pear trees to be produced for society (occuring where $MB_{Society} = MC$) is 4.

The second option for the Jones could be to impose a cost on the Smith family if they want to continue to get utility from their pear trees. Say, if the Jones family has a MC of $25 for each pear tree produced, it allows them to plant 3 pear trees a year (Jones' MB = MC). However, if the cost is imposed on the Smiths, the optimal quantity of pear trees produced a year will increase to 4 (Jones' MB + Smiths' MB = MC). By internalizing the externality, both the Smith family and the Jones family increase their overall utility by increasing production from 3 pear trees a year to 4. It should be noted that $5 is the maximum price the Smiths are willing to pay for an additional, fourth, pear tree, which implies their marginal benefit to plant a fifth pear tree is 0.

Criticism

Ronald Coase's work emphasised a problem in applying the Coase theorem: transactions are "often extremely costly, sufficiently costly at any rate to prevent many transactions that would be carried out in a world in which the pricing system worked without cost." (Coase, 1960—first paragraph of section VI.) This isn't a criticism of the theorem itself, since the theorem considers only those situations in which there are no transaction costs. Instead, it is an objection to applications of the theorem that neglect this crucial assumption.

So, a key criticism is that the theorem is almost always inapplicable in economic reality, because real-world transaction costs are rarely low enough to allow for efficient bargaining. (That was the conclusion of Coase's original paper, making him the first 'critic' of using the theorem as a practical solution.) Neo-Keynesian economist James Meade argued that even in a simple case of a beekeeper's bees pollinating a nearby farmer's crops, Coasean bargaining is inefficient (though beekeepers and farmers do make contracts and have for some time).

Chicago school anarcho-capitalist economist David D. Friedman has argued that the fact that an "economist as distinguished as Meade assumed an externality problem was insoluble save for government intervention suggests...the range of problems to which the Coasian solution is relevant may be greater than many would at first guess." Friedman is scathing of most critical attacks on the Coase theorem.

In many cases of externalities, the parties might be a single large factory versus a thousand landowners nearby. In such situations, say the critics, not only do transaction costs rise extraordinarily high, but bargaining is hindered by the basic incentive to free-ride and poorly defined property rights—classic public good problems.

A third critique can be found in the work of the critical legal scholar Duncan Kennedy, who argues that the initial allocation always matters in reality. This is because psychological studies indicate that asking prices often exceed offer prices, due to the so-called endowment effect. In other words, a person who already has an entitlement is likely to request more to give it up than would a person who started off without the entitlement.

Unconstrained Coasean bargaining ex post may lead to a hold-up problem ex ante. Thus, even though it is often claimed that Coasean bargaining is an alternative to Pigouvian taxation, it has been argued that in a hold-up situation Coasean bargaining may actually justify Pigouvian taxation. Alternatively, it may be efficient to forbid renegotiation. Yet, there are situations in which a ban on contract renegotiation is not desirable.

New institutional economist Steven N. S. Cheung thinks that private property rights are institutions that arise to reduce transaction costs. The existence of private property rights implies that transaction costs are non-zero. If transaction costs are really zero, any property rights system will result in identical and efficient resource allocation, and the assumption of private property rights is not necessary. Therefore, zero transaction costs and private property rights cannot logically coexist.

In 2009, in their seminal JEI article, Hahnel and Sheeran highlight several major misinterpretations and common assumptions, which when accounted for substantially reduce the applicability of Coase's theorem to real world policy and economic problems. First, they recognize that the solution between a single polluter and single victim is a negotiation—not a market. As such, it is subject to the extensive work on bargaining games, negotiation, and game theory (specifically a "divide the pie" game under incomplete information). This typically yields a broad range of potential negotiated solutions, making it unlikely that the efficient outcome will be the one selected. Rather it is more likely to be determined by a host of factors including the structure of the negotiations, discount rates and other factors of relative bargaining strength (cf. Ariel Rubenstein).

If the negotiation is not a single shot game, then reputation effects may also occur, which can dramatically distort outcomes and may even lead to failed negotiation (cf. David M. Kreps, also the chainstore paradox). Second, the information assumptions required to apply Coase's theorem correctly to yield an efficient result are complete information—in other words that both sides lack private information, that their true costs are completely known not only to themselves but to each other, and that this knowledge state is also common knowledge. When this is not the case, Coasian solutions predictably yield highly inefficient results because of perverse incentives—not "mere" transaction costs.

If the polluter has the ownership rights, it is incentivized to overstate its benefits from polluting, if the victim has the ownership rights, (s)he has the incentive to also misrepresent her/his damages. As a result, under incomplete information (probably the only state of knowledge for most real world negotiations), Coaseian yield predictably inefficient results. Third, if there are multiple victims, victims who would be required to pay have incentive to pretend that they are not harmed (freeriding) or understate their harm. If the polluter is required to pay, victims overpresent, overestimate their damage, and/or hold out.

Hahnel and Sheeran emphasize that these failures are not due to behavioral issues or irrationality (although these are also quite prevalent (ultimatum game, cognitive biases), are not due to transaction costs (although these are also quite prevalent), and are not due to absorbing states and inability to pay, rather it is due to fundamental theoretical requirements of Coase's theorem (necessary conditions) that are typically grossly misunderstood, and that when not present systematically eliminate the ability of Coaseian approaches to obtain efficient outcomes—locking in inefficient ones. Hahnel and Sheeran conclude that it is highly unlikely that conditions required for an efficient Coaseian solution will exist in any real-world economic situations.

Another criticism is that the relative value determinations of the parties cannot reflect the actual values sought by the parties unless the parties start off at equal economic positions. In reality, the parties are more likely to start off at economically disparate positions. The result is that a dollar may have more relative worth to the victim than the polluter. Additionally, Coase's theorem assumes that anything of value can be characterized in economic terms. But some attributes of property simply cannot be reduced to monetary figures.

Using a game-theoretic model, it has been argued that sometimes it is easier to reach an agreement if the initial property rights are unclear.

Private Solution (Coase Theorem)

- Externalities emerge because property rights are not well defined.
- Establish property rights to create markets for pollution.
- Consider example of pollution in a river.
  - If consumer owns river, in competitive equilibrium, firms pay d for every unit of pollution emitted.
  - Marginal cost of production is now c(x) + d, leading to 1st best.
- The *Coase Theorem*: Social Efficiency is obtained when there are well-defined property rights and costless bargaining.
- Government Intervention?
  - Only enforce property rights.
- Consider the example of upstream steel firm & downstream fishery.
  - Suppose Property Rights is with the Fishery.
  - Through a process of bargaining, the steel firm will bribe the fishery to arrive at the socially optimal level.
  - After the point, where *MD* exceeds (*PMB* - *PMC*), the steel firm cannot come up with a large enough bribe to expand production further.

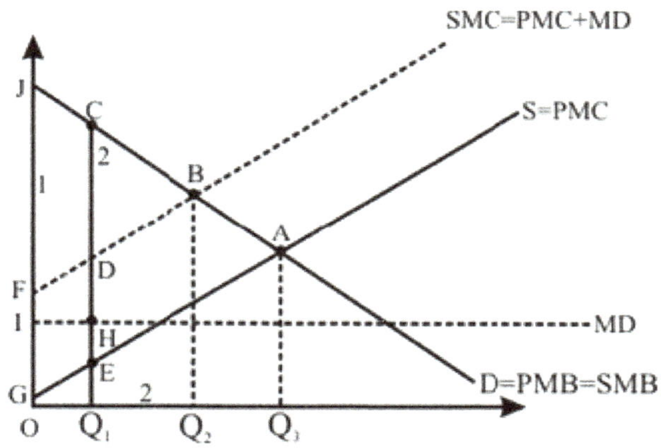

Gain to steel plant=GHCJ
Loss to fishery IH10
Compensate by bribing surplus to society: JCDF
Similarly for unit 2

- Give Property rights to A(steel plant) or B(Fishery).
- If the B had property rights, it would impose zero steel production.

  ∵ Steel production maker Fishery worse off.

- But there is room for bargaining. From the 1st unit of steel produced steel plant gets a surplus of JCEG (PMB-PMC) Fishery suffers a damage of 01HQ$_1$.
- Thus if possible the steel firm will bribe the fishery in order to produce the first unit.
- The gain to the society is (PMB –PMC -MD)= JCDF [(JCEG -FDEG) at Q$_1$] Similarly for the 2nd unit. Gain to the society =DCB.
- This bargaining will continue until B, the socially efficient level.
- Through individual Negotiation it is possible to arrive at the social optimum.
- At pts after *B, MD > (PMB -PMC)* ⇒ the steel plant cannot bribe any more.

Coarse Theorem Symmetric Solution

- Another implication of the Coase Theorem is symmetric solution when the steel firm owns river.
  - The efficient solution does not depend on which party is assigned the property rights.
- Assignment of property rights affects distribution but not efficiency.
- Let's give the property rights to the steel firm over the amount of steel production.

The direction in which the bribes go does depend on the assignment, however.

Figure: Illustrates this scenario.

Symmetric solution when steel firm owns river.

Assignment of property rights affects distribution but not efficiency.

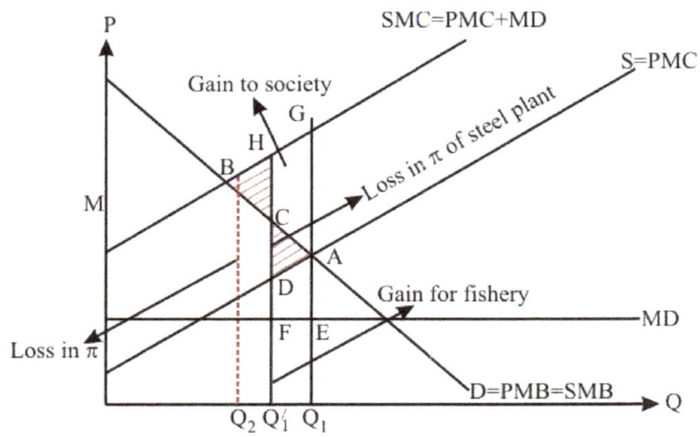

- Suppose property right given to the steel firm.
- Steel firm produce at A, $\because$ it is private optimum.
- The fishery gets a lot of surplus from cutting back steel production by 1 unit $= F\,E\,Q_1Q_1'$ (amount damage reduced by cutting back production).
- Steel plant suffers only modest loss in $\pi = PMB - PMC = ADC$.
- Thus fishery will bribe steel plant in to cutting back.
- The gain to the society is $ACHG.(SMC - PMB \text{ or } SMB - \text{loss of steel plant})$

Problems with Coasian Solutions

- There are several problems with the Coase Theorem, however.
  - The assignment problem
  - The holdout problem
  - The free rider problem
  - Transaction costs and negotiating problems
- The "assignment problem" relates to two issues:
  - It can be difficult to truly assign blame.
  - It is hard to value the marginal damage in reality.
- The "holdout problem" arises when the property rights in question are held by more than one party.
  - The shared property rights give each party power over all others.
  - This could lead to a breakdown in negotiations.
- The "free rider" problem: when an investment has a personal cost but a common benefit, individuals will under invest.
  - For example, if the steel firms were assigned property rights and you are the last (of many) fisherman to pay, the bribe is larger than the marginal damage to you personally.
- Finally, it is hard to negotiate when there are large numbers of individuals on one or both sides.
- Ex: air pollution would require millions of agents to coordinate and bargain
  - To reduce transactions costs, need an association to represent agents
  - Association is the government

In summary the coase solution is provocative and evitable for small problems but not very relevant for the most pressing environmental problems.

Public-sector Remedies for Externalities

- Public policy makes use of three instruments to address negative externalities:
  - Corrective taxation
  - Subsidies
  - Regulation

Pigovian Tax

A Pigovian tax (also spelled Pigouvian tax) is a tax levied on any market activity that generates negative externalities (costs not internalized in the market price). The tax is intended to correct an inefficient market outcome, and does so by being set equal to the social cost of the negative externalities. In the presence of negative externalities, the social cost of a market activity is not covered by the private cost of the activity. In such a case, the market outcome is not efficient and may lead to over-consumption of the product. An often-cited example of such an externality is environmental pollution.

In the presence of positive externalities, i.e., public benefits from a market activity, those who receive the benefit do not pay for it and the market may under-supply the product. Similar logic suggests the creation of a Pigovian subsidy to make the users pay for the extra benefit and spur more production. An example sometimes cited is a subsidy for provision of flu vaccine.

Pigovian taxes are named after English economist Arthur Pigou (1877-1959) who also developed the concept of economic externalities. William Baumol was instrumental in framing Pigou's work in modern economics in 1972.

Pigou's Original Argument

In 1920, British economist Arthur C. Pigou wrote *The Economics of Welfare*. In it, Pigou argues that industrialists seek their own marginal private interest. When the marginal social interest diverges from the marginal private interest, the industrialist has no incentive to internalize the cost of the marginal social cost. Conversely, Pigou argues, if an industry produces a marginal social benefit, the individuals receiving the benefit have no incentive to pay for that service. Pigou refers to these situations as incidental uncharged disservices and incidental uncharged services, respectively.

Pigou provides numerous illustrations of incidental uncharged disservices. For example, if a contractor builds a factory in the middle of a crowded neighborhood, the factory causes these incidental uncharged disservices: higher congestion, loss of light, and a loss of health for the neighbors. He also references businesses that sell alcohol. The sale of alcohol necessitates higher costs in policemen and prisons, Pigou argues, because of the crime associated with alcohol. In other words, the net private product of alcohol businesses is peculiarly large relative to the net social product of the same business. He suggests that this is why most countries tax alcohol businesses.

The divergence between the marginal private interest and the marginal social interest produces two primary results. First, as already noted, the party receiving the social benefit does not pay for it, and the one creating the social harm does not pay for it. Second, when the marginal social cost exceeds the private marginal benefit, the cost-creator over-produces the product. Ultimately, because non-pecuniary externalities overestimate the social value, they are over-produced.

To deal with over-production, Pigou recommends a tax placed on the offending producer. If the government can accurately gauge the social cost, the tax could equalize the marginal private cost and the marginal social cost. In more specific terms, the producer would have to pay for the non-pecuniary externality that it created. This would effectively reduce the quantity of the product produced, moving the economy back to a healthy equilibrium.

Working of the Pigovian Tax

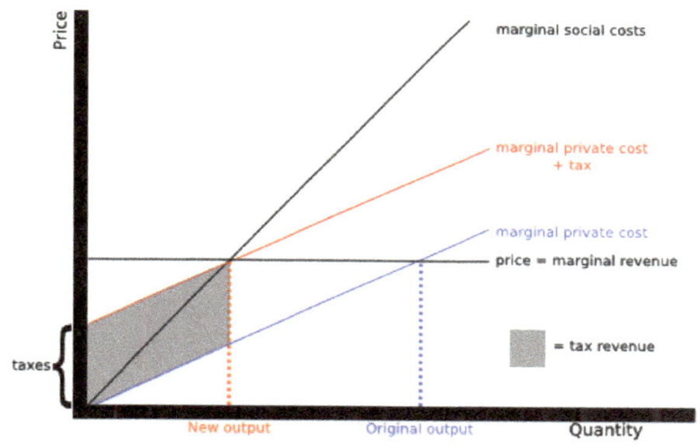

Pigovian tax effect on output

The diagram illustrates the working of a Pigovian tax. A tax shifts the marginal private cost curve up by the amount of the tax. If the tax is placed on the quantity of emissions from the factory, the producers have an incentive to reduce output to the socially optimum level. If the tax is placed on the percentage of emissions per unit of production, the factory has the incentive to change to cleaner processes or technology.

Lump-sum Tax Subsidy

In 1980, a new critique of Pigovian taxes emerged from Dennis Carlton and Glenn Loury. They argued that Pigovian taxes alone would not create an efficient outcome in the long-run, because the taxes controlled only the scale of the individual firms, not the number of firms in the particular industry. In the case of pollution, if the firms each produced a fraction of what they produced before, but the number of firms increased exponentially, the amount of pollution would still increase. To prevent this, Carlton and Loury recommend a policy with the potential to regulate the number of firms in an industry: lump-sum taxes or lump-sum subsidies.

Carlton and Loury present four basic arguments in their article. First, Pigovian taxes work in the short-term, because the number of firms cannot vary. Second, Pigovian taxes do not work in the long-term because the number of firms can vary. Third, an industry with a specific number of firms and scale can achieve the long-run social optimum (LRSO). The best option is to add an entry tax for potential firms and a subsidy for current firms to restrict a movement in the number of firms. Fourth, it is possible for a tax policy to create a LRSO.

Robert Kohn responded to this article in "The Limitations of Pigouvian Taxes as a Long-Run Remedy for Externalities: Comment," saying that a Pigovian tax on pollution emissions can, in fact, create the long-run social optimum without a lump-sum tax-subsidy. Carlton and Loury responded the same month, clarifying that they were discussing a Pigovian tax on output; whereas, Kohn was discussing a Pigovian tax on emissions. Carlton and Loury provide numerical proofs as to why these are different. Ultimately, they argue that there are some cases in which a single tax on emissions will produce the LRSO and others in which a single tax on output will attain the LRSO. Either case only works with the taxes properly determined.

Double-dividend Hypothesis

The double-dividend hypothesis proposes that a revenue-neutral substitution of environmental taxes for revenue-raising taxes might offer two benefits. The idea was first advanced by Tullock (1967) in a paper titled 'Excess Benefit'. The first benefit (or dividend) is the benefit or welfare gain resulting from an improvement in the environment (less pollution), and the second dividend or benefit is due to a reduction in the distortions of the revenue-raising tax system, which also produces an improvement in welfare. This idea received scant attention until the early 1990s, when the economics of climate change attracted attention to the topic of environmental taxes. The term 'double dividend' became widely used following its introduction by David Pearce in 1991. Pearce noted that estimates of the marginal excess burden (marginal distortionary cost) of existing levels of taxation in the US economy are between 20 and 50 cents per dollar of revenue collected. Because the revenue from the carbon tax would be recycled (used to lower preexisting and distorting taxes), the policy would be revenue-neutral, and the secondary benefit from revenue recycling would justify an even higher carbon tax. It is generally accepted now that the magnitude of the "revenue-recycling" benefit is lower than the 20–50 cents per dollar of revenue, but there are differing views on whether the second effect is positive or negative. The line of argument suggesting that the second "benefit" is negative proposes a previously unrecognized "tax interaction effect" (Bovenberg and de Mooij 1994).

In a 1997 paper, Don Fullerton and Gilbert E. Metcalf evaluated the double dividend hypothesis. They define the double-dividend hypothesis as the theory that environmental taxes can improve the environment and increase economic efficiency simultaneously. Either motivation can legitimately support a tax reform. The first dividend intuitively makes sense: decreasing pollutant emissions improves the environment. The improvement in economic efficiency results from a shift away from distorting taxes such as the income tax. Fullerton and Metcalf note that for every $1 extracted in taxes, a $1.35 burden falls on the economy. In a sense, the private sector must swallow a 35 cent excess burden for no particular reason. The second dividend aims to eliminate some of this excess burden.

Tempting as it may be to try, Fullerton and Metcalf argue, the validity of the double-dividend theory cannot be established as a whole. An observer must evaluate each circumstance individually. Fullerton and Metcalf do provide guidelines for this analysis. Two questions help shape this analysis: what is the status quo? What are the specifics of the reform? The amount and nature of the current taxes, permits, and regulations greatly influence the results of the additional tax. Also, where the tax revenue goes greatly affects the success of the tax.

Secondly, Fullerton and Metcalf say the previous literature on Pigovian taxes focused too heavily on the revenue dividend and too lightly on the environmental dividend of environmental taxes. Their predecessors naively value revenue too much, Fullerton and Metcalf argue, because they fail to recognize that all taxes impose costs on someone. These taxes could outweigh the environmental benefit. Thus, the government must use the Pigovian tax revenue to lower another tax if it wants to minimize the economic damage of a tax.

Fullerton and Metcalf also mention that the effectiveness of any sort of Pigovian tax depends on whether it supplements or replaces an existing pollution regulation. If the tax replaces a pollution regulation, it will most likely be environmentally neutral, even if it is revenue-positive. If it supplements the regulation, it may or may not be environmentally and revenue-neutral, depending on the effectiveness of the original regulation. The status quo substantially affects the outcome of a proposed tax.

Pigovian Tax and Distortionary Taxation

A. Lans Bovenberg and Ruud A. Mooij argue that there is a first-best case scenario and a second-best case scenario in their article "Environmental Levies and Distortionary Taxation." In the first-best case, the government does not need to get revenue from distortionary taxes such as the income tax, and the Pigovian tax can create the long-run social optimum. In the real world, second-best case, the status quo includes an income tax that distorts the labor supply. In this situation, Bovenberg and Mooij write that the best tax comes in below the level of the Pigovian tax.

Bovenberg and Mooij establish that households consume a dirty good (D) and a clean good (C). If the government taxes D, it can use the earned revenue to lower the labor income tax. At the same time, the tax levied on the firm will increase the price of D. The lowered income tax and the higher consumer prices even each other out, stabilizing the real net wage. But because C's price has not changed and it can substitute for D, consumers will buy C instead of D. Suddenly the government's environmental tax base has eroded and its revenue with it. The government then cannot afford to keep the labor income tax down. Bovenberg and Mooij posit that the increase in the price of goods will outweigh the slight decrease in the income tax. Labor and leisure become more interchangeable the lower the real net wage (or after-tax wage) falls. With this decrease in the real net wage, more people leave the job market. Ultimately, labor bears the cost of all public goods.

Goulder, Parry, and Burtraw agree that the net social welfare after the implementation of a tax hinges on the preexisting tax rate. Don Fullerton agreed with this analysis in 1997 in his article "Environmental Levies and Distortionary Taxation: Comment." He added that lowering the income tax and taxing the dirty good equates with raising the labor tax and subsidizing the clean product. These two polices create the same effects, Fullerton says.

In 1998, Fullerton and Gilbert E. Metcalf explain this theory more thoroughly. They begin by defining terms. The gross wage reflects the pre-tax wage a laborer receives. The simplest form of the net wage is the pre-tax wage minus the income tax. In reality, however, the net wage is the gross wage times one minus the tax rate, all divided by the price of consumption goods. With the status quo income tax, deadweight loss exists. Any addition to the price of consumption goods or an increase in the income tax extends the deadweight loss further. Either of these scenarios lowers the net wage, reducing the supply of labor offered. Supply of labor decreases because of the labor/leisure interchange. If someone gets paid very little, he or she may decide it is no longer worth his or her time to continue in that job. Thus, employment decreases. If the Pigovian tax, which increases the price of consumption goods, replaces the income tax, Fullerton argues that the net wage is not affected.

This rejection of the double dividend hypothesis found in the "tax interaction" literature was met with surprise and skepticism among economists for a variety of reasons. There are multiple sources of ambiguity, differing definitions of what constitutes a 'double dividend', and confusion caused when comparing models with direct versus indirect tax programs, reliance on comparisons with an unreliable benchmark, and misinterpretation of notation in the literature.

Although the central question for the double dividend hypothesis and the tax interaction literature has been whether the welfare gains from environmental taxation in a second-best world are larger or smaller than in a first-best setting, the Tax Interaction literature takes this central question and frames it indirectly, by asking whether the second-best optimal environmental tax is higher or lower than the first-best Pigouvian rate. This question, too, is not answered directly, because the first-best Pigouvian rate is replaced by a definition of marginal social damages, the value of which changes with the tax level and tax program normalization. This becomes an unreliable and shifting benchmark (Jaeger 2011).

In retrospect, three factors contributed to misleading interpretations in the TI literature: an algebraic error, the use of an unreliable benchmark, and unrecognized compounding or double taxation. As a result, the conclusion that a large, previously unnoticed distortionary tax interaction effect existed can be seen as partly due to misinterpretations (Jaeger 2013). Despite these sources of confusion, it remains the case that a) the possibility of a double dividend depends on specifics specific to the demands and the economy in which an environmental tax is being considered, and b) that the efficiency gains with revenue recycling will be greater, potentially significantly greater, than when revenues are not collected and used to reduce pre-existing revenue-raising taxes. Various research studies using numerical models find evidence in support of the double dividend hypothesis (Jorgensen et al., 2013).

Despite recent controversy on this topic, the conclusions that can be drawn are in keeping with economic intuition. Environmental and revenue-raising taxes are complementary tools for achieving two different kinds of government goals: the provision of public goods with revenue-motivated taxes and the protection of environmental quality with corrective taxes. Indeed, the joint pursuit of these two goals through taxation can enable government to justify doing more of each by making the optimal environmental tax higher than it would be otherwise, and by lowering the distortionary cost of financing the provision of public goods.

Alternatives

The Pigovian tax is a method commonly used by governments as it has relatively low transaction costs associated with implementation. Other methods such as command and control regulations or subsidies assume that the government has a complete knowledge of the market, which is almost never the case, and can often lead to inefficiencies and market failure through rent seeking behavior by individuals and firms.

No Intervention (Direct Negotiation between Parties)

Economist Ronald Coase argued that individuals can come to an agreement with an efficient result without the need for a third party when transaction costs are low. He says it is less expensive and less difficult for two neighbors to come to an agreement about a fence, the amount of noise, or the amount of smoke than it is for these two neighbors to approach a third party to solve the situation for them. Even when several parties are involved, outside interference could result in an inefficient outcome.

Yet, in dynamic settings Coasean bargaining ex post may lead to inefficient investments ex ante (the so-called hold-up problem). For this reason, some authors have argued that unconstrained Coasean bargaining may actually justify Pigouvian taxation.

Firm Limits

Instead of taxing the negative externality producer, government could regulate the production of that negative externality. Fullerton and Metcalf argue that restricting the amount of pollution that all firms in an industry can produce will indirectly reduce the output of all firms. This comprehensive supply reduction will automatically raise the consumption price of the good. These types of command-and-control restrictions stimulate cartel-like profits. Fullerton and Metcalf assert that production costs do not change, and assert that the companies can earn profits over and above what is earned before the regulations even with selling a lower quantity of goods. If the production cost of all firms increased simultaneously due to a regulation, the firms may be able to increase the price uniformly. They do not consider the elasticity of products and that's effect on the quantity of demand and the industry's final profits.

Cap and Trade

Another alternative to applying Pigovian taxation is for government to place a limit on the total amount of the production of the output causing the negative externality and create a market for rights to generate that specific output. In the United States since the late 1970s, and in other developed nations since the 1980s, the concept of a market for "pollution rights" has emerged. Giving out the rights for free (or at less than market price) allows polluters to lose less profit or even gain profits (by selling their rights) relative to the unaltered market case.

Goulder, Perry, and Burtraw suggest that selling permits to firms is the best option, but recognize that many firms in the status quo are grandfathered in, meaning they are given exemptions. The authors include an example of the U.S. regulations in coal-fired electrical power plants that require the reduction of 10 million tons of sulfur dioxide emissions. They estimate that more than half of the $907 million preexisting taxes could have been eliminated by auctioning off the permits rather than grandfathering them.

Criticisms

Most of the criticism of the Pigovian tax relates to the determination of the tax and the implementation. Pigou and Friedrich Hayek point out that the assumption that the government can determine the marginal social cost of a negative externality and convert that amount into a monetary value is a weakness of the Pigovian tax. William Baumol suggests that the measurement of social cost is almost impossible. Ronald Coase argues that all social costs are reciprocal in nature, so, once the tax is set, it must not be changed. Others point out that political factors can complicate the implementation of a Pigovian tax.

Measurement Problem

Arthur Pigou said: "It must be confessed, however, that we seldom know enough to decide in what fields and to what extent the State, on account of [the gaps between private and public costs] could interfere with individual choice." In other words, the economist's blackboard "model" assumes knowledge we don't possess – it's a model with assumed "givens" which are in fact *not* given to anyone. Friedrich Hayek would argue that this is knowledge which could not be provided as a "given" by any "method" yet discovered, due to insuperable cognitive limits.

William Baumol as well as Polodoo (2008) have argued that it is extraordinarily difficult to measure the social costs of any externality, especially because many costs are psychological and individual. Even if a measurement of the psychological effect of some externality did exist, it would be impossible to collect that data for all individuals affected and then find the optimum output level. Since it is not possible to find the optimum output level, it is not possible to find the optimum Pigovian tax level to achieve that optimum. In the end, Baumol argues that the best solution is to set a minimum standard of acceptability for negative externalities, and create tax systems to achieve those minimum standards. Baumol points out that government committees have a tradition of agreeing on minimum standards, so the practicality of this solution is reasonable.

Peter Boettke brings forth that "The Pigouvian remedy was to bring marginal private costs (subjectively understood) into line with marginal social costs (objectively understood). The problem, James M. Buchanan pointed out, was that the analyst had to specify the conditions under which objectively measurable costs could be ascertained by economic and policy actors. In general competitive equilibrium there are also no deviations between marginal private costs and marginal social costs. In other words, Buchanan (like Ronald Coase) pointed out that Pigovian tax remedies are either possible and redundant, or impossible to set because the conditions presupposed for their establishment either eliminate their necessity or (if absent) preclude their enactment." In other words, "Karen I. Vaughn has pointed out the dilemma involved in this situation. To calculate the appropriate corrective tax, the policymaker must know the equilibrium price; yet the situation demanding correction implies a disequilibrium situation."

Reciprocal Cost Problem

Ronald Coase argues that the tax placed on an industry creating a negative externality should not be changed after it is implemented. The crux of his argument is that all social costs are reciprocal in nature. Coase argues that a factory emitting smoke is not entirely responsible for the social harm of smoky air. If the factory were not there, no one would suffer from smoky air, and if the people were not there, no one would suffer from smoky air. Because of this reciprocity of harm, Coase argues that neither party bears sole responsibility for the social harm, so neither party should pay the full cost.

The social harm gets worse, Coase argues, if only one offender pays for the social harm. If the smoke-emitting factory must pay dearly for all its smoke, it will reduce its quantity of production or buy the necessary technology to reduce its smoke rate. With the advent of clean air, neighbors may move into the area. This immediately increases the marginal social cost of smoke, which would require a tax increase on the factory. Essentially, each time the tax increases, the population increases and the marginal cost of the status quo increases again, so the factory is punished for making conditions good enough that people want to move there.

One complexity of this situation is the multiple local maxima, or the interchangeable best-case scenarios. It all hinges on the numbers. If the cost of abating all smoke is more than the cost to move the neighbors out, the neighbors should move out and let the factory continue emitting smoke. On the other hand, if it costs less to abate the smoke than to move the neighbors, then the factory ought to pay the tax or buy the clean technology to provide clean air for the surrounding residents. Once the optimum solution is implemented, Coase argues that the tax should not change, regardless of changing circumstances. In this case, if a tax is imposed on the factory and some more neighbors move in, the factory tax should not increase.

Political Problem

Political factors such as lobbying of government by polluters may also tend to reduce the level of the tax levied, which will tend to reduce the mitigating effect of the tax; lobbying of government by special interests who calculate the negative utility of the externality higher than others may also tend to increase the level of the tax levied, which will tend to result in a sub-optimal level of production.

Political factors can result in complementary problems when pollution opponents assert irrationally high levels of harm or operate from a hidden agenda of extirpating the polluting agent regardless of the prospects for regulating it to cause minimal harm; regulators are then driven to set absurdly high tax levels, possibly high enough to effectively prohibit operation.

Similarly, lobbyists whose agendas are entirely orthogonal to pollution reduction per se might intervene with regulators to drive tax rates higher or lower, thus preventing optimal operation of the tax. Likely instances of such include organizations intending to lower the polluter's market value as part of a pending plan to buy out its parent entity. Alternatively there might be efforts to drive the polluter's market value higher prior to its sale. Familiar real-world examples of groups intervening for reason unrelated to pollution reduction include opponents of the polluter's (or the polluter's parent organization's) labor practices and groups with seemingly religious opposition to anything connected to nuclear energy.

Earl A. Thompson and Ronald Batchelder cited one political problem with Pigovian taxes being that if a firm can influence the tax rate or regulations put on it, the results will not be as certain as Pigou and Baumol suggested. Baumol responded to this, saying that almost all discussions on Pigovian taxes include the assumption of pure competition. This certainly does alter the scenario, but the literature had not ignored it; it had merely used a different set of assumptions.

Thomas A. Barthold argues in 1994 that actual policy decisions often come from budget requirements, not concern for the environment. The taxes do not always parallel raw economic theory because social benefits and costs are hard to measure. He uses the 1989 Montreal Protocol as an example. President George H. W. Bush signed this protocol that allowed either a permit auction or a tax on ozone-depleting chemicals. Barthold attributes the decision to implement the tax to the pressure on the Ways and Means committee to come up with more consistent revenue.

The tax policy also did not accord with basic common sense economic principles. For one, it makes sense to impose a tax on the industry that creates the pollution problem, on the activity that emits the harmful chemicals. This particular activity happened to be the use of automobiles with leaky compressor systems, but because of the high administration cost of taxing that many people, the government decided to tax the producers of those chemicals, though they contributed nothing to the actual problems of chlorofluorocarbons in the atmosphere.

Another evidence of the alternative motivations for this policy is the fact that the base tax increases annually. Does the harm from chlorofluorocarbons increase every year and in the same increment? Who is to say that $1.37 per pound of chlorofluorocarbons is an accurate description of the marginal social cost of pollution? The conspicuous hike in the tax in 1992 that equalized the Energy Policy Act's budget ignited Barthold's suspicions. Additionally, exporting firms should not receive exemptions from environmental taxes simply because they are exporting goods. If the motivation for this tax was simply the first dividend, environmental improvement, then all firms, whether or not they export, would be taxed.

Aside from this frustration, Barthold noted that politicians often prefer regulations with obvious benefits and hidden costs over regulations with hidden benefits and obvious costs. This is one reason why politicians often prefer to hand out permits to firms rather than impose a tax on them, even though the tax is more economically efficient. Free permits create winners of grandfathered firms and losers of the consumer who has to pay more for the same product. According to Barthold, taxation makes losers of the factory producers and indirect winners of the consumers.

Corrective Taxation

- The government can impose a "Pigouvian" tax on the steel firm, which lower its output and reduces deadweight loss.
- Impose tax t = MD (Q*).
- If the per-unit tax equals the marginal damage, the firm will cut back to that point.

  B where it is most optimal to produce in the presence of externalities.

A Pigovian tax (also spelled Pigouvian tax) is a tax levied on a market activity that generates negative externalities.

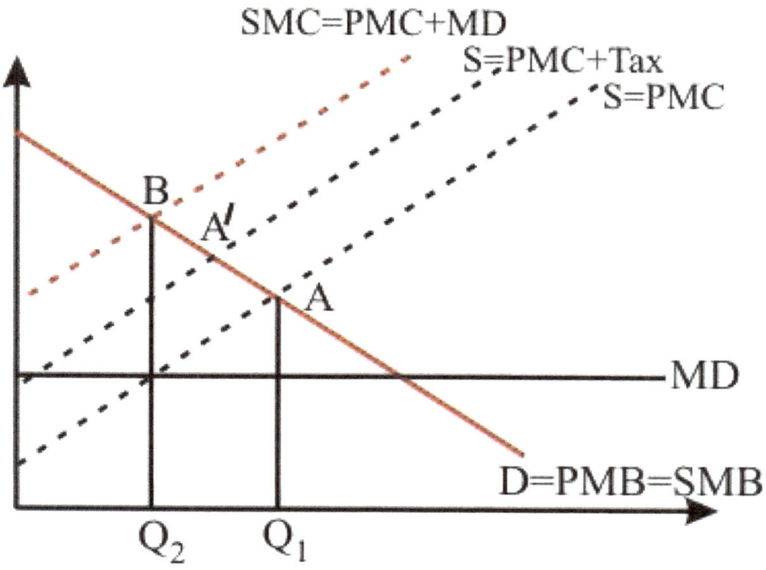

- The steel plant initially produces at A, Q_1.
- Imposing a tax shifts PMC upwards & ↓ steel production.
- Q_2 is achieved.
- The Pigouvian tax essentially shifts the private marginal cost.
- The firm cuts back output, which moves the economy to the socially optimal level when there is a negative externality.
- The steel firm's privately optimal production solves

$$PMB = PMC + tax$$

- When the tax equals MD, this becomes:

$$PMB = PMC + MD = SMC$$

This determines the efficient level of production.

Subsidies

- The government can impose a "Pigouvian" subsidy on producers of positive externalities, which increases its output.
- If the subsidy equals the external marginal benefit at the socially optimal quantity, the firm will increase production to that point.

Example: oil exploration has positive externality.

Figure: Illustrates such a subsidy.

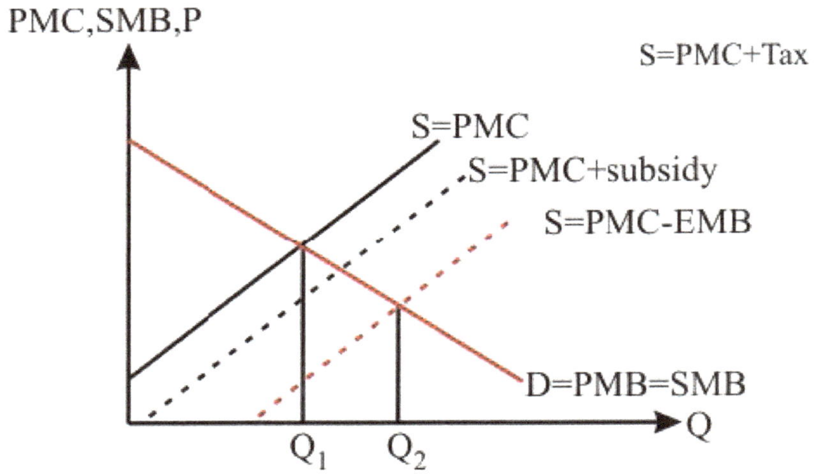

- The firm initially chooses Q_1 maximizing π.
- Providing a subsidy shifts the PMC downward.
- Providing subsidy $= EMB$ shifts the PMC downwards to SMC.
- The firm expands output, shifting the economy towards the social optimal when there is a positive externality.

$$PMC = PMC - subsidy$$

- When the subsidy equals EMB, this becomes:

$$PMB = PMC - EMB = SMC$$

- This determines the efficient level of production. Q_2 is achieved.

Pigouvian Tax/Subsidy

- Restores Pareto efficiency and maximizes social welfare.
- Practical limitations:
  - Must know marginal damage function to set t.
  - Difficult to measure the marginal damage in practice.

Regulation

- Finally, the government can impose quantity regulation, rather than relying on the price mechanism.
- Same outcome as Pigouvian taxation: move people to social optimal.

For example, consider the steel firm in Figure.

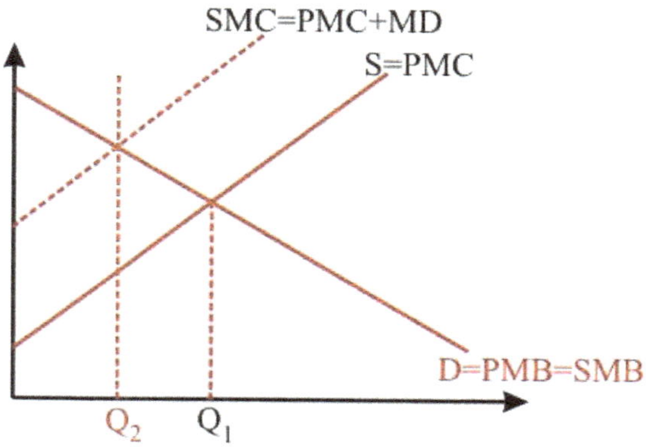

- The firm has incentive to produce at Q_1
- Yet the government simply requires it to produce at Q_2
- Advantages:
  - Ease of enforcement
  - Expedience
- Disadvantages:
  - Dynamics: no incentive to innovate
  - Allocative inefficiency with heterogeneity in cost of pollution reduction
- In an ideal world, Pigouvian taxation and quantity regulation give identical policy outcomes.
- In practice, there are complications that may make taxes a more effective means of addressing externalities.

Price vs. Quantity Approach

- The key goal is, for any reduction in pollution, to find the least-cost means of achieving that reduction.
- One approach could simply be to reduce output.
- Another approach would be to adopt pollution-reduction technology.
- So far we have examined reductions in output say, steel production. Now we examine *pollution reduction*, by the steel firm.
- We do this exercise to see why policy makers prefer tax in some situations and Quantity Regulation in others.
- For example: If the government wants to reduce the emission of Sulphur Dioxide, it could simply put a cap on the amount of Sculpture Dioxide produced. This can be achieved in multiple ways.

Model of Pollution Reduction

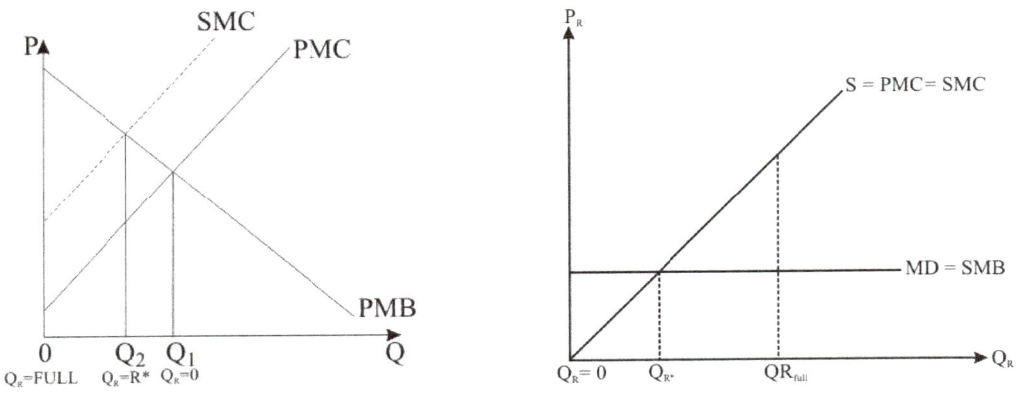

a b

- The good that is being created is pollution reduction, the x-axis measure pollution reduction as we move from left to right.
- Pollution Reduction has a price associated with it, P_R
- On its own steel company would set $Q_R = 0, Q_{steel} = Q_1$
- Such an action maximizes profits for the steel plant.
- The steel firm's MB from pollution reduction is 0.Hence PMB is represented by the horizontal axis
- While it faces increasing marginal costs from reducing its pollution level
- Since the firm pays for the pollution reduction and there is no externality in the process of pollution reduction, the social cost is same as private cost $\Rightarrow SMC = PMC$
- While the benefit of pollution Reduction is 0 to the firm, society benefits by MD
  - The private market outcome is zero pollution reduction, while the socially efficient level is higher.
  - The optimal tax would simply be MD-the firm would reduce pollution levels to R*, because its MC is less than the tax up until that point, but no further.
- Thus optimal level of pollution reduction is : R* where $PMC = SMC = SMB$
- At some level the firm would achieve full pollution Reduction
- The X- axis also measures pollution levels as we move from right to left, i.e. From R_{full} towards 0.
- Is, quantity regulation simpler- just mandate pollution reduction of R*?

In this case taxation is easier ∵ the government just needs to know MD (a constant) regulation implies the government must also know the exact shape of PMC to solve PMC=MD & set

Q_R^* . However since MD is not constant in general, both tax & quantity regulation are challenging. If MD is not constant the government must know the slope of both MD & PMC.

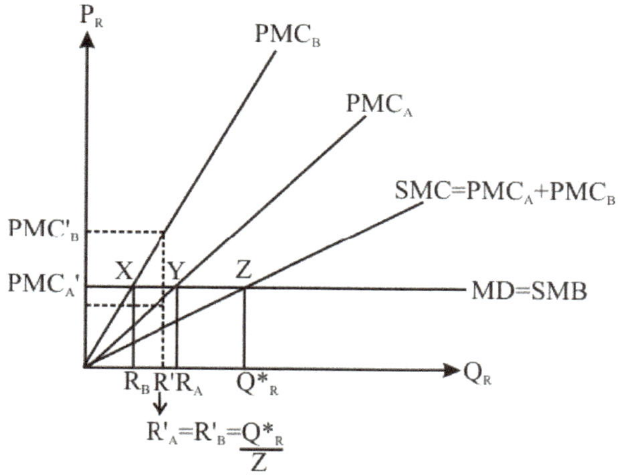

Two Firms Emit Pollution

In figure

- Two firms emit pollution.
- Firm B is old and has a relatively inefficient pollution reduction technology $\Rightarrow$ steep PMC of pollution reduction.
- Firm A is new and more efficient.
- For any given output level of pollution Reduction, $PMC_B > PMC_A$.
- To get total MC, we sum PMC_s horizontally.
- The SMB curve is same as before.
- The efficient level of pollution reduction is also same as before

$$\Sigma MC = MB(MD)(at\ po\text{int}\ z)$$

MD is the marginal damage averted by additional pollution reduction. This is the social MB of pollution reduction. Here we have drawn it as horizontal for simplicity. Generally it is downward sloping due to diminishing returns.

Quantity regulation could result in equal reduction in pollution by both firms such that

$$R_1 + R_2 = R^*$$

– This could happen if government just cares about total reduction R*, and not how it is divided between the firms.

- Pollution reduction in this way is clearly inefficient since firm B is worse at reducing pollution.

- So total social cost of reducing pollution is higher than the cost would be if A reduced more.

- If we could make firm A reduce more, we could lower the total social cost.
- Efficient regulation is where the MC of pollution reduction for each firm equal SMB.

$$Q\left(\sum_i PMC_i\right) = Q(SMB) \quad \Rightarrow Q^* = \sum Qi^*$$

$$PMC_i = SMB \Rightarrow Q_1^*$$

- Imposing a Pigouvian tax equal to MD, induces these levels of output.

  Taxes are preferred here: government just needs to know MD, not MC and the firms can flexibly choose their optimal amount of reduction (allowing them to choose according to true MC). No need to distribute Q_R^A & Q_R^B.

- This fig shows that price regulation through taxes is more efficient than quantity regulation.

Price vs. Quantity Approach

- Rescuing quantity regulation: Use tradable permits.
  - Cap total amount of pollution.
  - Issue permits that allow firms to pollute.
  - Allow firms to trade permits to pollute.
  - Hybrid of Regulation and Coasian solution.
  - Both allocative and productive efficiency will be achieved.
  - Also have dynamic incentives to innovate because each firm is bearing a marginal cost of pollution.

Assigning Permits

- Initially the permits might be assigned as quantity regulation was assigned.
  - This means that initially $R_A = R_B$.
  - But now Firm B has an interest in buying some of Firm *A*'s permits, reducing its emissions costs PMC_B ($>PMC_A$). Both sides could be made better off by Firm *A* selling a permit to Firm *B*, and then Firm *A* simply reducing its pollution level.
  - This trading process will continue until $PMC_B = PMC_A$

Policy without Uncertainly

- Let q denote pollution reduction starting from private market equation where q = o

- Let $B(Q)$ denote social benefits of pollution reduction.
- Let $C(Q)$ denote social costs.
- In the simple model in graph:
- MB of pollution reduction is constant $B'(Q) = d$..
- MC is given by the loss in surplus from producing 1 less car (1 unit less steel). More generally MC should be interpreted as cost of reducing pollution through cheapest method. (eg. Cleaner plants).
- In competitive equilibrium PMB of pollution reduction $= 0 \Rightarrow$ level of pollution Reduction is $Q_R = 0$
- Social optimum: max $B(Q) = C(Q)$ FOC $\Rightarrow B'(Q) = C'(Q)$
- With no uncertainty, could obtain optimum with either quantity or price policy Quantity: regulate amount Q^*
- Price: set price for pollution reduction $P^* = C'(Q)$.

Optimal Policy with Uncertainly

- Now suppose that there is uncertainty about the MC of reducing pollution.
- Cost is now $C(Q,\theta)$ with θ unknown.(Uncertainty about cost).
- Marginal cost lies between MC_{LB}, MC_{UB} with mean MC_{mean}

$$MC \in [MC_{LB}, MC_{UB}]$$

$$MC_{mean} = Mean[MC]$$

- Objective: maximize expected social welfare.
- Formally choose one of two options, P or Q directly

$$\rightarrow \max\{E_\theta[B(Q) - C(Q,\theta)], E_\theta[B(Q(P)) - C(Q(P),\theta)]\}$$

- Choice depends on the steepness of the MB curve.
- Price mechanism (taxes) is identical to quantity mechanism (permits) in above model.
- Weitzman (1974): with uncertainty, the government may not always know how costly it is for a firm to reduce its pollution levels.
  - price and quantity no longer equivalent

Optimal Policy with Uncertainty

MB flat, Q Regulation:

Example: Global Warning

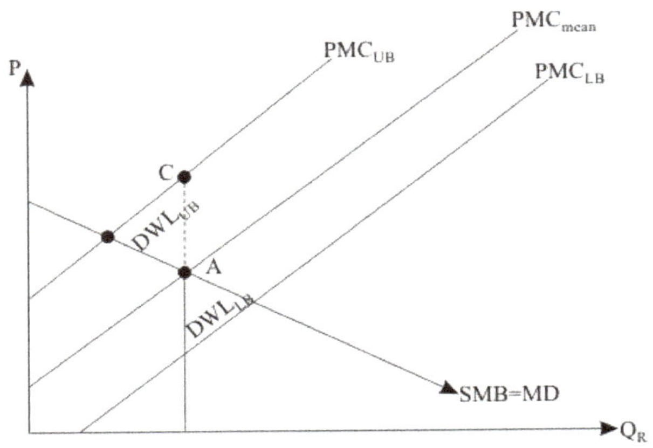

- First assume that SMB is downward sloping but fairly flat (this could arise for global warming for example (does not change a lot with pollution reduction)
- In addition suppose the government's best guess of the costs is MC_{mean}
- But it is possible for actual cost to firm $= PMC_{UB}$
- Regulation mandates Q_R^*
- Suppose the MC is PMC_{UB}, there is a large $DWL = ABC$

MB Flat, P Regulation (Tax)

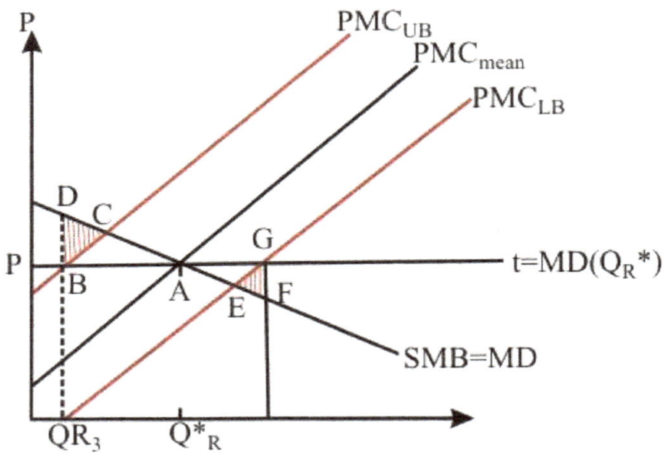

- If instead the government levied a tax, it would equal MD at $Q_R = Q_R^*$

  $(recall\ t = MD(Q^*))$
- Again actual $MC = PMC_{UB}$
- The result is a much smaller DWL $= BDC(SMB = PMC_{UB})$
- Or $DWL = EFG\ if\ PMC_{true} = PMC_{LB}$

Model with Uncertainty and locally steep Benefits.

MB Steep, Quantity Regulation

Example: Nuclear Leakage

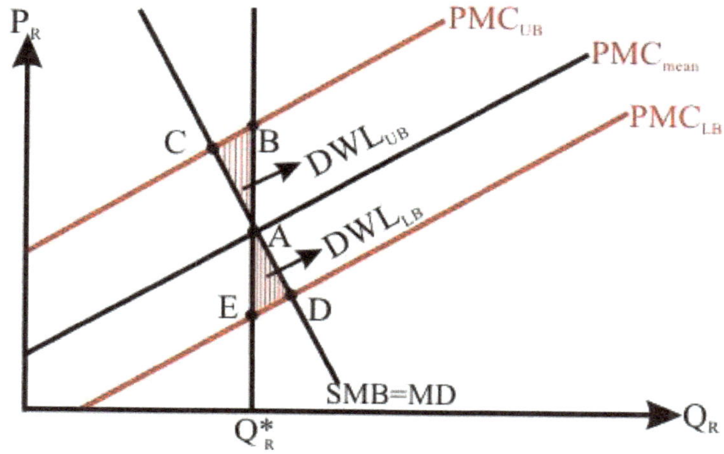

Figure a

- Assume SMB is downward sloping and fairly steep.
- (This for example in case of nuclear leakage).
- Suppose government's best guess about PMC is PMC_{mean}
- But actual is PMC_{UB}
- Regulation mandates Q_R^*
- $DWL = ABC$, small

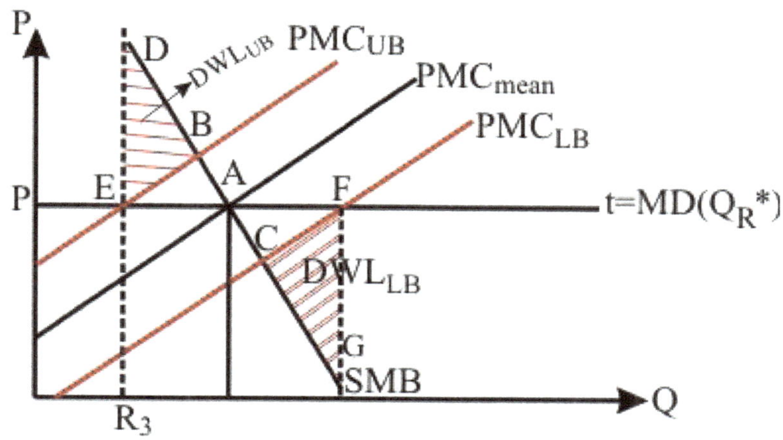

Figure b

MB Steep, Price Regulation

- If instead the government levied a tax it would equal MD at $Q_R = Q_R^*(SMB = PMC_{mean})$
- If $PMC_{true} = PMC_{UB}, DWL = \Delta BED$, much highter than ΔABC in figure

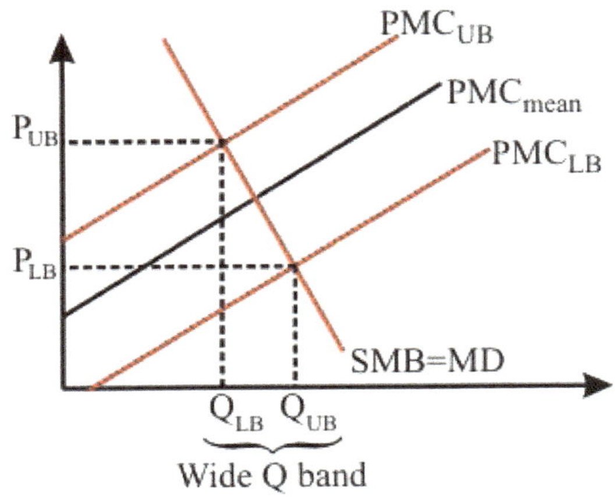

Steep MB

Figure a

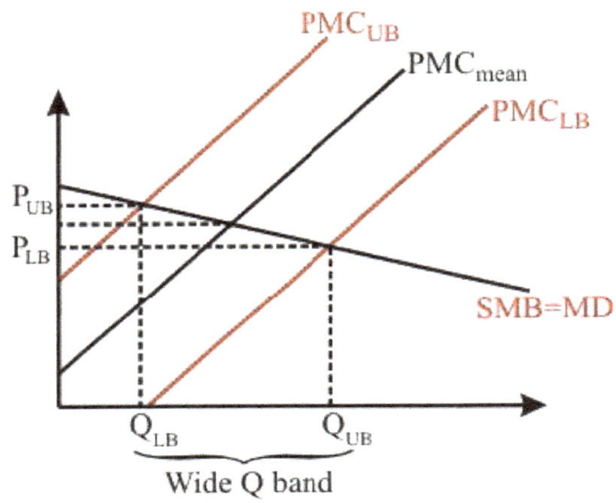

Flat MB

Figure b

- These figures show the implications for choice of quantity regulation versus corrective taxes.
  - The key issue is whether the government wants to get the amount of pollution reduction correct, or to minimize social (same as firm here) costs.
  - Quantity regulation assures the desired level of pollution reduction. When it is important to get the right level (such as with nuclear leakage), this instrument works well.
- However, corrective taxation protects firms against large cost overruns.

Weitzman: Uncertainty about Benefits

- Now suppose that there is uncertainty about the marginal benefits of reducing pollution but that the costs are known.

- For a given p, the government knows the Q that will result exactly since p = C' (Q).
- Since the government knows the true c' (Q), it can either choose P or Q and the firm would be minimizing costs (social costs minimized) always. So the society always minimizes costs.
- More generally, uncertainty matters only when it is about the cost/benefit schedule for the agent who chooses level of pollution reduction.
- If consumer chooses level of pollution reduction, then only uncertainty about marginal benefits matters

Recap of Externalities: Problems and Solutions

- Externality theory
- Private-sector solutions
- Public-sector solutions
- Distinctions between price and quantity approaches to addressing externalities

Number of Cigarettes Smoked in the US

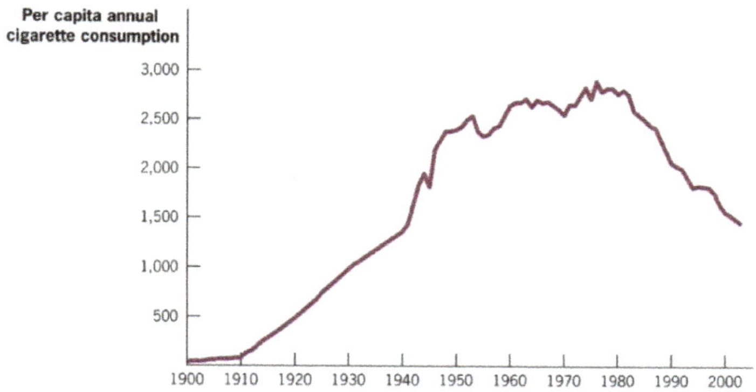

Figure: shows that the number of cigarettes smoked has declined substantially in the United States over time.

- Smoking still causes more than 440,000 deaths each year
- Four times as much as AIDS, motor vehicle accidents, homicide, and suicide combined.
- Smoking is estimated to be the leading cause of death throughout the world by 2030

An Application: Economics of Smoking

What is the role for government intervention in the case of a decision like smoking?

The Economics of Smoking

- Smoking is bad.

  - In standard utility-maximization, any damage individuals do to themselves from dangerous activities results from a rational tradeoff of benefits against potential costs.

- Smoking is addictive.
  - "Rational addicts" understand that each cigarette that they smoke today increases their addiction.
  - Smokers consider *not* only the cost of today's pack of cigarettes, but the cost of all additional future packs that will now be purchased because their addiction is deepened.
  - Smokers also understand that smoking doesn't just reduce health through the current cigarette, but all future cigarettes that will be consumed because of the addiction.
- With this model, smoking remains a rational choice.

The Externalities of Smoking

- Smoking generates negative externalities due to higher health costs.
- Smoking-related disease increases U.S. medical costs by 5% of the total costs, annually.
- If insurance companies can make *actuarial adjustments*, they simply charge smokers higher rates.
  - Such adjustments internalize the medical cost externality from smoking. In a simple model, there are no health externalities because smokers pay for the high medical costs through higher premiums.
- Actuarial adjustments are often *not* the case with employer health insurance, however.
  - In this case, the externality is financial, *not* physical. This is an externality because the social marginal benefit from an individual's cigarette consumption is below the private marginal benefit–the individual's coworkers have to pay higher premiums.
  - In addition to higher health costs to the private sector, individuals who receive government insurance exert a negative externality onto taxpayers.
- Smoking generates negative externalities due to lower workplace productivity and more frequent absences.
- Firms may be able to adjust wages to compensate for this type of problem.
  - If workers' wages adjust to compensate for their lower expected productivity, then the externality is internalized, akin to the adjustments in health premiums.
- Smoking generates *positive* externalities to taxpayers due to the early deaths of smokers and lower payouts for some social insurance programs.

  - Often people contribute towards retirement benefits (pensions) during working life, but smokers may *not* be alive to collect benefits when they are old.
  - This is known as the "death benefit."

- Smoking generates negative externalities (mostly to other family members) through secondhand smoke.
  - Considerable medical uncertainty about the damages done from this.
  - Moreover, if the smoker maximizes family utility rather than individual utility, he rationally trades off the benefits to himself versus the harm to his family.
  - Evidence suggests family utility maximization is incomplete, however.

External Costs

  - Many studies have estimated the external costs of smoking from US data.
  - Taken together, the external costs of smoking are roughly 40¢ per pack of cigarettes in 2003 dollars.
  - Estimates of external costs of secondhand smoke vary widely, from 1¢ to $1.16 per pack.

Tax to Offset External Costs

  - The average federal plus state cigarette tax in the US is over $1 per pack, which takes care of the external costs imposed by smoking.

Should we care Only about Externalities, or do "Internalities" also Matter?

- Traditional economics approach cares only about externalities that smokers impose on others.
- Model ignores some key features of the smoking decision that may motivate government intervention.
  - Youth smoking decisions
  - Inability of adults to quit
- Assumes Rationality: Problematic.
- Youth smoking decisions: 75% of adults who smoke began smoking before their 19th birthday- the legal smoking age in the US.
- It is *not* clear at what age rational decision making sets in.
- Younger people may be unable to make rational tradeoffs between current benefits of smoking and future costs.
- Suggestive that teen who smoke may *not* account for the long-run implications of addiction; they are overly optimistic.

- Among high school seniors who smoked more than 1 pack per day:
  - Among those who said they would *not* be smoking 5 years later, 74% still were.
  - Among those who said they would be smoking 5 years later, 72% still were.
- Many adults who smoke would like to quit, but are unable to do so.
  - 80% of adults who smoke express a desire to quit, but many fewer actually succeed.
  - Over 80% of smokers try to quit in a typical year, and the average smoker tries every 8.5 months.
  - 54% of serious attempts to quit fail within one week.
- Smokers may face a *self-control problem*, an inability to carry out optimal strategies for consumption.
- Economic theory assumes that individuals *not* only can maximize their utility, but carry out these optimal plans.
- Psychology contradicts this assumption: individuals are often unable to carry out *long-term plans* when there are *short-term costs* of doing so.
- Thus if rationality fails, there might be a case for government intervention.
- Evidence of irrational behavior has been found in
  - Smoking
  - Retirement savings
  - Diet and/or exercise.
- Evidence for self-control problems includes laboratory experiments and real-life institutional features.
  - In experiments, individuals reveal they are willing to be patient in the future, but impatient in the present.
  - For example, in one experiment, individuals preferred a check for $100 today versus one for $200 in the future.
  - Yet the same people preferred a check for $200 eight years from now versus a check for $100 six years from now.
  - Time inconsistency/hyperbolic preferences.
- The real-life evidence comes from the demand for *commitment devices*, used to fight off their bad instincts.
  - Smokers regularly set up systems to restrain themselves, such as betting with others or telling people about their decision.

- Expensive memberships at health clubs to commit themselves to exercise.
- Forced Savings : Like buying illiquid assets: Land.
- Student behavior: self proclaimed submission deadlines.

Nudge? Implications for Government Policy

- The lacks of self-control and irrationalities have implications for government policy.
- For smokers who make mistakes (rather than deliberate choices), the damage from smoking could be viewed as an *internality*–the damage people do to themselves through adverse behavior.
- The internality justifies government intervention in the same way an externality does.
- The market failure is the cost imposed on a person's long-run well-being generated by his or her short-run impatience or irrationality.

Implications for Government Policy

- External costs of smoking were roughly 40¢ per pack.
- Tax offsets External costs.
- But internal costs are much larger:
  - Smoker lives about 6 fewer years than a nonsmoker.
- Government has several policy tools for addressing "internalities"
  - Information/outreach campaigns–these have reduced the smoking rate a lot over the last 30 years.
  - Reducing access to cigarettes for teenagers.
  - Taxation–elasticity of demand for cigarettes is around -0.5, and higher for youth smokers. This implies that if cigarette taxes raise the gross price of cigarettes by 1%, demand for cigarettes would fall by 0.5%.

References

- Tietenberg, T. H. (1974-06-01). "On Taxation and the Control of Externalities: Comment". The American Economic Review. 64 (3): 462–466. ISSN 0002-8282. JSTOR 1808900. doi:10.2307/1808900
- Barry Commoner "Frail Reeds in a Harsh World". New York: The American Museum of Natural History. Natural History. Journal of the American Museum of Natural History, Vol. LXXVIII No. 2, February, 1969, p. 44
- Stern, Nicholas (2006). "Introduction". The Economics of Climate Change The Stern Review (PDF). Cambridge University Press. ISBN 978-0-521-70080-1
- "Spash, C. L. (2007) The economics of climate change impacts à la Stern: Novel and nuanced or rhetorically restricted? Ecological Economics 63(4): 706–13" (PDF). Archived from the original (PDF) on 2014-02-02. Retrieved 2012-12-23

- Brown, John Prather (1973). "Toward an Economic Theory of Liability". Journal of Legal Studies. 2 (2): 323–349. doi:10.1086/467501
- Costanza, Robert; Segura,Olman; Olsen, Juan Martinez-Alier (1996). Getting Down to Earth: Practical Applications of Ecological Economics. Washington, D.C.: Island Press. ISBN 1559635037
- Spash, Clive L. (16 July 2010). "The brave new world of carbon trading". New Political Economy. Taylor and Francis Online. 15 (2): 169–95. doi:10.1080/13563460903556049. Copy also available at "Archived copy" (PDF). Archived from the original (PDF) on 2013-05-10. Retrieved 2013-09-13
- Carlton, Dennis W.; Loury, Glenn C. (1980). "The Limitations of Pigouvian Taxes as a Long-Run Remedy for Externalities". Quarterly Journal of Economics. 95 (3): 559–566. doi:10.2307/1885093. JSTOR 1885093
- Boettke, Peter (2012). Living Economics. The Independent Institute, Universidad Francisco Marroquin. pp. 254–255. ISBN 9781598130751
- Gilles, Stephen G. (1994). "The Invisible Hand Formula". Virginia Law Review. Virginia Law Review. 80 (5): 1015–1054. JSTOR 1073624. doi:10.2307/1073624
- Kohn, Robert E. (1986). "The Limitations of Pigouvian Taxes as a Long-Run Remedy for Externalities: Comment". Quarterly Journal of Economics. 101 (3): 625–630. doi:10.2307/1885700
- Wright, Richard W. (2003). "Hand, Posner, and the Myth of the 'Hand Formula'". Theoretical Inquiries in Law. 4: 145. doi:10.2139/ssrn.362800

4

Public Goods: An Overview

An important question in public economics revolves around the concept of public goods. Should public goods be accounted as part of subsidies and benefits provided by the government? Public economics is best understood in confluence with the major topics listed in the following chapter.

Public Good

- Some markets do *not* work very well because the good in question has *public good* characteristics to it.
- For example, in Dhaka, Bangladesh, public trash collection is fairly inefficient, but attempts at privatization have *not* fared any better.
- The key problem with private collection of garbage is the *free rider problem*– with a private, voluntary system, each resident could simply sneak his garbage into his neighbor's garbage and avoid making payments.
- Eventually, everyone would figure this out, and no one would be willing to pay trash collection voluntarily.
- In fact, most residents have figured out the incentive to "free ride." Only 50 of 1,100 neighborhoods have private garbage collection.
- In this chapter we first define public goods and determine the optimal level of provision.
- We then turn to the question whether and to what extent should the government be involved in the provision of public goods.
- It also explores the notion of "crowd-out" where public provision simply substitutes for already existing private provision of a good.

The role of public goods is important in economics. The subsequent lessons explore issues related to:

Cost-benefit analysis

Political economy

State and local government

Education

Government Intervention

- Private market provides a Pareto efficient outcome under three conditions
  - No externalities

1. Markets may be incomplete due to lack of prices (e.g. pollution)
   - Achieving efficient Coasian solution requires an organization to coordinate individuals .that is, a government
   - This is why govt. funds public goods (highways, education, defense)
   - Questions: What public goods to provide and how to correct externalities?
   - Perfect information
2. When some agents have more information asymmetry than others, markets fail
   - Ex. 1: Adverse selection in health insurance
   - Healthy people drop out of private market! unraveling
   - Mandated coverage could make everyone better off
   - Ex. 2: credit constraints and subsidies for education
   - Ex. 3: Markets for intergenerational goods
   - Future generations' interests may not be fully reflected in market outcomes
   - Perfect competition
3. When markets are not competitive, there is role for govt. regulation
   - Ex: natural monopolies such as electricity and telephones
   - This topic is traditionally left to courses on industrial organization and is not covered in this course
   - But taking the methodological approach of public economics to problems traditionally analyzed in IO is a very promising area

- Individual Failures

4. Recent addition to the list of potential failures that motivate government intervention: people are not fully rational
   - Government intervention (e.g. by forcing saving via social security) may be desirable
5. In case of "individual" failure rather than a traditional market failure
   - Conceptual challenge: how to avoid paternalism critique

  - Why does govt. know better what's desirable for you (e.g. wearing a seatbelt, not smoking, saving more)
  - Difficult but central issues for policy design
  - Efficient markets often deliver very large rewards to small set of people (top incomes)
- First Welfare Theorem tells us when the government should intervene
- Redistribution Concerns
- Instances when government might intervene.

Why Limit Government Intervention?

- One solution to these issues would be for the government to oversee all production and allocation in the economy (socialism).
- Serious problems with this solution
  - Information: how does government aggregate preferences and technology to choose optimal production and allocation?
  - Government policies inherently distort incentives (behavioral responses in private sector)
  - Politicians are not necessarily benevolent planner in reality; face incentive constraints themselves
- Creates sharp tradeoffs between costs and benefits of government intervention
- Providing more public goods requires higher taxes and distorts consumption decisions
- Redistribution distorts incentives to work

In economics, a public good is a good that is both non-excludable and non-rivalrous in that individuals cannot be effectively excluded from use and where use by one individual does not reduce availability to others. Gravelle and Rees: "The defining characteristic of a public good is that consumption of it by one individual does not actually or potentially reduce the amount available to be consumed by another individual." In a non-economic sense, the term is often used to describe something that is useful for the public generally, such as education and infrastructure, although these are not "public goods" in the economic sense. This is in contrast to a common good which is non-excludable but is rivalrous to a certain degree.

Public goods include fresh air, knowledge, official statistics, national security, common language(s), flood control systems, lighthouses, and street lighting. Public goods that are available everywhere are sometimes referred to as global public goods. There is an important conceptual difference between the sense of 'a' public good, or public 'goods' in economics, and the more generalized idea of 'the public good' (or common good, or public interest),"'the' public good is a shorthand signal for shared benefit at a societal level (philosophical/political) sense should not be reduced to the established specific (economic) sense of 'a' public good."

Many public goods may at times be subject to excessive use resulting in negative externalities affecting all users; for example air pollution and traffic congestion. Public goods problems are often closely related to the "free-rider" problem, in which people not paying for the good may continue to access it. Thus, the good may be under-produced, overused or degraded. Public goods may also become subject to restrictions on access and may then be considered to be club goods or private goods; exclusion mechanisms include copyright, patents, congestion pricing, and pay television.

There is a good deal of debate and literature on how to measure the significance of public goods problems in an economy, and to identify the best remedies.

Terminology, and Types of Goods

Paul A. Samuelson is usually credited as the first economist to develop the theory of public goods. In his classic 1954 paper *The Pure Theory of Public Expenditure*, he defined a public good, or as he called it in the paper a "collective consumption good", as follows:

[goods] which all enjoy in common in the sense that each individual's consumption of such a good leads to no subtractions from any other individual's consumption of that good...

This is the property that has become known as *non-rivalry*. In addition a *pure public good* exhibits a second property called *non-excludability*: that is, it is impossible to exclude any individuals from consuming the good.

The opposite of a public good is a *private good*, which does not possess these properties. A loaf of bread, for example, is a private good; its owner can exclude others from using it, and once it has been consumed, it cannot be used again.

A good that is rivalrous but *non-excludable* is sometimes called a *common-pool resource*. Such goods raise similar issues to public goods: the mirror to the *public goods problem* for this case is sometimes called the "tragedy of the commons". For example, it is so difficult to enforce restrictions on deep sea fishing that the world's fish stocks can be seen as a non-excludable resource, but one which is finite and diminishing.

Definition Matrix

	Excludable	Non-excludable
Rivalrous	**Private goods** food, clothing, cars, parking spaces	**Common-pool resources** fish stocks, timber, coal
Non-rivalrous	**Club goods** cinemas, private parks, satellite television	Public goods free-to-air television, air, national defense

V. Ostrom and E. Ostrom proposed additional modifications to the classification of goods to identify fundamental differences that affect the incentives facing individuals (1) Replacing the term "rivalry of consumption" with "subtractability of use." (2) Conceptualizing subtractability of use and excludability to vary from low to high rather than characterizing them as either present or absent. (3) Overtly adding a very important fourth type of good—common-pool resources—that shares the attribute of subtractability with private goods and difficulty of exclusion with public goods. Forests, water systems, fisheries, and the global atmosphere are all common-pool resources of immense importance for the survival of humans on this earth. (4) Changing the name of a "club" good to a "toll" good since many goods that share these characteristics are provided by small scale public as well as private associations.

Challenges in Identifying Public Goods

The definition of non-excludability states that it is impossible to exclude individuals from consumption. Technology now allows radio or TV broadcasts to be encrypted such that persons without a special decoder are excluded from the broadcast. Many forms of information goods have characteristics of public goods. For example, a poem can be read by many people without reducing the consumption of that good by others; in this sense, it is non-rivalrous. Similarly, the information in most patents can be used by any party without reducing consumption of that good by others. Official statistics provide a clear example of information goods that are public goods, since they are created to be non-excludable. Creative works may be excludable in some circumstances, however: the individual who wrote the poem may decline to share it with others by not publishing it. Copyrights and patents both encourage the creation of such non-rival goods by providing temporary monopolies, or, in the terminology of public goods, providing a legal mechanism to enforce excludability for a limited period of time. For public goods, the "lost revenue" of the producer of the good is not part of the definition: a public good is a good whose consumption does not reduce any other's consumption of that good.

Debate has been generated among economists whether such a category of "public goods" exists. Steven Shavell has suggested the following:

when professional economists talk about public goods they do *not* mean that there are a general category of goods that share the same economic characteristics, manifest the same dysfunctions, and that may thus benefit from pretty similar corrective solutions...there is merely an infinite series of particular problems (some of overproduction, some of underproduction, and so on), each with a particular solution that cannot be deduced from the theory, but that instead would depend on local empirical factors.

Common confusion is that public goods are goods provided by the public sector. Although it is often the case that government is involved in producing public goods, this is not necessarily the case. Public goods may be *naturally* available. They may be produced by private individuals and firms, by non-state collective action, or they may not be produced at all.

The theoretical concept of public goods does not distinguish with regard to the geographical region in which a good may be produced or consumed. However, some theorists such as Inge Kaul use the term "global public good" for public goods which is non-rival and non-excludable throughout the whole world, as opposed to a public good which exists in just one national area. Knowledge has been held to be an example of a global public good, but also as a commons, the knowledge commons.

Graphically, non-rivalry means that if each of several individuals has a demand curve for a public good, then the individual demand curves are summed vertically to get the aggregate demand curve for the public good. This is in contrast to the procedure for deriving the aggregate demand for a private good, where individual demands are summed horizontally.

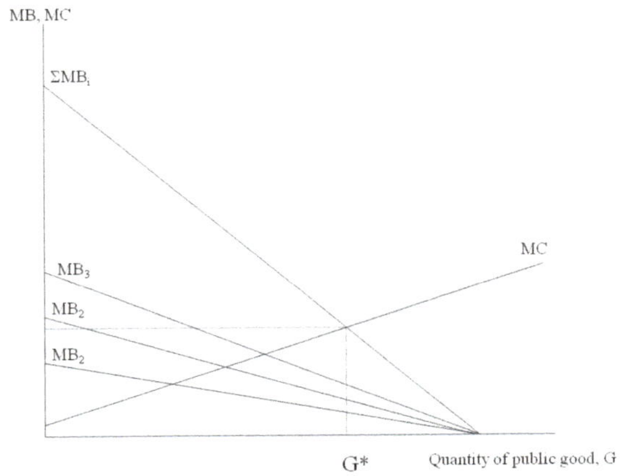

Aggregate demand (ΣMB) is the sum of individual demands (MBi)

Social goods

Social goods are defined as public goods that could be delivered as private goods, but are usually delivered by the government for various reasons, including social policy, and funded via public funds like taxes. Note that some writers have used the term "public good" to refer only to non-excludable "pure public goods" and refer to excludable public goods as "club goods".

Examples

Common examples of public goods include: defence, public fireworks, lighthouses, clean air and other environmental goods, and information goods, such as official statistics, software development, authorship, and invention. Some goods, like orphan drugs, require special governmental incentives to be produced, but can't be classified as public goods since they don't fulfill the above requirements (non-excludable and non-rivalrous.) Law enforcement, streets, libraries, museums, and education are commonly misclassified as public goods, but they are technically classified in economic terms as quasi-public goods because excludability *is* possible, but they do still fit some of the characteristics of public goods.

The provision of a lighthouse is a standard example of a public good, since it is difficult to exclude ships from using its services. No ship's use detracts from that of others, but since most of the benefit of a lighthouse accrues to ships using particular ports, lighthouse maintenance can be profitably bundled with port fees (Ronald Coase, *The Lighthouse in Economics* 1974). This has been sufficient to fund actual lighthouses.

Technological progress can create new public goods. The most simple examples are street lights, which are relatively recent inventions (by historical standards). One person's enjoyment of them does not detract from other persons' enjoyment, and it currently would be prohibitively expensive to charge individuals separately for the amount of light they presumably use. Official statistics are another example. The government's ability to collect, process and provide high-quality information to guide decision-making at all levels has been strongly advanced by technological progress. On the other hand, a public good's status may change over time. Technological progress can significantly impact excludability of traditional public goods: encryption allows broadcasters to sell individual access to their programming. The costs for electronic road pricing have fallen dramatically, paving the way for detailed billing based on actual use.

Some question as to whether defense is a public good. Murray Rothbard argues, "'national defense' is surely not an absolute good with only one unit of supply. It consists of specific resources committed in certain definite and concrete ways—and these resources are necessarily scarce. A ring of defense bases around New York, for example, cuts down the amount possibly available around San Francisco." Jeffrey Rogers Hummel and Don Lavoie note, "Americans in Alaska and Hawaii could very easily be excluded from the U.S. government's defense perimeter, and doing so might enhance the military value of at least conventional U.S. forces to Americans in the other forty-eight states. But, in general, an additional ICBM in the U.S. arsenal can simultaneously protect everyone within the country without diminishing its services".

Public goods are not restricted to human beings. Indeed, it is one aspect of the study of cooperation in biology.

Free Rider Problem

Public goods provide a very important example of market failure, in which market-like behavior of individual gain-seeking does not produce efficient results. The production of public goods results in positive externalities which are not remunerated. If private organizations do not reap all the benefits of a public good which they have produced, their incentives to produce it voluntarily might be insufficient. Consumers can take advantage of public goods without contributing sufficiently to their creation. This is called the free rider problem, or occasionally, the "easy rider problem" (because consumers' contributions will be small but non-zero). If too many consumers decide to "free-ride", private costs exceed private benefits and the incentive to provide the good or service through the market disappears. The market thus fails to provide a good or service for which there is a need.

The free rider problem depends on a conception of the human being as *homo economicus*: purely rational and also purely selfish—extremely individualistic, considering only those benefits and costs that directly affect him or her. Public goods give such a person an incentive to be a free rider.

For example, consider national defense, a standard example of a pure public good. Suppose *homo economicus* thinks about exerting some extra effort to defend the nation. The benefits to the individual of this effort would be very low, since the benefits would be distributed among all of the millions of other people in the country. There is also a very high possibility that he or she could get injured or killed during the course of his or her military service.

On the other hand, the free rider knows that he or she cannot be excluded from the benefits of national defense, regardless of whether he or she contributes to it. There is also no way that these benefits can be split up and distributed as individual parcels to people. The free rider would not voluntarily exert any extra effort, unless there is some inherent pleasure or material reward for doing so (for example, money paid by the government, as with an all-volunteer army or mercenaries). The free-riding problem is even more complicated than it was thought to be until recently. Any time non-excludability results in failure to pay the true marginal value (often called the "demand revelation problem"), it will also result in failure to generate proper income levels, since households will not give up valuable leisure if they cannot individually increment a good. This implies that, for public goods without strong special interest support, under-provision is likely since benefit-cost analyses are being conducted at the wrong income levels, and all of the ungenerated income would have been spent on the public good, apart from general equilibrium considerations.

In the case of information goods, an inventor of a new product may benefit all of society, but hardly anyone is willing to pay for the invention if they can benefit from it for free. In the case of an information good, however, because of its characteristics of non-excludability and also because of almost zero reproduction costs, commoditization is difficult and not always efficient even from a neoclassical economic point of view.

Economic and Political Solutions

Assurance Contracts

An assurance contract is a contract in which participants make a binding pledge to contribute to building a public good, contingent on a quorum of a predetermined size being reached. Otherwise the good is not provided and any monetary contributions are refunded.

A dominant assurance contract is a variation in which an entrepreneur creates the contract and refunds the initial pledge plus an additional sum of money if the quorum is not reached. (The entrepreneur profits by collecting a fee if the quorum is reached and the good is provided.) In game-theoretic terms this makes pledging to build the public good a dominant strategy: the best move is to pledge to the contract regardless of the actions of others.

Coasian Solution

A *Coasian solution*, named for the economist Ronald Coase, proposes that potential beneficiaries of a public good can negotiate to pool their resources and create it, based on each party's self-interested willingness to pay. His treatise, "The Problem of Social Cost" (1960), argued that if the transaction costs between potential beneficiaries of a public good are low—that it is easy for potential beneficiaries to find each other and organize a pooling their resources based upon the good's value to each of them—that public goods could be produced without government action.

Much later, Coase himself wrote that while what had become known as the Coase Theorem had explored the implications of zero transaction costs, he had actually intended to use this construct as a stepping-stone to understand the real world of positive transaction costs, corporations, legal systems and government actions.,

I examined what would happen in a world in which transaction costs were assumed to be zero. My aim in doing so was not to describe what life would be like in such a world but to provide a simple setting in which to develop the analysis and, what was even more important, to make clear the fundamental role which transaction costs do, and should, play in the fashioning of the institutions which make up the economic system.

and,

The world of zero transaction costs has often been described as a Coasian world. Nothing could be further from the truth. It is the world of modern economic theory, one which I was hoping to persuade economists to leave. What I did in "The Problem of Social Cost" was simply to shed light on some of its properties. I argued in such a world the allocation of resources would be independent of the legal position, a result which Stigler dubbed the "Coase theorem."

Thus, while Coase himself appears to have considered the "Coase theorem" and Coasian solutions as simplified constructs to ultimately consider the real 20th-century world of governments and laws and corporations, these concepts have become attached to a world where transaction costs were much lower, and government intervention would unquestionably be less necessary. Is there room in the 21st century for something closer to this ideal?

A minor alternative, especially for information goods, is for the producer to refuse to release a good to the public until payment to cover costs is met. Author Stephen King, for instance, authored chapters of a new novel downloadable for free on his website while stating that he would not release subsequent chapters unless a certain amount of money was raised. Sometimes dubbed *holding for ransom*, this method of public goods production is a modern application of the street performer protocol for public goods production. Unlike assurance contracts, its success relies largely on social norms to ensure (to some extent) that the threshold is reached and partial contributions are not wasted.

One of the purest Coasian solutions today is the new phenomenon of Internet crowdfunding. Here rules are enforced by computer algorithms and legal contracts as well as social pressure. For example, on the Kickstarter site, each funder authorizes a credit card purchase to buy a new product or receive other promised benefits, but no money changes hands until the funding goal is met. Because automation and the Internet so reduce the transaction costs for pooling resources, project goals of only a few hundred dollars are frequently crowdfunded, far below the costs of soliciting traditional investors. Other crowdfunded projects have raised over a million dollars, like the Arkyd-100 space satellite telescope funded on Kickstarter in June 2013. It would seem to be a clear instance of a Coase solution when a public good that always required government sponsorship in the 20th century can be efficiently organized from 18,000 individuals' self-interest (including rewards such as an orbital "selfie", and five minutes of observation time donated in their name to find potential killer asteroids).

Government Provision

If voluntary provision of public goods will not work, then the obvious solution is making their provision involuntary. This saves each of us from our own tendency to be a free rider, while also assuring us that no one else will be allowed to free ride. One frequently proposed solution to the problem is for governments or states to impose taxation to fund the production of public goods. This does not actually solve the theoretical problem because *good government* is itself a public good. Thus it is difficult to ensure the government has an incentive to provide the optimum amount even if it were possible for the government to determine precisely what amount would be optimum. These issues are studied by public choice theory and public finance.

Sometimes the government provides public goods using "unfunded mandates". An example is the requirement that every car be fit with a catalytic converter. This may be executed in the private sector, but the end result is predetermined by the state: the individually involuntary provision of the public good clean air. Unfunded mandates have also been imposed by the U.S. federal government on the state and local governments, as with the Americans with Disabilities Act, for example.

Regardless the role of the government is provide vital goods to all individuals, some of which they cannot obtain on themselves. In order to ensure that government services are properly funded taxes and other government controlled entities are enforced. Although enforced taxes deter the free-rider problem many contend that some goods should be excluded and made into private goods. However, this not possible with all goods such as pure public goods that are inseparable and inclusive, thus require "provision by public means". In short, the government has a responsibility to ensure that the social welfare of individuals is met as opposed to privatized goods.

Subsidies and Joint Products

A government may subsidize production of a public good in the private sector. Unlike government provision, subsidies may result in some form of a competitive market. The potential for cronyism (for example, an alliance between political insiders and the businesses receiving subsidies) can be limited with secret bidding for the subsidies or application of the subsidies following clear general principles. Depending on the nature of a public good and a related subsidy, principal–agent problems can arise between the citizens and the government or between the government and the subsidized producers; this effect and counter-measures taken to address it can diminish the benefits of the subsidy.

Subsidies can also be used in areas with a potential for non-individualism: For instance, a state may subsidize devices to reduce air pollution and appeal to citizens to cover the remaining costs.

Similarly, a joint-product model analyzes the collaborative effect of joining a private good to a public good. For example, a tax deduction (private good) can be *tied* to a donation to a charity (public good). It can be shown that the provision of the public good increases when tied to the private good, as long as the private good is provided by a monopoly (otherwise the private good would be provided by competitors without the link to the public good).

Privileged Group

The study of collective action shows that public goods are still produced when one individual benefits more from the public good than it costs him to produce it; examples include benefits from individual use, intrinsic motivation to produce, and business models based on selling complement goods. A group that contains such individuals is called a privileged group. A historical example could be a downtown entrepreneur who erects a street light in front of his shop to attract customers; even though there are positive external benefits to neighboring nonpaying businesses, the added customers to the paying shop provide enough revenue to cover the costs of the street light.

The existence of privileged groups may not be a complete solution to the free rider problem, however, as underproduction of the public good may still result. The street light builder, for instance, would not consider the added benefit to neighboring businesses when determining whether to erect his street light, making it possible that the street light isn't built when the cost of building is too high for the single entrepreneur even when the total benefit to all the businesses combined exceeds the cost.

An example of the privileged group solution could be the Linux community, assuming that users derive more benefit from contributing than it costs them to do it.

Another example is those musicians and writers who create music and writings for their own personal enjoyment, and publish because they enjoy having an audience. Financial incentives are not necessary to ensure the creation of these public goods. Whether this creates the correct production level of writings and music is an open question.

Merging Free Riders

Another method of overcoming the free rider problem is to simply eliminate the profit incentive for free riding by buying out all the potential free riders. A property developer that owned an entire city street, for instance, would not need to worry about free riders when erecting street lights since he owns every business that could benefit from the street light without paying. Implicitly, then, the property developer would erect street lights until the marginal social benefit met the marginal social cost. In this case, they are equivalent to the private marginal benefits and costs.

While the purchase of all potential free riders may solve the problem of underproduction due to free riders in smaller markets, it may simultaneously introduce the problem of underproduction due to monopoly. Additionally, some markets are simply too large to make a buyout of all beneficiaries feasible – this is particularly visible with public goods that affect everyone in a country.

Introducing an Exclusion Mechanism (Club Goods)

Another solution, which has evolved for information goods, is to introduce exclusion mechanisms which turn public goods into club goods. One well-known example is copyright and patent laws. These laws, which in the 20th century came to be called intellectual property laws, attempt to remove the natural non-excludability by prohibiting reproduction of the good. Although they can address the free rider problem, the downside of these laws is that they imply private monopoly power and thus are not Pareto-optimal.

For example, in the United States, the patent rights given to pharmaceutical companies encourage them to charge high prices (above marginal cost) and to advertise to convince patients to persuade their doctors to prescribe the drugs. Likewise, copyright provides an incentive for a publisher to act like The Dog in the Manger, taking older works out of print so as not to cannibalize revenue from the publisher's own new works.

The laws also end up encouraging patent and copyright owners to sue even mild imitators in court and to lobby for the extension of the term of the exclusive rights in a form of rent seeking.

These problems with the club-good mechanism arise because the underlying marginal cost of giving the good to more people is low or zero, but, because of the limits of price discrimination those who are unwilling or unable to pay a profit-maximizing price do not gain access to the good.

If the costs of the exclusion mechanism are not higher than the gain from the collaboration, club goods can emerge naturally. James M. Buchanan showed in his seminal paper that clubs can be an efficient alternative to government interventions.

On the other hand, the inefficiencies and inequities of club goods exclusions sometimes cause potentially excludable club goods to be treated as public goods, and their production financed by some other mechanism. Examples of such "natural" club goods include natural monopolies with very high fixed costs, private golf courses, cinemas, cable television and social clubs. This explains why many such goods are often provided or subsidized by governments, co-operatives or volunteer associations, rather than being left to be supplied by profit-minded entrepreneurs. These goods are often known as *social goods*.

Joseph Schumpeter claimed that the "excess profits", or profits over normal profit, generated by the copyright or patent monopoly will attract competitors that will make technological innovations and thereby end the monopoly. This is a continual process referred to as "Schumpeterian creative destruction", and its applicability to different types of public goods is a source of some controversy. The supporters of the theory point to the case of Microsoft, for example, which has been increasing its prices (or lowering its products' quality), predicting that these practices will make increased market shares for Linux and Apple largely inevitable.

A nation can be seen as a club whose members are its citizens. Government would then be the manager of this club. This is further studied in the Theory of the State.

Altruistic Solutions

Social Norms

If enough people do not think like free-riders, the private and voluntary provision of public goods may be successful. For example, a free rider might come to a public park to enjoy its beauty, yet discard litter that makes it less enjoyable for others. More public-spirited individuals don't do this (they might even pick up existing litter) – why? There could be several reasons. Perhaps they have lived nearby for years and derive pleasure from helping their community, or at least would feel ashamed if their neighbors or friends saw them. Perhaps they are emotionally attached to the environment, or the park is a national treasure; littering it would offend their patriotism. To the extent that most people behave like this (for any reason), a public good is produced: everyone enjoys a clean park, without the government needing to spend tax money on maintenance crews.

Good or bad social behavior is contagious: people unconsciously adapt their behavior to that of their peers. Even people who engaged in free-riding by littering elsewhere are less likely to if they see others hold on to their trash.

Social norms can also be observed everywhere people interact, not only in physical spaces but in virtual communities on the Internet. Lawrence Lessig describes how social norms can regulate behavior in cyberspace: through an individual's perceptions from the (physical or virtual) surrounding community. For example, if a disabled person boards a crowded bus, everyone expects that some able-bodied person will volunteer their seat. The same social norm, although executed in a different environment, can also be applied to the Internet. If a user enters a discussion in a chat room and continues to use all capital letters or make personal attacks ("flames") when addressing other users, the culprit may realize he or she has been blocked by other participants. As in real life, users learning to adapt to the social norms of cyberspace communities provide a public good—here, not suffering disruptive online behavior—for all the participants.

Social Sanctions (Punishment)

Experimental literature suggests that free riding can be overcome without any state intervention. Peer-to-peer punishment, that is, members sanction those members that do not contribute to the public good at a cost, is sufficient to establish and maintain cooperation. Such punishment is often considered altruistic, because it comes at a cost to the punisher, however, the exact nature remains to be explored. Whether costly punishment can explain cooperation is disputed. Recent research finds that costly punishment is less effective in real world environments. For example, punishment works relatively badly under imperfect information, where people cannot observe the behavior of other perfectly.

Voluntary Organizations

Organizations such as the Red Cross, public radio and television or a volunteer fire department provide public goods to the majority at the expense of a minority who voluntarily participate or contribute funds. Contributions to online collaborative media like Wikipedia and other wiki projects, and free software projects such as Linux are another example of relatively few contributors providing a public good (information) freely to all readers or software users.

Proposed explanations for altruistic behavior include biological altruism and reciprocal altruism. For example, voluntary groups such as labor unions and charities often have a federated structure, probably in part because voluntary collaboration emerges more readily in smaller social groups than in large ones.

While both biological and reciprocal altruism are observed in other animals, our species' complex social behaviors take these raw materials much farther. Philanthropy by wealthy individuals—some, such as Andrew Carnegie giving away their entire vast fortunes—have historically provided a multitude of public goods for others. One major impact was the Rockefeller Foundation's development of the "Green Revolution" hybrid grains that probably saved many millions of people from starvation in the 1970s. Christian missionaries, who typically spend large parts of their lives in remote, often dangerous places, have had disproportionate impact compared with their numbers worldwide for centuries. Communist revolutionaries in the 20th century had similar dedication and outsized impacts. International relief organizations such as Doctors Without Borders, Save the Children and Amnesty International have benefited millions, while also occasionally costing workers their lives. For better and for worse, humans can conceive of, and sacrifice for, an almost infinite variety of causes in addition to their biological kin. Reciprocal altruism that leads a vampire bat to regurgitate blood to feed a few others in its colony who fed it on previous nights when it flew back hungry, motivates humans to build lifelong careers in huge multinational corporations and lubricates vast systems of banking and trade and production between hundreds or thousands of actors worldwide.

Religions and Ideologies

Voluntary altruistic organizations often motivate their members by encouraging deep-seated personal beliefs, whether religious or other (such as social justice or environmentalism) that are taken "on faith" more than proved by rational argument. When individuals resist temptations to free riding (e.g., stealing) because they hold these beliefs (or because they fear the disapproval of others who do), they provide others with public goods that might be difficult or impossible to "produce" by administrative coercion alone.

"The noblest motive is the public good." Thomas Jefferson Building, Library of Congress.

One proposed explanation for the ubiquity of religious belief in human societies is multi-level selection: altruists often lose out within groups, but groups with more altruists win. A group whose members believe a "practical reality" that motivates altruistic behavior may out-compete other groups whose members' perception of "factual reality" causes them to behave selfishly. A classic example is a soldier's willingness to fight for his tribe or country. Another example given in evolutionary biologist David Sloan Wilson's *Darwin's Cathedral* is the early Christian church under the late Roman Empire; because Roman society was highly individualistic, during frequent epidemics many of the sick died not of the diseases *per se* but for lack of basic nursing. Christians, who believed in an afterlife, were willing to nurse the sick despite the risks. Although the death rate among the nurses was high, the average Christian had a *much better chance* of surviving an epidemic than other Romans did, and the community prospered.

Religious and non-religious traditions and ideologies (such as nationalism and patriotism) are in full view when a society is in crisis and public goods such as defense are most needed. Wartime leaders invoke their God's protection and claim that their society's most hallowed traditions are at stake. For example, according to President Abraham Lincoln's Gettysburg Address during the American Civil War, the Union was fighting so "that government of the people, by the people, for the people, shall not perish from the earth". Such voluntary, if exaggerated, exhortations complement forcible measures—taxation and conscription—to motivate people to make sacrifices for their cause.

Efficient Production Levels of Public Goods

The Pareto optimum provision of a public good in a society is at the level where the combined sum of the marginal rate of substitution between private goods and a given public good of all individuals is equal to the marginal rate of transformation. This contrasts to the Pareto optimality condition of private goods, in which each consumers marginal rate of substitution is equal; as is the societies marginal rate of transformation.

When should a public good be provided? Take, for example, a community of just two consumers and the government is considering whether or not to build a public park. Arthur is prepared to pay up to $200 for its use, while Julia is willing to pay up to $100. The total value to the two individuals of having the park is $300. If it can be produced for $225, there is a $75 gain on its production since it provides services that the community values at $300 at a cost of only $225.

Regardless of the method of providing public goods, the efficient level of such provision is still being subjected to economic analysis. For instance, the Samuelson condition calculates the efficient level of public goods production to be where the ratio of the marginal social cost of public and private goods production equals the ratio of the marginal social benefit of public and private goods production.

"If the amount of a public good can be varied continuously, the optimal quantity to produce is that quantity for which the marginal cost of the last unit is just equal to the sum of the prices that all consumers would be willing to pay for that unit." This equilibrium guarantees that the last unit of the public good costs as much to produce as the value that it gives to all of its consumers.

Ownership

An important question regarding public goods is whether they should be owned by the public or the private sector. Economic theorists such as Hart (1995) argue that ownership matters for investment incentives when contracts are incomplete. The incomplete contracting paradigm has been applied to public goods by Besley and Ghatak (2001). They consider the government and a non-governmental organization (NGO) who can both make investments to provide a public good. Who should be the owner of the public good, the government or the NGO? Besley and Ghatak show that the party who has a larger valuation for the public good should be the owner, regardless of whether the government or the NGO has a better investment technology. This result contrasts with the case of private goods studied by Hart (1995), where the party with the better investment technology should be the owner. However, more recently it has been shown that the investment technology matters also in the public-good case when a party is indispensable or when there are bargaining frictions between the government and the NGO.

Private Good

These cheeses are private goods. They are rivalrous, as the same piece of cheese can only be consumed once. They are also excludable, as it is well possible to prevent someone from consuming the cheese - simply by denying to sell it to them.

A private good is defined in economics as "an item that yields positive benefits to people" that is excludable, i.e. its owners can exercise private property rights, preventing those who have not paid for it from using the good or consuming its benefits; and rivalrous, i.e. consumption by one necessarily prevents that of another. A private good, as an economic resource is scarce, which can cause competition for it. The market demand curve for a private good is a horizontal summation of individual demand curves.

Unlike public goods, private goods are less likely to have the free rider problem. Assuming a private good is valued positively by everyone, the efficiency of obtaining the good is obstructed by its rivalry, that is simultaneous consumption of a rivalrous good is theoretically impossible; the feasibility of obtaining the good is made difficult by its excludability, that is people have to pay for it to enjoy its benefits.

One of the most common ways of looking at goods in the economy is by examining the level of competition in obtaining a given good, and the possibility of excluding its consumption; one cannot, for example, prevent another from enjoying a beautiful view, or clean air.

Definition Matrix

	Excludable	Non-excludable
Rivalrous	Private goods food, clothing, cars, parking spaces	**Common-pool resources** fish stocks, timber, coal
Non-rivalrous	**Club goods** cinemas, private parks, satellite television	**Public goods** free-to-air television, air, national defense

Example of a Private Good

An example of the private good is bread: bread eaten by a given person cannot be consumed by another (rivalry), and it is easy for a baker to refuse to trade a loaf (exclusive).

To illustrate the horizontal summation characteristic, assume there are only two people in this economy and that:

- Person A will purchase: 0 loaves of bread at $4, 1 loaf of bread at $3, 2 loaves of bread at $2, and 3 loaves of bread at $1
- Person B will purchase: 0 loaves of bread at $6, 1 loaf of bread at $5, 2 loaves of bread at $4, 3 loaves of bread at $3, 4 loaves of bread at $2, and 5 loaves of bread at $1

As a result, a new market demand curve can be derived with the following results:

Price per loaf of bread	**Loaves of bread**		
	Person A	Person B	Total
$6	0	0	0
$5	0	1	1
$4	0	2	2

\$3	1	3	4
\$2	2	4	6
\$1	3	5	8

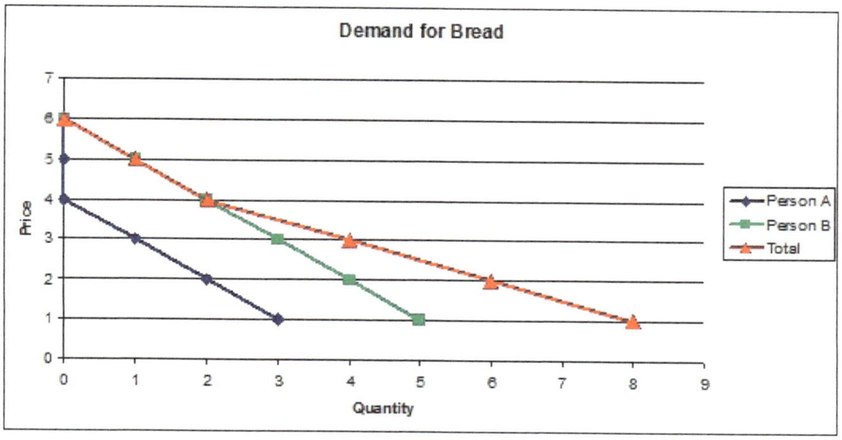

Optimal Provision of Private Goods

- In the case of private goods, equilibrium is determined by the interplay of supply and demand.
- As prices adjust, each person changes his quantity consumed according to own preferences.
- For a private good, *consumers demand different quantities at the same market price.*

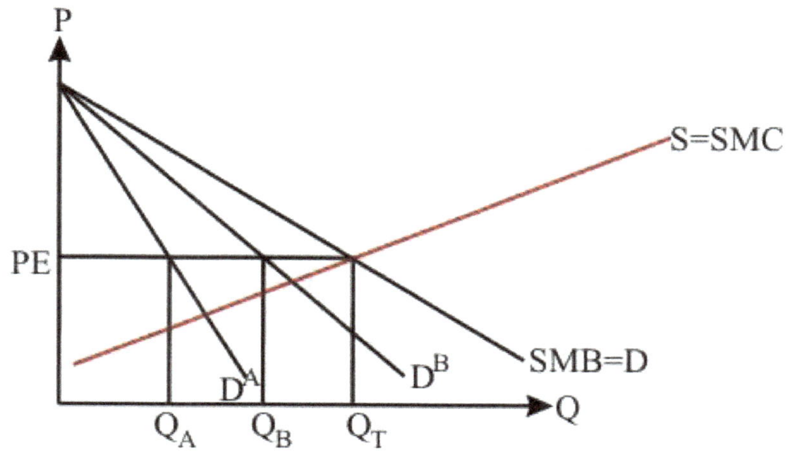

- Consider a private good B and the market for it.
- The alternative use of money is buying the numeraire $x(\Rightarrow P_x = 1)$.
- D^A & D^B are individual dd curves for A &B respectively coming from private preferences of A & B.

- Adding up A & B's dd for good Y we get SMB, which is same as the demand curve.
- Market supply is S.
- Competitive equilibrium price PE. Q^T is the market clearing quantity, But A & B derive their demand from the individual demand curve. Q_A & Q_B
- The private market equilibrium in this case is socially efficient.
- The *MRS* for any quantity of Y equals the *SMB* of that quantity–the marginal value to society equals the marginal value to any individual in the perfectly competitive market.

Optimal Provision of Public Goods

- Now consider the market for military spending as opposed to Food spending.
- Demand for a public good is determined by the Willingness To Pay
- That is, holding quantity fixed, what is each person"s willingness to pay?

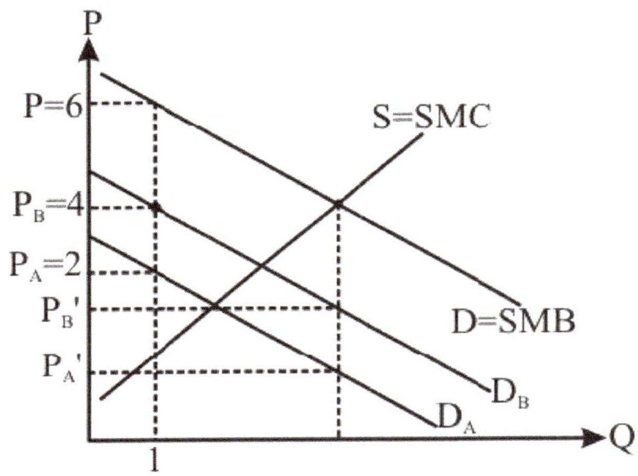

Demand for a Public Good

- $D_A \rightarrow$ A's demand curve for Missiles
- $D_B \rightarrow$ B's demand curve for Missiles
- We want to know if individuals are willing to pay for missiles.
- Suppose we need 1 missile
- A is willing to pass P_A for 1 missile
- B is willing to pass P_A for 1 missile
- Adding the two willingness to pay we get, $P = P_A + P_B$
- For the 5th missile , A is willing to pay P_A'

- For the 5th missile, B is willing to pay P_B
- For the 5th missile Total $WTP = P_A' + P_B'$
- Adding A & B"s WTP for each quantity of the public good we get, society"s Demand curve or society"s WTP.
- $S = SMC$ is the market supply curve
- Competitive equilibrium = 5 missiles, B & A consume 5 missiles each.

Unlike the case of private goods, where aggregate demand is found by summing the individual demands horizontally, with public goods, aggregate demand is found by summing individual demand curve *vertically*.

Samuelson Rule: Optimal Provision of Public Goods

- Private Goods: social efficiency is maximized when the marginal costs are set equal to the marginal rate of substitution for each individual
- Public Goods: social efficiency is maximized when the marginal costs are set equal to the sum of the marginal rates of substitution (rather than each individual's MRS).
- Two goods P and G
- Two individuals

  A&B

$$u_A(P,G); u_B(P.G)\} \; p = private\ good$$
$$\& \; a = numeraire$$

- To A: The marginal public good is worth

$$\frac{Mu_G{}^A}{Mu_P^A} = MRS_{G,P}^A$$

- To B : $\dfrac{Mu_G{}^B}{Mu_P^B} = MRS_{G,P}^B$

Now $MRS_{G,P}$ = Marginal benefit derived from consumption of G.

$$\Rightarrow MRS_{G,P}^A = MB_A$$
$$MRS_{G,P}{}^B = MB_B$$

⇒ The social marginal benefit from the next unit of public good G is $MB_A + MB_B$

$$= \sum_i MRS_{G,P} \qquad i = A, B$$

The social MC is the same as before: derived from the production function of G.

MC_G

Efficiency requires $SMB = SMC$

Samuelson Rule (1954)} ⇒ $\sum_i MRS_{G,P} = SMC = MC_G = MRT_{G,P}$ as opposed to private good case when $MRS_i^Y = MC^Y$

This is because the good is nonrival:

$$\sum_h MRS_{GX}^h = MRT_{GX}$$

- Since a unit can be consumed by all consumers, society would like the producer to take into account all consumers" preferences.
- This is because the good is *non-rival.*
- Excludability plays no role in the analysis. Only relevant for determining feasible provision mechanisms

Free Rider Problem

- All of the individual members of a group can benefit from the efforts of each member and all can benefit substantially from collective action.
- For example, if each of us pollutes less, we all benefit from the reduction of harmful gases in the air we breathe.
- If all of us prefer the state of less pollution over the state of pollution, then the provision of cleaner air is a collective good for us.
- Unfortunately, my polluting less does not matter enough for anyone -- especially me -- to notice. Therefore, I may not contribute my share toward not polluting.
- I may be a *free ride* on the beneficial actions of others.

Private Provision of Public Goods

In general, the private sector *under-provides public goods* because of the *free rider problem.*

Private-sector Underprovision: A Numerical Example

- Consider two people, A and B, with identical preferences

- Two consumption goods – private and public, Roads and Cars.
- Set the prices of each good at 1.
- A and B benefit equally from Road that is provided by either of them since road is a public good.
- Each person chooses combinations of Car and Roads in which his own *MRS*
- equals the ratio of price.
- Recall that marginal utilities diminish with increasing consumption of a good.
- In this example, optimal provision would require that Roads are consumed until their utility equals *half* the marginal utility of Cars.
- Thus, each individually buys too much Car privately & provides too few roads privately.
- Strong positive externality in private provision of roads → leads to underprovision

The Free Rider Problem in Practice

- There are some interesting examples of the free-rider problem in practice.
  - Many users of file sharing services, like youtube, *never* contribute uploaded files; they only download files.
  - To overcome this problem some of these services though give download priority to those who contribute.

Private Provision of Public Goods: Experiments Testing Free Rider Behavior

Marwell and Ames 1981

- Groups of 5 subjects, each given 10 tokens.
- Can invest tokens in either an individual or group account.
- Money deposited in own account returned 1-1. Money deposited in the public account was first pooled, then multiplied by some factor greater than one, and then distributed equally among all subjects.
- Thus tokens given to group account paid out money at higher rate but the group sum was divided equally between all contributors irrespective of their donation to the fund
- Nash equilibrium is 100% individual contribution but Pareto efficient outcome is 100% group contribution.
- Rationality implies that all subjects will follow the individual strategy.
- For empirical evidence: Compute fraction invested in group account under various treatments.

- Experiment run on various groups of high school and college students & economics PhD students.
- Finding: 40 to 60% of tokens were still invested in the public good.
- Only one group free-rode a lot: 1st year econ graduate students (20% donation rate).
- Stephen Marglin, The Dismal Science: Thinking like an economist undermines community
- Two follow up questions:
  - What is a "fair" investment in the public good?

75 percent of the noneconomists answered "1/2 or more", 25 percent answered "all."

  - Are you concerned about "fairness" in making your investment decision?

Almost all noneconomists answered "yes."

- More than one-third of the economists either refused to answer the question regarding what is fair.
- Those who did respond were much more likely to say that little or no contribution was „fair."
- They were about half as likely as other subjects to indicate „concerned with fairness" in making their decisions.
- Criticism
  - Difference in age
  - Difference in gender composition of their group of economics graduate students
- These experiments may be of limited applicability or fail external validity:
  - Individuals may behave differently in a contrived laboratory setting.
  - The stakes are often small, so the cost of being altruistic is low.
  - College undergraduates may not be representative of the population more generally.

Free Rider Problem

In economics, the free rider problem occurs when those who benefit from resources, goods, or services do not pay for them, which results in an underprovision of those goods or services. The free rider problem is the question of how to limit free riding and its negative effects in these situations. The free rider problem may occur when property rights are not clearly defined and imposed.

The free rider problem is common with goods which are non-excludable, including public goods and situations of the Tragedy of the Commons.

Although the term "free rider" was first used in economic theory of public goods, similar concepts have been applied to other contexts, including collective bargaining, antitrust law, psychology and political science. For example, some individuals in a team or community may reduce their contributions or performance if they believe that one or more other members of the group may free ride.

The Economic Problem with Free Riding

Free riding is a problem of economic inefficiency when it leads to the under-production or over-consumption of a good. For example, when people are asked how much they value a particular public good, with that value measured in terms of how much money they would be willing to pay, their tendency is to under report their valuations.

Goods which are subject to free riding are usually characterized by the inability to exclude non-payers. This problem is sometimes compounded by the fact that common-property goods are characterized by rival consumption. Not only can consumers of common-property goods benefit without payment, but consumption by one imposes an opportunity cost on others. This will lead to overconsumption and even possibly exhaustion or destruction of the common-property good. If too many people start to free ride, a system or service will eventually not have enough resources to operate.

The other problem of free-riding is experienced when the production of goods does not consider the external costs, particularly the use of ecosystem services.

Possible Solutions

Government is the primary agency that societies utilize to address the free rider problem. Regulation is a form of action taken by governments to resolve free rider problems to prevent environmental degradation or excessive resource use. Practical tacts include compulsory participation (taxation) or a form of regulation and linking the public good to a desirable private good (getting people to pay voluntarily). Governments have imposed taxes when not enough people have voluntarily paid for a public good or service, and some governments have turned a public good into a private one.

Optimality Condition

- First Best if G is Private good: $MRS^{h}_{G,X} = MRT_{G,X}$
- Decentralized market equilibrium will implement such an allocation
- First Best if G is Public good:

$$\sum_{h} MRS^{h}_{GX} = MRT_{GX}$$

- Decentralized private provision is suboptimal
  - Market outcome is inefficient; underprovision of G

When is Private Provision Likely to Overcome the Free Rider Problem?

- While the free-rider problem clearly exists, there are also examples where the private market is able to overcome this problem to some extent.
- Examples of private provision of a public good
  - Privately financed highways.
- But the private market may still fall short of the socially optimal amount.

Can Private Providers Overcome the Free Rider Problem?

- Gurgaon was widely regarded as an economic wasteland. In 1979, the state of Haryana created Gurgaon by dividing a longstanding political district on the outskirts of New Delhi. One half went to Faridabad, which had an active municipal government, direct rail access to the capital, fertile farmland and a strong industrial base. The other half, Gurgaon, had rocky soil, no local government, no railway link and almost no industrial base.
- Gurgaon's disadvantages turned out to be advantages, none more important, initially, than the absence of a district wide government, which meant less red tape capable of choking development.
- Gurgaon has no publicly provided "functioning citywide sewer or drainage system; reliable electricity or water; public sidewalks, adequate parking, decent roads or any citywide system of public transportation."
- Not only are services such as roads and utilities poor, the private oases don't internalize all the externalities so there are problems with common resources such as the water table. It would also be more efficient to have centralized sewage and electricity.

Business Improvement Districts

- BID in New York
  - The quality of city streets is a public good.
  - During the 1980s, New York City had high crime. The city had lost all hopes of cleaning up Times Square.
  - In 1992, local businessmen started a BID–a legal entity to provide security and sanitation, with fees collected from local businesses.
- New York law makes participation of businesses compulsory if BID organizers can get 60% of local businesses to join, allowing the organizers to overcome the free-rider problem.
  - The BID was a success in New York City.
- BID in Massachusetts
  - Law allows businesses to "opt-out" of a BID within 30 days of the BID approval by the local government.

- This deters formation of BIDs in the first place, because there are fixed costs of doing so.
- As a consequence, only 2 BIDs have been formed in Massachusetts.

When is Private Provision Likely to Overcome the Free Rider Problem?

- Under what circumstances are private market forces likely to solve the free rider problem?
  - Intense preferences.
  - Altruism.
  - Utility from one's own contribution to the public good.

Some Individuals Care more than others

- When some individuals have especially high demand for a public good, private provision may emerge (but not necessarily provide efficiently).
- The key intuition is that the decision to provide a public good is a function of the enjoyment that the individual gets from the total amount of the public good, net of cost.
  - If a person gets a lot of enjoyment, or has a lot of money, he will choose to purchase more of the public good even though it benefits others.
- Olson and Zeckhauser (1966) studied the financing of NATO (North Atlantic Treaty Organization), which was a voluntary organization at the time.
  - Although countries had an incentive to free-ride on the contributions of others, the largest nations (such as the United States) did contribute.
  - Higher incomes or stronger tastes can mitigate the free rider problem to some extent, but are unlikely to solve it completely. Thus, underprovision is still likely to occur.

Altruism

- Another reason is that there is evidence that many individuals are *altruistic*, caring about the outcomes of others as well as themselves.
- Once again consider the experiment by Marwell and Ames 1981; a wide majority did contribute to the group fund.
- Some real-world evidence is consistent with altruism in private support of public goods.
  - Brunner (1998) found that the number of public radio listeners who contribute decreases only modestly as the total number of listeners increases.

Warm Glow

- A final reason is that that individuals may provide for a public good is due to warm glow.

- The *warm glow model* is a model of public good provision in which individuals care about both the total amount of the public good and their particular contributions as well.

- For example, they may get some psychological benefit from knowing they helped a worthy cause.
- In this case, the public good becomes more like a private good, though it does not fully solve the underprovision problems.

Private Sector under Provision

In general decentralized private mechanism under provides public goods. Consider two goods P and G and two individuals A&B, as before.

Here we analyze the case of private sector under provision and pareto efficiency more formally.

Two individuals A & B

$$u_A(P,G), u_B(P,G) \left\{ \begin{array}{l} p = \text{private good} \\ \& \text{ a numeraire} \end{array} \right.$$

⟶ Private good P & a pure public good G.

⟶ Price of each good normalized to 1. (1-1 transformation technology).

⟶Each household starts with endowment of good P.

⟶ Out of Y^h individual h contributes G^h to public good funding.

⟶ $\Rightarrow$ total funding $= \Sigma_h G^h = G$ available for every one

⟶Consumption units are one –to-one with respect to expenditure since price = 1

⟶Consumption of private good $= P^h = Y^h - G^h$ for h.

⟶ Individual h solves max $u^h\left(P^h, G\right)$

⟶ Max $U^h(P^h, G^1 + G^2 + \cdots + G^H)$

Subject to $P^h + G^h = Y^h$

Nash equilibrium outcome is given by : $u_p^h = u_G^h$

$MU_G^h = MU_P^h$ i.e. $MRS_{G,P}^h = 1$

⟶ Rule for optimal public good provision, Samuelson rule, is not satisfied.

⟶ Pareto improvement possible if each person invested $1/H$ more Rupees in the public good.

→ Each person contributing $1/H \Rightarrow$ total contribution = $H * \frac{1}{H} = 1$

→ Assuming an additive utility function, with 1 more unit of G, net welfare change for h is:

ΔW (for household h) $= -u_P^h(1/H) + u_G^h =$ (gain in utility from 1 extra unit of public good) + (1/H) (Fall in utility from giving up 1/H amount of private good)

Pareto Improvement

$$\Rightarrow \Delta w = -u_P^h \left(\frac{1}{H}\right) + u_G^h$$

$$= -u_G^h\left(1/H\right) + \underbrace{u_G^h = u_G^h\left(1 - 1/H\right) > 0}_{} \quad \Rightarrow \Delta w > 0 \Rightarrow \text{welfare improvement}$$

Decentralized Private provision suboptimal

$\Rightarrow$ Market outcome is inefficient and there is under provision of G.

Lindahl Tax

A Lindahl tax is a form of taxation conceived by Erik Lindahl in which individuals pay for public goods according to their marginal benefits. In other words, they pay according to the amount of satisfaction or utility they derive from the consumption of an additional unit of the public good.

It can be seen as an individual's share of the collective tax burden of an economy. The optimal level of a public good is that quantity at which the willingness to pay for one more unit of the good, taken in totality for all the individuals is equal to the marginal cost of supplying that good. Lindahl tax is the optimal quantity times the willingness to pay for one more unit of that good at this quantity.

History

Erik Lindahl was deeply influenced by his professor and mentor Knut Wicksell and proposed a method for financing public goods in order to show that consensus politics is possible. As people are different in nature, their preferences are different, and consensus requires each individual to pay a somewhat different tax for every service, or good that he consumes. If each person's tax price is set equal to the marginal benefits received at the ideal service level, each person is made better off by provision of the public good and may accordingly agree to have that service level provided.

Lindahl Equilibrium

A Lindahl equilibrium is a state of economic equilibrium under a Lindahl tax as well as a method for finding the optimum level for the supply of public goods or services that happens when the total per-unit price paid by each individual equals the total per-unit cost of the public good. It can be shown that an equilibrium exists for different environments. Therefore, the Lindahl equilibrium describes how efficiency can be sustained in an economy with personalised prices. Leif Johansen gave the complete interpretation of the concept of "Lindahl equilibrium", which assumes that household consumption decisions are based on the share of the cost they must provide for the supply of the particular public good.

The importance of Lindahl equilibrium is that it fulfills the Samuelson condition and is therefore Pareto efficient, despite the good in question being a public one. It also demonstrates how efficiency can be reached in an economy with public goods by the use of personalised prices. The personalised prices equate the individual valuation for a public good to the cost of the public good.

Criticism

Lindahl pricing and taxation requires the knowledge of the demand functions for each individual for all private and public goods. When information about marginal benefits is available only from the individuals themselves, they tend to under report their valuation for a particular good, this gives rise to a "preference revelation problem". Each individual can lower his tax cost by under reporting his benefits derived from the public good or service. This informational problem shows that survey-based Lindahl taxation is not incentive compatible. Incentives to understate or under report one's true benefits under Lindahl taxation resemble those of a traditional public goods game.

Preference revelation mechanisms can be used to solve that problem, although none of these has been shown to completely and satisfactorily address it. The Vickrey–Clarke–Groves mechanism is an example of this, ensuring true values are revealed and that a public good is provided only when it should be. The allocation of cost is taken as given and the consumers will report their net benefits (benefits-cost) the public good will be provided if the sum of the net benefits of all consumers is positive. If the public good is provided side payments will be made reflecting the fact that truth telling is costly. The side payments internalize the net benefit of the public good to other players. The side payments must be financed from outside the mechanism. In reality, preference revelation is difficult as the size of the population makes it costly both in terms of money and time.

A second drawback to Lindahl prices is that they may be unfair. Consider a television broadcast antenna that is arbitrarily placed in an area. Those living near the antenna will receive a clear signal while those living farther away will receive a less clear signal. Those living close to the antenna will have a relatively low marginal value for additional wattage (thus paying a lower Lindahl price) compared to those living farther away (thus paying a higher Lindahl price).

Mathematical Representation

We assume that there are two goods in an economy:the first one is a "public good", and the second is "everything else". The price of the public good can be assumed to be P_{public} and the price of everything else can be P_{else}.

- $\alpha * P_{(public)} / P_{(else)} = MRS_{(person1)}$

This is just the usual price ratio/marginal rate of substitution deal the only change is that we multiply P_{public} by α to allow for the price adjustment to the public good. Similarly, Person 2 will choose his bundle such that:

- $(1-\alpha) * P_{(public)} / P_{(else)} = MRS_{(person2)}$

Now we have both individuals' utility maximizing. We know that in a competitive equilibrium, the marginal cost ratio or price ratio should be equal to the marginal rate of transformation, or

- $MC_{(public)}/MC_{(else)}=[P_{(public)}/P_{(else)}]=MRT$

Properties of Lindahl Equilibria

Lindahl Conditions

    - Public good must be fully financed
    - All individuals must demand same quantity of G

- Samuelson Rule applies and outcome is Pareto efficient
- With identical individuals, simply set tax t = 1/H (H= total number of individuals/households) and ask individuals to voluntarily contribute to G
- With heterogeneity, efficient outcome can be attained with public goods through prices that are individual-specific

Lindahl Pricing: Intuition

- Ideally, the government could provide public goods through unanimous consent of its citizens.
- Lindahl pricing: Individuals report their willingness to pay for each quantity of the public good, and the government aggregates preferences to get social benefit.
- First, the government announces tax prices for the public good, that is, the share of the cost that each individual must bear.
- When a tax price is arrived at where both individuals want the same amount of the public good, the government has reached Lindahl equilibrium.
- Private goods: Individuals maximize utility by letting marginal rates of substitutions equal the relative price. Since in a competitive equilibrium all individuals face the same relative prices, the implication is that marginal rates of substitutions are equalized across all individuals, resulting in a pareto efficient allocation. All individuals face the same price, but may consume different quantities of goods.
    - Consumption differs price the same.
- Public goods: Individuals have to consume the same amount of public good, thus individuals cannot equalize their marginal rates of substitutions to the common relative price. If consumption of the good must be the same it is possible to vary prices across individuals to get efficiency.
    - Consumption same price differs.

Lindahl Equilibrium

How to achieve pareto efficiency through a Decentralized mechanism?

- Suppose individual h has to pay a share τ^h of the public good & can pick a level of G.
- individual h chooses G to maximize

$$\begin{bmatrix} u^h(P^h, G). \\ st. P^h + \tau^h G = Y^h \\ u^h(Y^h - \tau^h G, G) \end{bmatrix}$$

Without any public good his utility is $U(Y^h)$

First order condition for utility maximization for individual h:

$$\tau^h u_P^h = u_G^h$$

Demand for: $G^h = G^h(\tau^h, Y^h)$.

A Lindahl equilibrium satisfies the following conditions

- public good must be fully financed

$$\sum_h \tau^h = 1$$

- All individuals must demand same quantity of G.

Existence of prices, τ^h satisfied: (1) H equations

$$\underbrace{\underbrace{G^1 = G^1 = G^2 \ldots\ \ldots\ \ldots = G^H}_{(H-1)eq^{ns}} \ and \underbrace{\sum_h \tau^h = 1}_{1\,eq^n}}_{Total\ H\ equations}$$

& H unknowns (τ^h)

Samuelson rule applies and outcome is pareto efficient

$$\underbrace{\Sigma_h \frac{u_G^h}{u_P^h} = \Sigma \tau^h}_{From\ foc} \underbrace{=1}_{Lindahl\ condition}$$

With identical individuals simply set $\tau^h = 1/H$ and ask individuals to voluntarily contribute to G.

- With heterogeneity, efficient public good allocation can be attained through prices that are individual specific.

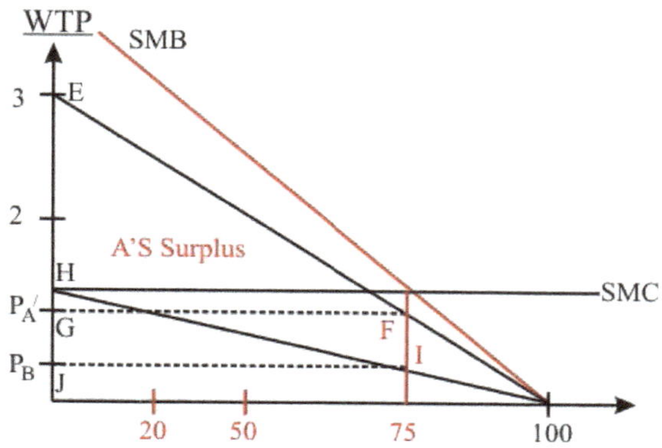

Suppose A's demand curve for public good is steep and B's demand curve for public good is flat.

Aggregate Demand:

$AD = (D_A + D_B)$ Vertical sum

With SMC =1 (remember price of G=1). It is beneficial to produce the good.

Suppose the socially efficient level of G is 75

This generates a tax price of $P_A = 0.75$ for A

This generates a tax price of $P_B = 0.25$ for B

A's Surplus =E F G

B's Surplus = H I J

The production at 75 is equilibrium for 2 reasons:

1. Both A & B are happy to pay those tax prices to get that quantity.
2. Government has covered the marginal cost of production by charging each person their marginal willingness to pay.

Lindahl Pricing: How Much Public Good to Provide

- The government chooses some initial tax share and informs consumers.
- Each person announces how much of the public good he or she wants at those tax prices.
- If everyone demands the same level of public good, then provide that level & split the cost according to tax share.
- If the individual announcements differ, the government raises the tax price for the person who wants more of the good, and lowers it for the person who wants less.
- Provision decision effectively secured through unanimity.

Properties of Lindahl Equilibria

- Lindahl pricing corresponds to the concept of benefit taxation, which occurs when individuals are being taxed for a public good according to their valuation of the benefit they receive i.e. τ^h paid by individual h is the MB that she derives from G.

The Lindahl equation is a set of shares $\tau^h\{\tau^h,\tau^2\dots..\tau^H\}$ and a public good provision G^* such that

$$\Sigma_h \tau^h = 1$$

$$G^* = B_1^*(\tau^1) = B_2^*(\tau^2) = \cdots B_H^*(\tau^H)$$

Household 1's best response function can be thought of as demand curve for G at different τ^h.

Graphical Representation of Lindahl Equilibrium

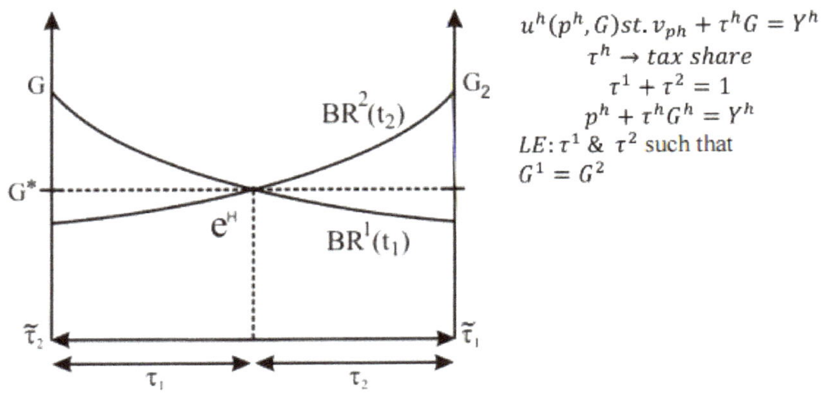

$\tau_1 + \tau_2 = 1$ (Total cost of producing G)

- With Lindahl pricing, the government does not need to know the utility functions of individual voters: it gets the voters to reveal their preferences by stating their willingness to pay for different levels of the public good.

Lindahl Equilibrium: Challenges

Lindahl equation leaves every one better off.

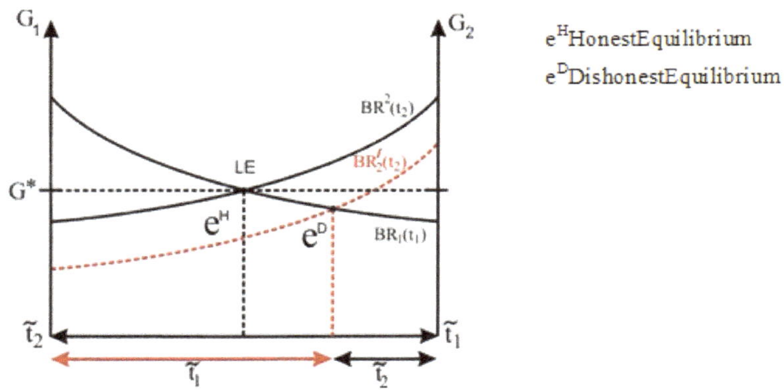

By Lunder reporting preference for G, individual 2 secures a lower tax.

- Announcing and adjusting tax shares with many consumers
- Incentive for truthful demand revelation
- Assumed max U taking τ as given – i.e. honest
- But τ^h depends on his reported demand, can increase U^h by strategically

Misrepresenting Demand

  - Assume 1 is honest, 2 knows this and BR^1 Honest eqm= e^H
  - Report BR^2 Instead of BR^2 (i.e.max U^2 given BR^1) Eqm= e^D

- Therefore should focus on mechanisms that are not open to strategic manipulation in this way if we want efficiency.

Lindahl Pricing: Practical Constraints

- Must be able to exclude a consumer from using the public good.
  - Does not work with non-excludable public good
  - Must be able to exclude since otherwise those with WTP=0 will also end up consuming
- Must know individual preferences to set personalized prices, τ^h
  - Preference revelation problem: Agents have no incentives to reveal their preferences. Individuals may behave strategically and pretend their willingness to pay is low in order to get others to bear a larger cost of the public good.
- Preference knowledge problem: It is hard for people to properly value goods they do not shop for on a regular basis.
- Preference aggregation problem: Aggregating millions of voters' preferences is difficult in reality. Direct democracy, whereby voters directly cast ballots in favour of or in opposition to particular public projects, is one way of aggregating preferences.
- Difference between Lindahl equilibria and standard equilibria:
  - No decentralized mechanism for deriving prices; no market forces that will generate the right price vector

Public Provision of Public Goods

- How do we actually determine level of PGs in practice?
  - Voting on bundles of PGs and taxes
  - Does voting lead to the first best solution?

Alternative Way of Financing Public Goods: Lotteries (Morgan 2000)

Benchmark model with quasi linear preferences :(No Lottery)

- 2 identical players
- Each with income Y^h, consuming private goods, P and public goods G.
- H's utility function is

$$U_h = P^h + f(G)$$

Where $f' > \& f' < 0$

Outcomes: Efficient $2f'(G) = 1$

And Private $f'(G) = 1$

- Private charities and Governments often use lotteries in lieu of voluntary contributions to finance public goods
- Lottery funding
  - Rather than buying public good directly, suppose each individual buys lottery tickets for a chance to win some prize
  - One person picked at random to win, probability of being picked equals the share of lottery tickets bought
  - Lottery revenues used to finance prize and public goods

Lottery Model

- h buys lottery tickets Z_h
- His probability of winning prize R is $\frac{Zh}{Z_h + Z_k}$

Note that G = $Z_h + Z_k - R$

- he's expected utility is

$$EU = P^h + f(G) + \frac{Z_h}{Z_h + Z_k}.R$$

Outcome: h then buys Z_h such that

$$f'(G) + \frac{Z_k}{(Z_h + Z_k)^2}R = 1$$

- When R=0, G is private provision level
- When R>0, G is more than private provision level, since $f'(G) < 0$

- The prize money provides an additional incentive to purchase public goods.
- More efficient as: Positive externality (G) offset by negative externality (Lottery).
- In practice, three problems emerge:
  - Determining the public's preferences.
  - Measuring costs and benefits.
  - Crowd-out.
- So how do we actually determine level of PGs in practice?
  - Voting on bundles of PGs and taxes.
  - Does voting lead to the first best solution?

Mechanisms for Aggregating Individual Preferences

- This section discusses how voting can serve to aggregate individual preferences into a social decision.
- For now, we focus on direct democracy, whereby voters directly cast ballots in favor of or in opposition to particular public projects.

Majority Voting: When it Works

- The Lindahl pricing scheme had a very high standard for coming to a consensus: only when citizens are unanimously in agreement would the government achieve Lindahl equilibrium.
- A common mechanism used to aggregate individual votes into a social decision is *majority voting*, in which individual policy options are put to a vote, and the option that receives the majority of votes is chosen.
- Majority voting does not always provide a consistent means of aggregating preferences.
- To be consistent, an aggregation mechanism must satisfy three goals:
  - *Dominance*: If one choice is preferred by all voters, then the aggregation mechanism must be such that this choice is made by society.
  - *Transitivity*: Choices must satisfy transitivity (If A>B & B>C, then A>C).

Independence of Irrelevant Alternatives: The introduction of a third choice does not change the ranking of the first two choices

Majority Voting

- It turns out that with these three conditions, majority voting can only produce a consistent aggregation of individual preferences if preferences are restricted to take a certain form.
- Taxes are Assumed to be Not-regressive

- Suppose a town is deciding on education taxes (and spending). There are 3 possibilities: high, medium, and low spending. There are also 3 groups, represented in equal proportions-low, middle & high income parents.
- Quality of Public schools < Quality of Private schools: implies they are not really substitutable since very different goods
- Low income parents have the highest stake since they will send their children to public schools: hence the above choice
- High income: just the opposite. They can put their children in private schools so don't care for public schools
- Mid Income: Moderate taxes since they still want to send their children to good public schools but at the same time choosing high means they will have to pay a lot, out of pocket. Then they might be better off sending children to private. So low is the next choice.
- Social ordering implies an unambiguous outcome: M Condorcet Paradox: where majority voting does not work.
- Now consider a different set of preferences as shown in table.
- Low income is same choice as before. Mid income is also same choice. But for the high income now, either no public school required, or if all public school then better be good
- Collective preferences can be cyclic (i.e. not transitive), even if the preferences of individual voters are not. This is paradoxical, because it means that majority wishes can be in conflict with each other. When this occurs, it is because the conflicting majorities are each made up of different groups of Individuals Condorcet Paradox: majority voting does not lead to a stable outcome.
- Condorcet's paradox, which shows that majority preferences can become intransitive with three or more options—it is possible for a certain electorate to express a preference for A over B, a preference for B over C, and a preference for C over A, all from the same set of ballots.

		Types of voters/individuals		
Preference Orderings		Low	Middle	High
	First	H	M	L
	Second	M	L	M
	Third	L	H	H

Majority vote share (number of times one outcome is preferred to another)

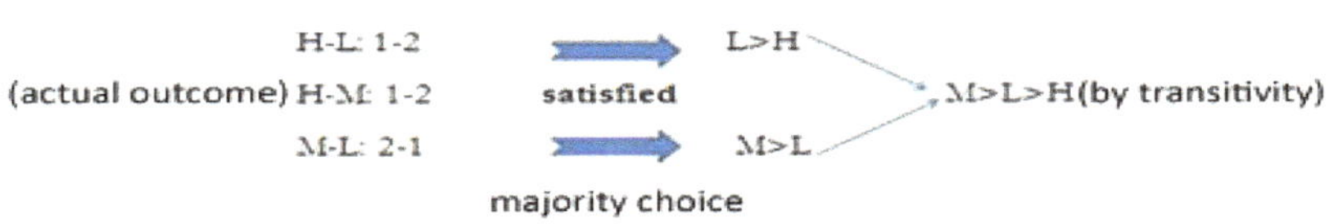

Table: Majority voting delivers a consistent outcome

Preference Orderings		Types of voters		
		Low	Middle	High
	First	H	M	L
	Second	M	L	H
	Third	L	H	M

H-L: 1-2 → L>H

H-M: 2-1 not satisfied → M>L>H

M-L: 2-1 → M>L

Cycling in social ordering: H > M > L > H

Table : Majority voting doesn't deliver a consistent outcome

Majority Voting: When it Doesn't Work

- In the example above the second set of outcomes is problematic because there is no clear winner. These results violate the principle of transitivity resulting in cycling–when majority voting does not deliver a consistent aggregation of individual preferences.
- Note that the failure to get a consistent winner from majority voting does not reflect a failure on the part of individuals–each group has a sensible set of preferences.
- The problem is aggregation–we are unable to use voting to aggregate these individual preferences into a consistent social outcome. Public good provision by Banerjee & Somanathan, 2003 (caste heterogeneity).
- This creates the problem of the *agenda setter*, the person who decides the sequencing of the votes.
- In the second situation, he can affect the outcome.
  - For low spending to win, for example, first set up a vote between H and M. H wins. Then a vote between L and H means L will win.
  - Any outcome can win with appropriate ordering: so the agenda setter will follow the order that leads to his preferred outcome.

Arrow's Impossibility Theorem

In social choice theory, Arrow's impossibility theorem, the general possibility theorem or Arrow's paradox is an impossibility theorem stating that when voters have three or more distinct alternatives (options), no ranked order voting system can convert the ranked preferences of individuals into a community-wide (complete and transitive) ranking while also meeting a pre-specified set of criteria: *unrestricted domain*, *non-dictatorship*, *Pareto efficiency*, and *independence of irrelevant alternatives*. The theorem is often cited in discussions of voting theory as it is further interpreted by the Gibbard–Satterthwaite theorem.

The theorem is named after economist Kenneth Arrow, who demonstrated the theorem in his doctoral thesis and popularized it in his 1951 book *Social Choice and Individual Values*. The original paper was titled "A Difficulty in the Concept of Social Welfare".

In short, the theorem states that no rank-order voting system can be designed that always satisfies these three "fairness" criteria:

- If every voter prefers alternative X over alternative Y, then the group prefers X over Y.
- If every voter's preference between X and Y remains unchanged, then the group's preference between X and Y will also remain unchanged (even if voters' preferences between other pairs like X and Z, Y and Z, or Z and W change).
- There is no "dictator": no single voter possesses the power to always determine the group's preference.

Cardinal voting systems are not covered by the theorem, as they convey more information than rank orders. Arrow originally rejected cardinal utility as a meaningful tool for expressing social welfare, and so focused his theorem on preference rankings, but later stated that a cardinal score system with three or four classes "is probably the best".

The theorem can also be sidestepped by weakening the notion of independence.

The axiomatic approach Arrow adopted can treat all conceivable rules (that are based on preferences) within one unified framework. In that sense, the approach is qualitatively different from the earlier one in voting theory, in which rules were investigated one by one. One can therefore say that the contemporary paradigm of social choice theory started from this theorem.

The practical consequences of the theorem are debatable: Arrow has said "Most systems are not going to work badly all of the time. All I proved is that all can work badly at times."

Statement of the Theorem

The need to aggregate preferences occurs in many disciplines: in welfare economics, where one attempts to find an economic outcome which would be acceptable and stable; in decision theory, where a person has to make a rational choice based on several criteria; and most naturally in voting systems, which are mechanisms for extracting a decision from a multitude of voters' preferences.

The framework for Arrow's theorem assumes that we need to extract a preference order on a given set of options (outcomes). Each individual in the society (or equivalently, each decision criterion) gives a particular order of preferences on the set of outcomes. We are searching for a ranked voting system, called a *social welfare function* (*preference aggregation rule*), which transforms the set of preferences (*profile* of preferences) into a single global societal preference order. Arrow's theorem says that if the decision-making body has at least two members and at least three options to decide among, then it is impossible to design a social welfare function that satisfies all these conditions (assumed to be reasonable requirement of a fair voting system) at once:

Non-dictatorship

The social welfare function should account for the wishes of multiple voters. It cannot simply mimic the preferences of a single voter.

Unrestricted Domain, or Universality

For any set of individual voter preferences, the social welfare function should yield a unique and complete ranking of societal choices. Thus:

- It must do so in a manner that results in a complete ranking of preferences for society.
- It must deterministically provide the same ranking each time voters' preferences are presented the same way.

Independence of Irrelevant Alternatives (IIA)

The social preference between x and y should depend only on the individual preferences between x and y (*pairwise independence*). More generally, changes in individuals' rankings of *irrelevant* alternatives (ones outside a certain subset) should have no impact on the societal ranking of the subset. For example, the introduction of a third candidate to a two-candidate election should not affect the outcome of the election unless the third candidate wins.

Monotonicity, or Positive Association of Social and Individual Values

If any individual modifies his or her preference order by promoting a certain option, then the societal preference order should respond only by promoting that same option or not changing, never by placing it lower than before. An individual should not be able to hurt an option by ranking it *higher*.

Non-imposition, or Citizen Sovereignty

Every possible societal preference order should be achievable by some set of individual preference orders. This means that the social welfare function is surjective: It has an unrestricted target space.

A later (1963) version of Arrow's theorem replaced the monotonicity and non-imposition criteria with:

Pareto Efficiency, or Unanimity

If every individual prefers a certain option to another, then so must the resulting societal preference order. This, again, is a demand that the social welfare function will be minimally sensitive to the preference profile.

This later version is more general, having weaker conditions. The axioms of monotonicity, non-imposition, and IIA together imply Pareto efficiency, whereas Pareto efficiency (itself implying non-imposition) and IIA together do not imply monotonicity.

Independence of Irrelevant Alternatives (IIA)

The IIA condition has three purposes (or effects):

Normative

Irrelevant alternatives should not matter.

Practical

Use of minimal information.

Strategic

Providing the right incentives for the truthful revelation of individual preferences. Though the strategic property is conceptually different from IIA, it is closely related.

Arrow's death-of-a-candidate example (1963, page 26) suggests that the agenda (the set of feasible alternatives) shrinks from, say, X = {a, b, c} to S = {a, b} because of the death of candidate c. This example is misleading since it can give the reader an impression that IIA is a condition involving *two* agenda and *one* profile. The fact is that IIA involves just *one* agendum ({x, y} in case of pairwise independence) but *two* profiles. If the condition is applied to this confusing example, it requires this: Suppose an aggregation rule satisfying IIA chooses b from the agenda {a, b} when the profile is given by (cab, cba), that is, individual 1 prefers c to a to b, 2 prefers c to b to a. Then, it must still choose b from {a, b} if the profile were, say: (abc, bac); (acb, bca); (acb, cba); or (abc, cba).

Formal Statement of the Theorem

Let A be a set of outcomes, N a number of voters or decision criteria. We shall denote the set of all full linear orderings of A by L(A).

A (strict) social welfare function (preference aggregation rule) is a function which aggregates voters' preferences into a single preference order on A.

An N-tuple $(R_1, \ldots, R_N) \in L(A)^N$ of voters' preferences is called a *preference profile*. In its strongest and simplest form, Arrow's impossibility theorem states that whenever the set A of possible alternatives has more than 2 elements, then the following three conditions become incompatible:

Unanimity, or Weak Pareto Efficiency

If alternative, a, is ranked strictly higher than b for all orderings $R_1, \ldots, R_N$, then a is ranked strictly higher than b by $F(R_1, R_2, \ldots, R_N)$. (Note that unanimity implies non-imposition.)

Non-dictatorship

There is no individual, i whose strict preferences always prevail. That is, there is no $i \in \{1, \ldots, N\}$ such that for all $(R_1, \ldots, R_N) \in L(A)^N$, a ranked strictly higher than b by R_i implies a ranked strictly higher than b by $F(R_1, R_2, \ldots, R_N)$, for all a and b.

Independence of irrelevant alternatives

For two preference profiles $(R_1, \ldots, R_N)$ and $(S_1, \ldots, S_N)$ such that for all individuals, i, alternatives, a and b, have the same order in R_i as in S_i, alternatives, a and b, have the same order in $F(R_1, R_2, \ldots, R_N)$ as in $F(S_1, S_2, \ldots, S_N)$.

Informal Proof

Based on two proofs appearing in *Economic Theory*. For simplicity we have presented all rankings as if ties are impossible. A complete proof taking possible ties into account is not essentially different from the one given here, except that one ought to say "not above" instead of "below" or "not below" instead of "above" in some cases.

We will prove that any social choice system respecting unrestricted domain, unanimity, and independence of irrelevant alternatives (IIA) is a dictatorship. The key idea is to identify a *pivotal voter* whose ballot swings the societal outcome. We then prove that this voter is a partial dictator (in a specific technical sense, described below). Finally we conclude by showing that all of the partial dictators are the same person, hence this voter is a dictator.

Part One: There is a "Pivotal" Voter for B Over A

Say there are three choices for society, call them A, B, and C. Suppose first that everyone prefers option B the least: everyone prefers A to B, and everyone prefers C to B. By unanimity, society must also prefer both A and C to B. Call this situation *profile 0*.

On the other hand, if everyone preferred B to everything else, then society would have to prefer B to everything else by unanimity. Now arrange all the voters in some arbitrary but fixed order, and for each i let *profile i* be the same as *profile 0*, but move B to the top of the ballots for voters 1 through i. So *profile 1* has B at the top of the ballot for voter 1, but not for any of the others. *Profile 2* has B at the top for voters 1 and 2, but no others, and so on.

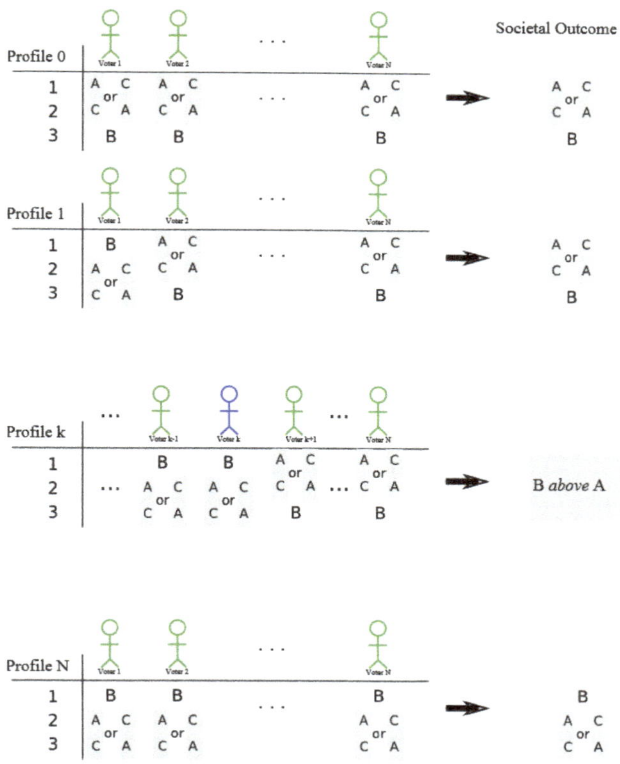

Part one: Successively move **B** from the bottom to the top of voters' ballots. The voter whose change results in **B** being ranked over **A** is the *pivotal voter for* **B** *over* **A**.

Since B eventually moves to the top of the societal preference, there must be some profile, number *k*, for which B moves above A in the societal rank. We call the voter whose ballot change causes this to happen the pivotal voter for B over A. Note that the pivotal voter for B over A is not, a priori, the same as the pivotal voter for A over B. In part three of the proof we will show that these do turn out to be the same.

Also note that by IIA the same argument applies if *profile o* is any profile in which A is ranked above B by every voter, and the pivotal voter for B over A will still be voter *k*. We will use this observation below.

Part Two: The Pivotal Voter for B Over A is a Dictator for B Over C

In this part of the argument we refer to voter *k*, the pivotal voter for B over A, as *pivotal voter* for simplicity. We will show that pivotal voter dictates society's decision for B over C. That is, we show that no matter how the rest of society votes, if Pivotal Voter ranks B over C, then that is the societal outcome. Note again that the dictator for B over C is not a priori the same as that for C over B. In part three of the proof we will see that these turn out to be the same too.

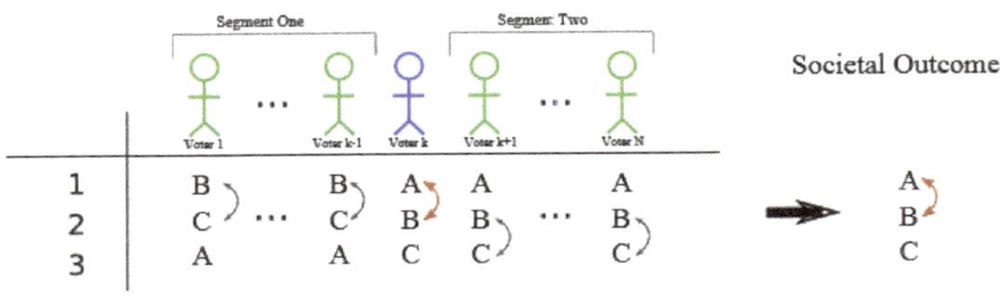

Part two: Switching A and B on the ballot of voter *k* causes the same switch to the societal outcome, by part one of the argument. Making any or all of the indicated switches to the other ballots has no effect on the outcome.

In the following, we call voters 1 through *k* – *1*, *segment one*, and voters *k* + *1* through *N*, *segment two*. To begin, suppose that the ballots are as follows:

- Every voter in segment one ranks B above C and C above A.
- Pivotal voter ranks A above B and B above C.
- Every voter in segment two ranks A above B and B above C.

Then by the argument in part one (and the last observation in that part), the societal outcome must rank A above B. This is because, except for a repositioning of C, this profile is the same as *profile k* – *1* from part one. Furthermore, by unanimity the societal outcome must rank B above C. Therefore, we know the outcome in this case completely.

Now suppose that pivotal voter moves B above A, but keeps C in the same position and imagine that any number (or all!) of the other voters change their ballots to move B below C, without changing the position of A. Then aside from a repositioning of C this is the same as *profile k* from part one and hence the societal outcome ranks B above A. Furthermore, by IIA the societal outcome must rank A above C, as in the previous case. In particular, the societal outcome ranks B above C, even though Pivotal Voter may have been the *only* voter to rank B above C. By IIA, this conclusion holds independently of how A is positioned on the ballots, so pivotal voter is a dictator for B over C.

Part Three: There can be at Most one Dictator

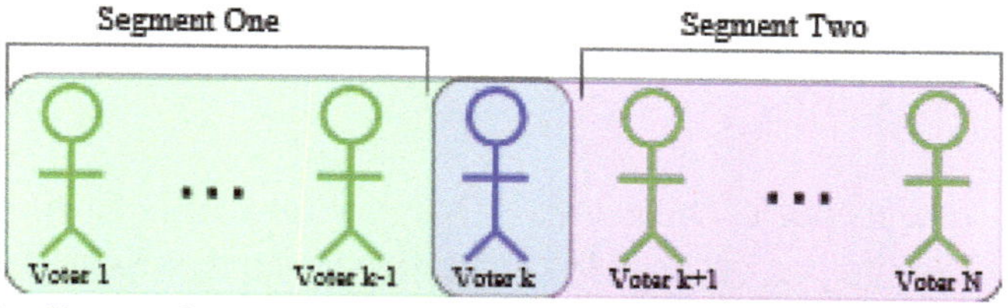

Part three: Since voter k is the dictator for B over C, the pivotal voter for B over C must appear among the first k voters. That is, *outside* of segment two. Likewise, the pivotal voter for C over B must appear among voters k through N. That is, outside of Segment One.

In this part of the argument we refer back to the original ordering of voters, and compare the positions of the different pivotal voters (identified by applying parts one and two to the other pairs of candidates). First, the pivotal voter for B over C must appear earlier (or at the same position) in the line than the dictator for B over C: As we consider the argument of part one applied to B and C, successively moving B to the top of voters' ballots, the pivot point where society ranks B above C must come at or before we reach the dictator for B over C. Likewise, reversing the roles of B and C, the pivotal voter for C over B must be at or later in line than the dictator for B over C. In short, if $k_{X/Y}$ denotes the position of the pivotal voter for X over Y (for any two candidates X and Y), then we have shown

$$k_{B/C} \leq k_{B/A} \leq k_{C/B}.$$

Now repeating the entire argument above with B and C switched, we also have

$$k_{C/B} \leq k_{B/C}.$$

Therefore, we have

$$k_{B/C} = k_{B/A} = k_{C/B}$$

and the same argument for other pairs shows that all the pivotal voters (and hence all the dictators) occur at the same position in the list of voters. This voter is the dictator for the whole election.

Interpretations of the Theorem

Although Arrow's theorem is a mathematical result, it is often expressed in a non-mathematical way with a statement such as *no voting method is fair*, *every ranked voting method is flawed*, or *the only voting method that isn't flawed is a dictatorship*. These statements are simplifications of Arrow's result which are not universally considered to be true. What Arrow's theorem does state is that a deterministic preferential voting mechanism—that is, one where a preference order is the only information in a vote, and any possible set of votes gives a unique result—cannot comply with all of the conditions given above simultaneously.

Various theorists have suggested weakening the IIA criterion as a way out of the paradox. Proponents of ranked voting methods contend that the IIA is an unreasonably strong criterion. It is the one breached in most useful voting systems. Advocates of this position point out that failure of the standard IIA criterion is trivially implied by the possibility of cyclic preferences. If voters cast ballots as follows:

- 1 vote for A > B > C
- 1 vote for B > C > A
- 1 vote for C > A > B

then the pairwise majority preference of the group is that A wins over B, B wins over C, and C wins over A: these yield rock-paper-scissors preferences for any pairwise comparison. In this circumstance, *any* aggregation rule that satisfies the very basic majoritarian requirement that a candidate who receives a majority of votes must win the election, will fail the IIA criterion, if social preference is required to be transitive (or acyclic). To see this, suppose that such a rule satisfies IIA. Since majority preferences are respected, the society prefers A to B (two votes for A > B and one for B > A), B to C, and C to A. Thus a cycle is generated, which contradicts the assumption that social preference is transitive.

So, what Arrow's theorem really shows is that any majority-wins voting system is a non-trivial game, and that game theory should be used to predict the outcome of most voting mechanisms. This could be seen as a discouraging result, because a game need not have efficient equilibria; e.g., a ballot could result in an alternative nobody really wanted in the first place, yet everybody voted for.

Remark: Scalar Rankings from a Vector of Attributes and the IIA Property

The IIA property might not be satisfied in human decision-making of realistic complexity because the *scalar* preference ranking is effectively derived from the weighting—not usually explicit—of a *vector* of attributes (one book dealing with the Arrow theorem invites the reader to consider the related problem of creating a scalar measure for the track and field decathlon event—e.g. how does one make scoring 600 points in the discus event "commensurable" with scoring 600 points in the 1500 m race) and this scalar ranking can depend sensitively on the weighting of different attributes, with the tacit weighting itself affected by the context and contrast created by apparently "irrelevant" choices. Edward MacNeal discusses this sensitivity problem with respect to the ranking of "most livable city" in the chapter "Surveys" of his book *MathSemantics: making numbers talk sense* (1994).

Other Possibilities

In an attempt to escape from the negative conclusion of Arrow's theorem, social choice theorists have investigated various possibilities ("ways out"). These investigations can be divided into the following two:

- those investigating functions whose domain, like that of Arrow's social welfare functions, consists of profiles of preferences;
- those investigating other kinds of rules.

Approaches Investigating Functions of Preference Profiles

This section includes approaches that deal with:

- aggregation rules (functions that map each preference profile into a social preference), and
- other functions, such as functions that map each preference profile into an alternative.

Since these two approaches often overlap, we discuss them at the same time. What is characteristic of these approaches is that they investigate various possibilities by eliminating or weakening or replacing one or more conditions (criteria) that Arrow imposed.

Infinitely many Individuals

Several theorists (e.g., Kirman and Sondermann) point out that when one drops the assumption that there are only finitely many individuals, one can find aggregation rules that satisfy all of Arrow's other conditions.

However, such aggregation rules are practically of limited interest, since they are based on ultrafilters, highly non-constructive mathematical objects. In particular, Kirman and Sondermann argue that there is an "invisible dictator" behind such a rule. Mihara shows that such a rule violates algorithmic computability. These results can be seen to establish the robustness of Arrow's theorem.

Limiting the Number of Alternatives

When there are only two alternatives to choose from, May's theorem shows that only simple majority rule satisfies a certain set of criteria (e.g., equal treatment of individuals and of alternatives; increased support for a winning alternative should not make it into a losing one). On the other hand, when there are at least three alternatives, Arrow's theorem points out the difficulty of collective decision making. Why is there such a sharp difference between the case of less than three alternatives and that of at least three alternatives?

Nakamura's theorem (about the core of simple games) gives an answer more generally. It establishes that if the number of alternatives is less than a certain integer called the Nakamura number, then the rule in question will identify "best" alternatives without any problem; if the number of alternatives is greater or equal to the Nakamura number, then the rule will not always work, since for some profile a voting paradox (a cycle such as alternative A socially preferred to alternative B, B to C, and C to A) will arise. Since the Nakamura number of majority rule is 3 (except the case of four individuals), one can conclude from Nakamura's theorem that majority rule can deal with up to two alternatives rationally. Some super-majority rules (such as those requiring 2/3 of the votes) can have a Nakamura number greater than 3, but such rules violate other conditions given by Arrow.

Pairwise Voting

A common way "around" Arrow's paradox is limiting the alternative set to two alternatives. Thus, whenever more than two alternatives should be put to the test, it seems very tempting to use a mechanism that pairs them and votes by pairs. As tempting as this mechanism seems at first glance, it is generally far from satisfying even Pareto efficiency, not to mention IIA. The specific order by which the pairs are decided strongly influences the outcome. This is not necessarily a bad feature of the mechanism. Many sports use the tournament mechanism—essentially a pairing mechanism—to choose a winner. This gives considerable opportunity for weaker teams to win, thus adding interest and tension throughout the tournament. This means that the person controlling the order by which the choices are paired (the agenda maker) has great control over the outcome. In any case, when viewing the entire voting process as one game, Arrow's theorem still applies.

Domain Restrictions

Another approach is relaxing the universality condition, which means restricting the domain of aggregation rules. The best-known result along this line assumes "single peaked" preferences.

Duncan Black has shown that if there is only one dimension on which every individual has a "single-peaked" preference, then all of Arrow's conditions are met by majority rule. Suppose that there is some predetermined linear ordering of the alternative set. An individual's preference is *single-peaked* with respect to this ordering if he has some special place that he likes best along that line, and his dislike for an alternative grows larger as the alternative goes further away from that spot (i.e., the graph of his utility function has a single peak if alternatives are placed according to the linear ordering on the horizontal axis). For example, if voters were voting on where to set the volume for music, it would be reasonable to assume that each voter had their own ideal volume preference and that as the volume got progressively too loud or too quiet they would be increasingly dissatisfied. If the domain is restricted to profiles in which every individual has a single peaked preference with respect to the linear ordering, then *simple* aggregation rules, which includes majority rule, have an *acyclic* (defined below) social preference, hence "best" alternatives. In particular, when there are odd number of individuals, then the social preference becomes transitive, and the socially "best" alternative is equal to the median of all the peaks of the individuals (Black's median voter theorem). Under single-peaked preferences, the majority rule is in some respects the most natural voting mechanism.

One can define the notion of "single-peaked" preferences on higher-dimensional sets of alternatives. However, one can identify the "median" of the peaks only in exceptional cases. Instead, we typically have the destructive situation suggested by McKelvey's Chaos Theorem: for any x and y, one can find a sequence of alternatives such that x is beaten by x_1 by a majority, x_1 by x_2, up to x_k by y.

Relaxing Transitivity

By relaxing the transitivity of social preferences, we can find aggregation rules that satisfy Arrow's other conditions. If we impose *neutrality* (equal treatment of alternatives) on such rules, however, there exists an individual who has a "veto". So the possibility provided by this approach is also very limited.

First, suppose that a social preference is *quasi-transitive* (instead of transitive); this means that the strict preference $\succ$ ("better than") is transitive: if $x \succ y$ and $y \succ z$, , then $x \succ z$. . Then, there do exist non-dictatorial aggregation rules satisfying Arrow's conditions, but such rules are *oligarchic*. This means that there exists a coalition L such that L is *decisive* (if every member in L prefers x to y, then the society prefers x to y), and each member in L *has a veto* (if she prefers x to y, then the society cannot prefer y to x).

Second, suppose that a social preference is *acyclic* (instead of transitive): there do not exist alternatives $x_1,\ldots,x_k$ that form a *cycle* ($x_1 \succ x_2, x_2 \succ x_3, \ldots, x_{k-1} \succ x_k, x_k \succ x_1$). Then, provided that there are at least as many alternatives as individuals, an aggregation rule satisfying Arrow's other conditions is *collegial*. This means that there are individuals who belong to the intersection ("collegium") of all decisive coalitions. If there is someone who has a veto, then he belongs to the collegium. If the rule is assumed to be neutral, then it does have someone who has a veto.

Finally, Brown's theorem left open the case of acyclic social preferences where the number of alternatives is less than the number of individuals. One can give a definite answer for that case using the *Nakamura number*.

Relaxing IIA

There are numerous examples of aggregation rules satisfying Arrow's conditions except IIA. The Borda rule is one of them. These rules, however, are susceptible to *strategic manipulation* by individuals.

Relaxing the Pareto Criterion

Wilson (1972) shows that if an aggregation rule is non-imposed and non-null, then there is either a dictator or an inverse dictator, provided that Arrow's conditions other than Pareto are also satisfied. Here, an *inverse dictator* is an individual i such that whenever i prefers x to y, then the society prefers y to x.

Remark

Amartya Sen offered both relaxation of transitivity and removal of the Pareto principle. He demonstrated another interesting impossibility result, known as the "impossibility of the Paretian Liberal". Sen went on to argue that this demonstrates the futility of demanding Pareto optimality in relation to voting mechanisms.

Social Choice Instead of Social Preference

In social decision making, to rank all alternatives is not usually a goal. It often suffices to find some alternative. The approach focusing on choosing an alternative investigates either *social choice functions* (functions that map each preference profile into an alternative) or *social choice rules* (functions that map each preference profile into a subset of alternatives).

As for social choice functions, the Gibbard–Satterthwaite theorem is well-known, which states that if a social choice function whose range contains at least three alternatives is strategy-proof, then it is dictatorial.

As for social choice rules, we should assume there is a social preference behind them. That is, we should regard a rule as choosing the maximal elements ("best" alternatives) of some social preference. The set of maximal elements of a social preference is called the *core*. Conditions for existence of an alternative in the core have been investigated in two approaches. The first approach assumes that preferences are at least *acyclic* (which is necessary and sufficient for the preferences to have a maximal element on any *finite* subset). For this reason, it is closely related to relaxing transitivity. The second approach drops the assumption of acyclic preferences. Kumabe and Mihara adopt this approach. They make a more direct assumption that individual preferences have maximal elements, and examine conditions for the social preference to have a maximal element.

Rated Voting Systems and other Approaches

Arrow's framework assumes that individual and social preferences are "orderings" (i.e., satisfy completeness and transitivity) on the set of alternatives. This means that if the preferences are represented by a utility function, its value is an *ordinal* utility in the sense that it is meaningful so far as the greater value indicates the better alternative. For instance, having ordinal utilities of 4, 3, 2, 1 for alternatives a, b, c, d, respectively, is the same as having 1000, 100.01, 100, 0, which in turn is the same as having 99, 98, 1, .997. They all represent the ordering in which a is preferred to b to c to d. The assumption of *ordinal* preferences, which precludes *interpersonal comparisons* of utility, is an integral part of Arrow's theorem.

For various reasons, an approach based on cardinal utility, where the utility has a meaning beyond just giving a ranking of alternatives, is not common in contemporary economics. However, once one adopts that approach, one can take intensities of preferences into consideration, or one can compare (i) gains and losses of utility or (ii) levels of utility, across different individuals. In particular, Harsanyi (1955) gives a justification of utilitarianism (which evaluates alternatives in terms of the sum of individual utilities), originating from Jeremy Bentham. Hammond (1976) gives a justification of the maximin principle (which evaluates alternatives in terms of the utility of the worst-off individual), originating from John Rawls.

Not all voting methods use, as input, only an ordering of all candidates. Methods which don't, often called "rated" or "cardinal" (as opposed to "ranked", "ordinal", or "preferential") voting systems, can be viewed as using information that only cardinal utility can convey. In that case, it is not surprising if some of them satisfy all of Arrow's conditions that are reformulated. Range voting is such a method. Whether such a claim is correct depends on how each condition is reformulated. Other rated voting systems which pass certain generalizations of Arrow's criteria include approval voting and majority judgment. Note that Arrow's theorem does not apply to single-winner methods such as these, but the Gibbard–Satterthwaite theorem still does: no non-defective voting system is fully strategy-free, so the informal dictum that "no voting system is perfect" still has a mathematical basis.

Finally, though not an approach investigating some kind of rules, there is a criticism by James M. Buchanan, Charles Plott, and others. It argues that it is silly to think that there might be *social* preferences that are analogous to *individual* preferences. Arrow answers this sort of criticism seen in the early period, which come at least partly from misunderstanding.

A multi-pronged refutation of Arrow's theorem was published by philosophy Professor Howard DeLong in 1991.

He challenges the theorem on the basis that Arrow wrongly assumes Preference is transitive property and that Collective Preference is the same as summing up individual preferences. He also claims that Arrow's model fails to model democracy as it exists in the real world as the model ignores the possibility of consensual temporary dictatorships and the effect of allowing lotteries to decide tie breakers and to avoid the problem of the tyranny of the majority, the example used being a group of campers at a summer camp, 8 of whom prefer cake, 7 who prefer ice cream, but funds are limited to one choice or the other on a weekly basis. Under the collective preference of majority rule each week the group would select cake. By drawing lots the choices would more accurately reflect the preferences of the collective than the majority. DeLong also criticizes Arrow's model for being hedonistic and not incorporating a sense of morality and social justice.

Analogs to Arrow's Theorem

Some applications of Arrow's impossibility theorem have been made to domains other than social choice. For example, Stegenga argues that amalgamating evidence from multiple sources faces an impossibility result analogous to Arrow's theorem.

Arrow's Impossibility Theorem

- In fact, there is *no voting system* that will produce a consistent outcome here.
- Arrow's Impossibility Theorem: Condorect Paradox is a general problem
  - States that there is no social decision (voting) rule that converts individual preferences into a consistent aggregate function without either restricting preferences or imposing a dictatorship.
- Subsequent work: restricts space of preferences to make progress
- Two assumptions that ensure existence of equilibrium:
  - G unidimensional
  - Preferences over G are single-peaked.

Restricting Preferences to Solve the Impossibility Theorem

- To solve this problem *restrict preferences* to "single-peaked" preferences.
  - A "peak" in preferences is a point that is preferred to all its immediate neighbors. Utility falls in any direction away from this point.
  - Multi-peaked preferences means that utility may first rise, then fall, then rise again.
  - If preferences are single peaked, majority voting will yield a consistent outcome.

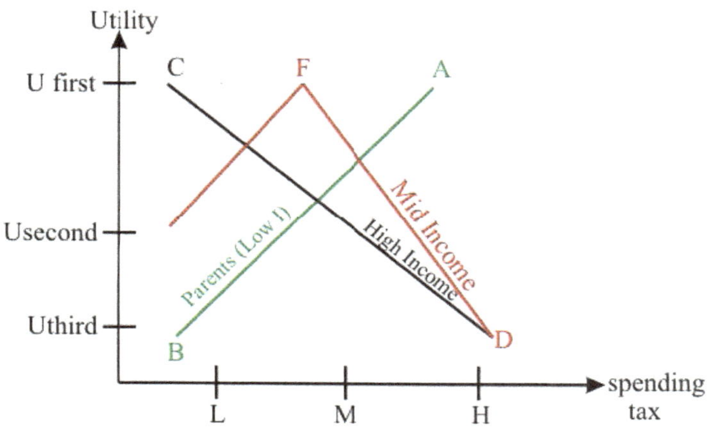

Panel A

- Panel A of figure corresponds to table. The low income group's preferences are reflected in the line A B.

- They get highest utility at the highest level of spending/ tax.
- At medium level of spending they get a medium utility and at the lowest level of spending they get the lowest utility.
- Here all preferences are single peaked (meaning a local maximum).
- For middle income, adjacent to the midpoint, utility is always falling as spending either rises or falls.
- Single peak of low income: high spending.
- Single peak of mid income: mid spending.
- Single peak of high income: low spending.
- Majority voting outcome: medium spending.

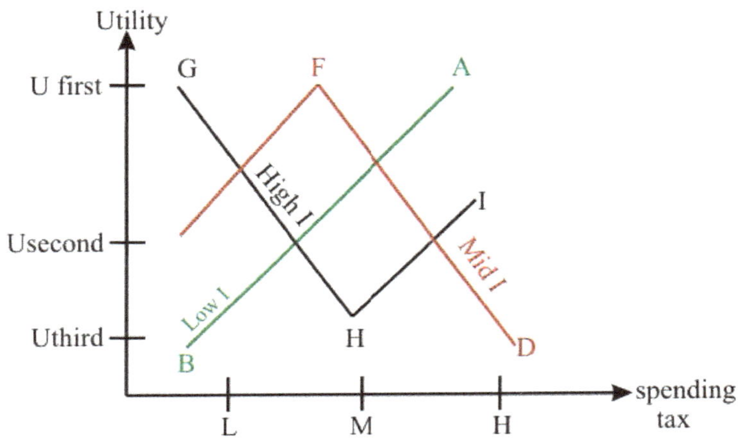

Panel-B

- Panel B of figure corresponds to table. The high income families have a peak at low spending, (Point G) where they have first choice & send their children to Private School. As spending their utility falls to point H, medium spending gives lowest utility. Unlike others however, their utility again as spending moves from medium to high creating a 2nd local maximum (or second peak). The failure of the single peaked preferences assumption in this case is what leads to the inability of majority voting to consistently aggregate preferences.

Summary of Impossibility Theorem

- With single-peaked preferences, majority voting rule produces a voting equilibrium (stable choice).
- The failure of these preferences for the "high income parents" in the second case is what leads to the inability of majority voting to consistently aggregate preferences.
- Single-peakedness is a reasonable assumption in most cases.

References

- West SA, Griffin AS, Gardner A (2007). "Evolutionary explanations for cooperation". Current Biology. 17 (16): R661–R672. PMID 17714660. doi:10.1016/j.cub.2007.06.004
- Demsetz, Harold (October 1970). "Full Access The Private Production of Public Goods". Journal of Law and Economics. 13 (2): 293–306. doi:10.1086/466695. JSTOR 229060
- Boyle, James (1996). Shamans, Software, and Spleens: Law and the Construction of the Information Society. Cambridge, Mass.: Harvard University Press. p. 268. ISBN 0-674-80522-4
- Morrell K & Harrington-Buhay N (2012). "What is governance in the public interest? The case of the 1995 property forum in post-conflict Nicaragua". Public Administration (journal). 90 (2): 412–28. doi:10.1111/j.1467-9299.2011.01977.x
- Fox, Glenn. "The Real Coase Theorems" (PDF). Cato Journal 27, Fall 2007. Cato Institute, Washington, D.C. Retrieved 17 February 2014
- Besley, Timothy; Ghatak, Maitreesh (2001). "Government Versus Private Ownership of Public Goods". The Quarterly Journal of Economics. 116 (4): 1343–1372. doi:10.1162/003355301753265598. ISSN 0033-5533
- Schmitz, Patrick W. (2015). "Government versus private ownership of public goods: The role of bargaining frictions". Journal of Public Economics. 132: 23–31. doi:10.1016/j.jpubeco.2015.09.009
- Hess, Charlotte; Ostrom, Elinor (2007). Understanding Knowledge as a Commons: From Theory to Practice. Cambridge: Massachusetts Institute of Technology. pp. 12–13. ISBN 978-0-262-08357-7
- Morrell K (2009). "Governance and the public good". Public Administration (journal). 87 (3): 538–56 (quote at p 543). doi:10.1111/j.1467-9299.2009.01756.x
- Hallgren, M.M.; McAdams, A.K. (1995). "A model for efficient aggregation of resources for economic public goods on the internet". The Journal of Electronic Publishing. 1. doi:10.3998/3336451.0001.125
- Campbell R. McConnell; Stanley L. Brue; Sean M. Flynn (2011). Economics: Principles, Problems, and Policies (19th ed.). McGraw-Hill/Irwin. p. 104. ISBN 978-0073511443
- Samuelson, Paul A. (1954). "The Pure Theory of Public Expenditure". Review of Economics and Statistics. 36 (4): 387–89. JSTOR 1925895. doi:10.2307/1925895
- Malkin, J.; Wildavasky, A. (1991). "Why the traditional distinction between public and private goods should be abandoned". Journal of Theoretical Politics. 3: 355–378. doi:10.1177/0951692891003004001
- Ray Powell (June 2008). "10: Private goods, public goods and externalities". AQA AS Economics (paperback ed.). Philip Allan. p. 352. ISBN 978-0-340-94750-0
- James M. Buchanan (February 1965). "An Economic Theory of Clubs". Economica. Blackwell Publishing. 32 (125): 1–14. JSTOR 2552442. doi:10.2307/2552442
- Arrow, Kenneth J. (1950). "A Difficulty in the Concept of Social Welfare" (PDF). Journal of Political Economy. 58 (4): 328–346. doi:10.1086/256963. JSTOR 1828886. Archived from the original (PDF) on 2011-07-20
- Arrow, Kenneth J.; Sen, Amartya K.; Suzumura, Kōtarō, eds. (2002). Handbook of social choice and welfare. 1. Amsterdam, Netherlands: Elsevier. ISBN 978-0-444-82914-6
- Elinor Ostrom; James Walker; Roy Gardner (June 1992). "Covenants With and without a Sword: Self-Governance Is Possible". American Political Science Review. 86 (2): 404–17. doi:10.2307/1964229

5

Issues in Public Goods Provision

Government intervention in the provision of public goods is based on certain theories. Median voter theory provides data that represents the majority of median voters, who are those whose preference towards a public good is at the middle level. There are certain shortcomings of this theory as it views voter preference as one-dimensional. This chapter discusses the methods of government intervention in a critical manner providing key analysis to the subject matter.

Median Voter Theorem

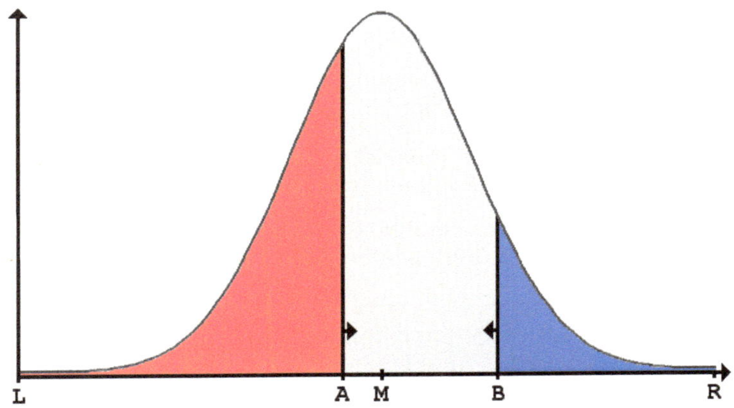

One possible model; here, if parties *A* and *B* want to catch the median voters, they should move towards the center. The red and blue areas represent the voters that *A* and *B* expect they have already captured.

The median voter theorem states that "a majority rule voting system will select the outcome most preferred by the median voter".

The median voter theorem makes two key assumptions. First, the theorem assumes that voters can place all election alternatives along a one-dimensional political spectrum. It seems plausible that voters could do this if they can clearly place political candidates on a left-to-right continuum, but this is often not the case as each party will have its own policy on each of many different issues. Similarly, in the case of a referendum, the alternatives on offer may cover more than one issue. Second, the theorem assumes that voters' preferences are single-peaked, which means that voters choose the alternative closest to their own view. This assumption predicts that the further away the outcome is from the voter's most preferred outcome, the less likely the voter is to select that alternative. It also assumes that voters always vote, regardless of how far the alternatives are from their own views. The median voter theorem implies that voters have an incentive to vote for their true preferences. Finally, the median voter theorem applies best to a majoritarian election system.

Explanations

To appreciate the logic of the median voter model, consider a setting where three individuals, Al, Bob, and Charlie, are to choose a restaurant for lunch. Al prefers a restaurant where lunch costs $5, Bob favors somewhat better fare at a restaurant serving $10 lunches, and Charlie wants a gourmet restaurant where lunch will cost around $20. Bob can be said to be the median voter, because there are exactly the same number of people who prefer a more expensive restaurant than Bob as there are who prefer a less expensive restaurant than Bob: here one each. For convenience assume that, given any two options, each member of the lunch group prefers restaurants with prices closer to their preferred restaurant to those that are farther from it. Now consider some majority decisions over alternative restaurants:

Options	Pattern of votes			Result
$20 vs. $5	A: 5	B: 5	C: 20	5
$10 vs. $20	A: 10	B: 10	C: 20	10
$10 vs. $5	A: 5	B: 10	C: 10	10

The weak form of the median voter theorem says the median voter always casts his or her vote for the policy that is adopted. Note that Bob always votes in favor of the outcome that wins the election. Note also that Bob's preferred $10 restaurant will defeat any other. If there is a median voter, his or her preferred policy will beat any other alternative in a pairwise vote. (The median voter's ideal point is always a Condorcet winner.) Consequently, once the median voter's preferred outcome is reached, it cannot be defeated by another in a pairwise majoritarian election. The strong form of the median voter theorem says the median voter always gets his most preferred policy.

The median voter theorem seems to explain some of the things that happen in majoritarian voting systems. First, it may explain why politicians tend to adopt similar platforms and campaign rhetoric. In order to win the majority vote, politicians must tailor their platforms to the median voter. For example, in the United States, the Democratic and Republican candidates typically move their campaign platforms towards the middle during congressional election campaigns. Just as sellers in a free market try to win over their competitors' customers by making slight changes to improve their products, so too do politicians deviate only slightly from their opponent's platform so as to gain votes.

Second, the median voter theorem reflects that radical candidates or parties rarely get elected. For example, a politician or party which is at an extreme end of the political spectrum will usually not get nearly as many votes as a more moderate party. Finally, the theorem may explain why two major political parties tend to emerge in majoritarian voting systems (Duverger's law). In the United States there are countless political parties, but only two established major parties play a part in almost every major election: the Democratic and Republican parties. According to the median voter theorem third parties will rarely, if ever, win elections for the same reason why extreme candidates do not tend to win. The major parties tend to co-opt the platforms of the minor parties in order to secure more votes. In many other long-established democratic countries there are several parties who each get a substantial share of the vote, although most of these have some form of proportional representation.

History

In his 1929 paper titled *Stability in Competition*, Harold Hotelling notes in passing that political candidates' platforms seem to converge during majoritarian elections. Hotelling compared political elections to businesses in the private sector. He postulated that just as there is often not much difference between the products of different competing companies, so, too, there is not a stark contrast between electoral platforms of different parties. This is because politicians, just like salesmen with consumers, seek to capture the majority of voters. Duncan Black, in his 1948 paper titled *On the Rationale of Group Decision-making*, provided a formal analysis of majority voting that made the theorem and its assumptions explicit. Black wrote that he saw a large gap in economic theory concerning how voting determines the outcome of decisions, including political decisions. Black's paper thus triggered research on how economics can explain voting systems. In 1957 with his paper titled *An Economic Theory of Political Action in Democracy*, Anthony Downs expounded upon the median voter theorem.

Accuracy

Several important economic studies strongly support the median voter theorem. For example, Holcombe analyzes the Bowen equilibrium level of education expenditures for 257 Michigan school districts and finds that the actual expenditures are only about 3% away from the estimated district average.

The theorem also explains the rise in government redistribution programs over the past few decades. Thomas Husted and Lawrence W. Kenny examined growth of redistribution programs especially between the years of 1950 and 1988. Tom Rice also writes that voters with the median income will take advantage of their status as deciders by electing politicians who will tax those who are earning more than the median voter, and then redistribute the money, including to those who are at the median. More specifically, Rice demonstrates that if a systematic closing of the gap between the median and mean income levels in the United States could be shown, more credibility could be given to the median voter theorem. Until the mid-1960s, Rice says that the gap between median and mean income levels tightened. Three main forces served to tighten this gap. First, the strength of the Democratic Party in the United States Congress in the decades leading up to the 1960s, as Democrats are more disposed to redistribution of wealth. Second, increased turnout at the polls, just as Husted and Kenny postulated, tightened the gap because an increase in voters means more individuals of lower income are voting. Finally, since unemployment, which causes median income families to fall below the median income, was relatively low compared to after the 1960s, this tightened the gap.

Limitations

The median voter theorem has several limitations. Keith Krehbiel postulates that there are many factors which prevent the political process from reaching maximum efficiency. Just as transaction costs prevent efficiency in market exchanges, the limitations of the majoritarian voting process stop it from reaching optimality. With the median voter theorem in particular, Krehbiel argues that voters' inability to directly amend legislation acts against the theorem. Sometimes, as Krehbiel writes, the policies being voted on are too complex to be placed within a one-dimensional continuum. Buchanan and Tollison also note that this is a problem for the median voter theorem, which assumes that decisions can be made on a one-dimensional field. If voters are considering more than one issue simultaneously, the median voter theorem is inapplicable. This may happen if, for example, voters may vote on a referendum regarding education spending and police spending simultaneously.

A larger problem for the median voter theorem, however, is the incentives structure for government representatives. Downs, in *A Theory of Bureaucracy*, writes that people's decisions are motivated by self-interest, an idea deeply rooted in the writings of Adam Smith. This holds for the government system as well, because it is composed of individuals who are self-interested. One cannot guarantee the degree to which a government representative will be committed to the public good, but it is certain that, to some degree, they will be committed to their own set of goals. These goals can include a desire to serve the public interest, but most often they include the desire for power, income, and prestige. To continue obtaining these things, then, officials must secure re-election. When representatives are constantly focused on becoming re-elected, this distorts the mandate they receive from their constituents: representatives will translate the wishes of their constituents into benefits for themselves. They will tend to vote for short-term policies that they hope will get them reelected.

Median Voter Theory

- When preferences are single-peaked, then majority voting will deliver a consistent aggregation of preferences of the individual voters.
- The Median Voter Theorem states that *majority voting* will yield the outcome preferred by the *median voter* if preferences are single peaked.
  - The median voter is the voter whose tastes are in the middle of the set of voters, so an equal number of other voters prefer more and prefer less of the public good.
- Voting equilibrium is characterized by preferred level of voter whose preferred level of PG spending is at the median of the distribution.
  - Compute preferred spending for each individual, G^h.
  - Majority voting will select median of distribution of G^h.

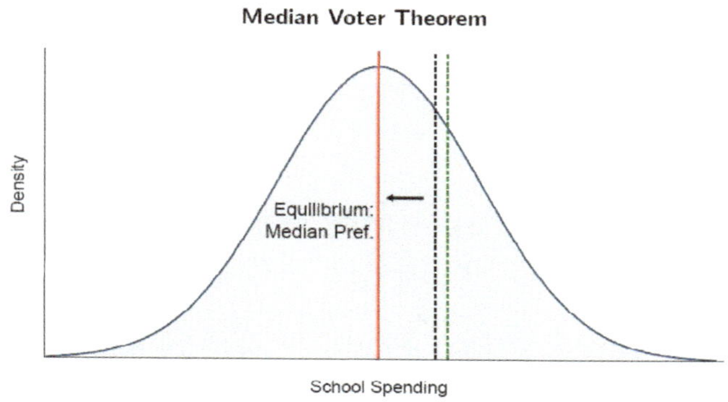

Potential Inefficiency of the Median Voter Outcome

- Thus, the voting would suggest that the government only needs to find the preferences of the median voter, and implement that level of public goods.
- In general, median voter equilibrium is not Pareto efficient:

  Suppose $\tau^h = 1/H$ for all h.

  Voting outcome: $MRS(G^{med}) = 1/H$.

  Samuelson rule: $\sum_h MRS(G^h)/H$ [Note that : $\sum_h MRS(G^h) = 1$].
- Difference between median and mean determines degree of inefficiency.

Inefficiency of the Median Voter Outcome

Intuition

- It does not account for *intensity of preferences*. So it does not follow that the social marginal benefits equal the social marginal cost.
  - For example, if small numbers of individuals derive enormous benefits from the public good, this should be accounted for in the total social marginal benefits.
  - But in Median voter rule this is not accounted for.
- For example, imagine that there are 1,001 voters in a town, who are considering building a Road that costs Rs40.040 (Rs40/person).
  - Assume all 1,001 voters have single-peaked preferences, so the median voter will determine the outcome.
- If 500 citizens value the Road at Rs100 each, and the other 501 value it at Rs0, then the social marginal benefit is Rs50,000, far greater than the cost.

However, the road doesn't get built.

Representative Democracy: Vote - Maximizing Politicians

- In practice, citizens do not vote on every bill; elect representatives to do so.
- In a standard (Hotelling) model, median voter theorem predicts that candidates will implement median voter's preferences when elected.
- Move toward centre to win election.
  - If politicians care about maximizing the number of votes they get, they choose the outcome preferred by the median voter.

Vote-Maximizing Politicians

- Suppose the public good in question is education;

- The key question is what fraction of the budget (say, 0% to 50%) should be spent on education?
- Voters are uniformly distributed on this continuum.
- Two parties, A and B, are running for office and vying to maximize their votes.

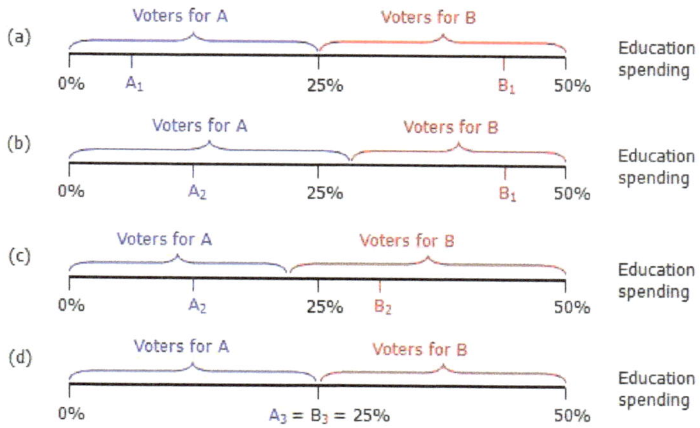

- A is trying to appeal to those who don't want much education spending, so he places himself at A1. While B chooses a much higher level of education, B1. In this case, the candidates split the vote equally.
- But now imagine that A changes his position to A2. By doing so, A now gets a majority of the votes.
- But now imagine that B changes his position to B2 in response to A2. By doing so, B now gets a majority of the votes.
- This process will continue until the median voter's preferences are arrived at.

Median Voter Choice: Evidence

- In a standard (Hotelling) model, median voter theorem predicts that candidates will implement median voter's preferences when elected.
- Does this happen in practice?
- Empirical Evidence:
  - Lee, Moretti, and Butler 2004 : Evidence on Congressional voting sharply contradicts prediction of median voter theory.
- Cannot rely on median voter logic to implement efficient choice even if mean and median are close.

Assumptions of the Median Voter Model

- The median voter model is a powerful tool, but relies on a number of assumptions worth mentioning:

- Single-dimensional voting: Voters only care about one issue.(but in practice the median voter in one issue could be different from the median voter in another issue).
- Only two candidates: With a 3rd candidate, there is no stable equilibrium.
- No ideology or influence: Assumes politicians only care about votes, not ideological positions.
- No selective voting: All citizens actually vote.
- No money as a tool of influence.
- Perfect information along three dimensions: voter knowledge of the issues, politician knowledge of the issues, and politician knowledge of voter preferences.

Crowding Out (Economics)

In economics, crowding out is argued by some economists to be a phenomenon that occurs when increased government involvement in a sector of the market economy substantially affects the remainder of the market, either on the supply or demand side of the market.

One type frequently discussed is when expansionary fiscal policy reduces investment spending by the private sector. The Government is "crowding out" investment because it is demanding more Loanable Funds and it is increasing interest rates from the borrowing, but that was broadened to multiple channels that might leave total output little changed or smaller.

Other economists use "crowding out" to refer to government providing a service or good that would otherwise be a business opportunity for private industry, and be subject only to the economic forces seen in voluntary exchange.

History

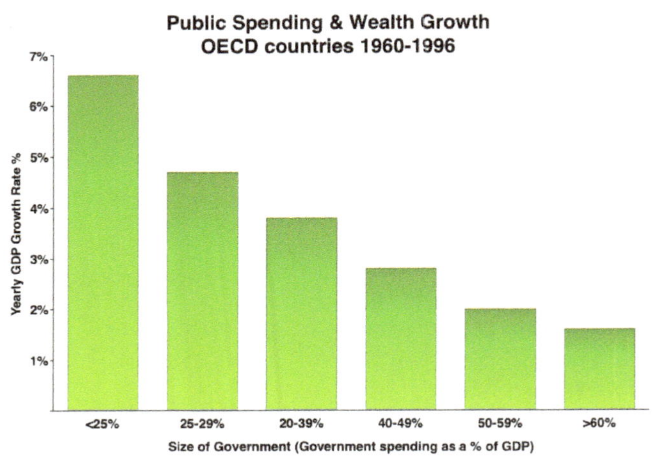

Public spending vs. GDP growth

The idea of the crowding out effect, though not the term itself, has been discussed since at least the 18th century. Economic historian Jim Tomlinson wrote in 2010: "All major economic crises in twentieth century Britain have reignited simmering debates about the impact of public sector expansion on economic performance. From the 'Geddes Axe' after the First World War, through Keynes' attack on the 'Treasury View' in the interwar years, down to the 'monetarist' assaults on the public sector of the 1970s and 1980s, it has been alleged that public sector growth in itself, but especially if funded by state borrowing, has detrimental effects on the national economy." Much of the debate in the 1970s was based on the assumption of a fixed supply of savings within a single country, but with the global capital markets of the 21st century "...international capital mobility completely undermines a simple model of crowding out".

Crowding out from Government Borrowing

One channel of crowding out is a reduction in private investment that occurs because of an increase in government borrowing. If an increase in government spending and/or a decrease in tax revenues leads to a deficit that is financed by increased borrowing, then the borrowing can increase interest rates, leading to a reduction in private investment. There is some controversy in modern macroeconomics on the subject, as different schools of economic thought differ on how households and financial markets would react to more government borrowing under various circumstances.

The extent to which crowding out occurs depends on the economic situation. If the economy is at capacity or full employment, then the government suddenly increasing its budget deficit (e.g., via stimulus programs) could create competition with the private sector for scarce funds available for investment, resulting in an increase in interest rates and reduced private investment or consumption. Thus the effect of the stimulus is offset by the effect of crowding out. On the other hand, if the economy is below capacity and there is a surplus of funds available for investment, an increase in the government's deficit does not result in competition with the private sector. In this scenario, the stimulus program would be much more effective. In sum, changing the government's budget deficit has a stronger impact on GDP when the economy is below capacity. In the aftermath of the 2008 subprime mortgage crisis, the U.S. economy remained well below capacity and there was a large surplus of funds available for investment, so increasing the budget deficit put funds to use that would otherwise have been idle.

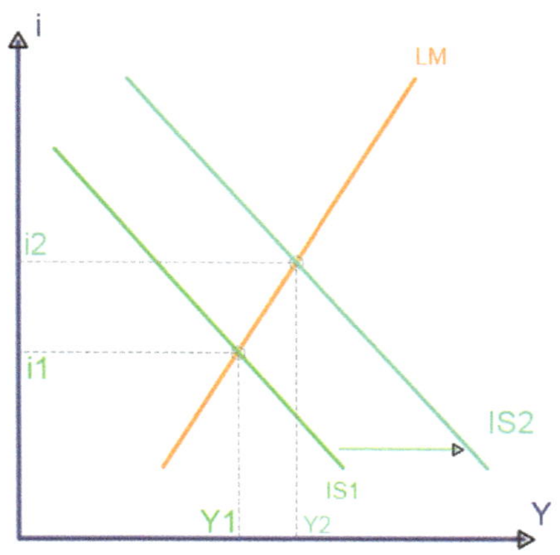

The **IS** curve moves to the right, causing higher interest rates (i) and expansion in the "real" economy (real GDP, or Y).

The macroeconomic theory behind crowding out provides some useful intuition. What happens is that an increase in the demand for loanable funds by the government (e.g. due to a deficit) shifts the loanable funds demand curve rightwards and upwards, increasing the real interest rate. A higher real interest rate increases the opportunity cost of borrowing money, decreasing the amount of interest-sensitive expenditures such as investment and consumption. Thus, the government has "crowded out" investment.

What Factors Determine how much Crowding out takes Place?

The extent to which interest rate adjustments dampen the output expansion induced by increased government spending is determined by:

- Income increases more than interest rates increase if the LM (Liquidity preference—Money supply) curve is flatter.
- Income increases less than interest rates increase if the IS (Investment—Saving) curve is flatter.
- Income and interest rates increase more the larger the multiplier, thus, the larger the horizontal shift in the IS curve.

In each case, the extent of crowding out is greater the more interest rate increases when government spending rises.

Economist Laura D'Andrea Tyson wrote in June 2012: "By itself an increase in the deficit, either in the form of an increase in government spending or a reduction in taxes, causes an increase in demand. But how this affects output, employment and growth depends on what happens to interest rates. When the economy is operating near capacity, government borrowing to finance an increase in the deficit causes interest rates to rise. Higher interest rates reduce or "crowd out" private investment, and this reduces growth. The "crowding out" argument explains why large and sustained government deficits take a toll on growth; they reduce capital formation. But this argument rests on how government deficits affect interest rates, and the relationship between government deficits and interest rates varies. When there is considerable excess capacity, an increase in government borrowing to finance an increase in the deficit does not lead to higher interest rates and does not crowd out private investment. Instead, the higher demand resulting from the increase in the deficit bolsters employment and output directly, and the resulting increase in income and economic activity in turn encourages or 'crowds in' additional private spending. The crowding-in argument is the right one for current economic conditions."

Two Extreme Cases

Liquidity Trap

If the economy is in a hypothesized liquidity trap, the "Liquidity-Money" (LM) curve is horizontal, an increase in government spending has its full multiplier effect on the equilibrium income. There is no change in the interest associated with the change in government spending, thus no investment spending cut off. Therefore, no dampening of the effects of increased government spending on income. If the demand for money is very sensitive to interest rates, so that the LM curve is almost horizontal, fiscal policy changes have a relatively large effect on output, while monetary policy changes have little effect on the equilibrium output. So, if the LM curve is horizontal, monetary policy has no impact on the equilibrium of the economy and the fiscal policy has a maximal effect.

The Classical Case and Crowding Out

If the LM curve is vertical, then an increase in government spending has no effect on the equilibrium income and only increases the interest rates. If the demand for money is not related to the interest rate, as the vertical LM curve implies, then there is unique level of income at which the money market is in equilibrium.

Thus, with vertical LM curve, an increase in government spending cannot change the equilibrium income and only raises the equilibrium interest rates. But if government spending is higher and the output is unchanged, there must be an offsetting reduction in private spending. In this case, the increase in interest rates crowds out an amount of private spending equal to increase in government spending. Thus, there is full crowding out if LM is vertical.

Crowding Out Sources

If increased borrowing leads to higher interest rates by creating a greater demand for money and loanable funds and hence a higher "price" (*ceteris paribus*), the private sector, which is sensitive to interest rates, will likely reduce investment due to a lower rate of return. This is the investment that is crowded out. The weakening of fixed investment and other interest-sensitive expenditure counteracts to varying extents the expansionary effect of government deficits. More importantly, a fall in fixed investment by business can hurt long-term economic growth of the supply side, i.e., the growth of potential output. Thus, the situation in which borrowing may lead to crowding out is that companies would like to expand productive capacity, but, because of high interest rates, cannot borrow funds with which to do so. According to American economist Jared Bernstein, writing in 2011, this scenario is "not a plausible story with excess capacity, the Fed funds [interest] rate at zero, and companies sitting on cash that they could invest with if they saw good reasons to do so." Another American economist, Paul Krugman, pointed out that, after the beginning of the recession in 2008, the federal government's borrowing increased by hundreds of billions of dollars, leading to warnings about crowding out, but instead interest rates had actually fallen. When aggregate demand is low, government spending tends to expand the market for private-sector products through the fiscal multiplier and thus stimulates – or "crowds in" – fixed investment (via the "accelerator effect"). This accelerator effect is most important when business suffers from unused industrial capacity, i.e., during a serious recession or a depression.

Crowding out can, in principle, be avoided if the deficit is financed by simply printing money, but this carries concerns of accelerating inflation.

Chartalist and Post-Keynesian economists question the crowding out thesis because government bonds sales have the actual effect of lowering short-term interest rates, not raising them, since the rate for short-term debt is always set by central banks. Additionally, private credit is not constrained by any "amount of funds" or "money supply" or similar concept. Rather, banks lend to any credit-worthy customer, constrained by their capitalization level and risk regulations. The resulting loan creates a deposit simultaneously, increasing the amount of endogenous money at that time. Crowding out is most plausibly effective when an economy is already at potential output or full employment. Then the government's expansionary fiscal policy encourages increased prices, which lead to an increased demand for money. This in turn leads to higher interest rates (*ceteris paribus*) and crowds out interest-sensitive spending. At potential output, businesses are in no need of markets, so that there is no room for an accelerator effect. More directly, if the economy stays at full employment gross domestic product, any increase in government purchases shifts resources away from the private sector. This phenomenon is sometimes called "real" crowding out.

Crowding out of another sort (often referred to as international crowding out) may occur due to the prevalence of floating exchange rates, as demonstrated by the Mundell-Fleming model. Government borrowing leads to higher interest rates, which attract inflows of money on the capital account from foreign financial markets into the domestic currency (i.e., into assets denominated in that currency). Under floating exchange rates, that leads to appreciation of the exchange rate and thus the "crowding out" of domestic exports (which become more expensive to those using foreign currency). This counteracts the demand-promoting effects of government deficits but has no obvious negative effect on long-term economic growth.

Crowding Out Demand

In terms of health economics, "crowding-out" refers to the phenomenon whereby new or expanded programs meant to cover the uninsured have the effect of prompting those already enrolled in private insurance to switch to the new program. This effect was seen, for example, in expansions to Medicaid and the State Children's Health Insurance Program (SCHIP) in the late 1990s.

Therefore, high takeup rates for new or expanded programs do not merely represent the previously uninsured, but also represent those who may have been forced to shift their health insurance from the private to the public sector. As a result of these shifts, it can be projected that healthcare improvements as a result of policy change may not be as robust. In the context of the CHIP debate, this assumption was challenged by projections produced by the Congressional Budget Office, which "scored" all versions of the CHIP reauthorization and included in those scores the best assumptions available regarding the impacts of increased funding for these programs. CBO assumed that many already eligible children would become enrolled as a result of the new funding and policies in CHIP reauthorization, but that some would be eligible for private insurance. The vast majority, even in states with enrollments of those above twice the poverty line (around $40,000 for a family of four), did not have access to age-appropriate health insurance for their children. New Jersey, supposedly the model for profligacy in SCHIP with eligibility that stretched to 350% of the federal poverty level, testified that it could identify 14% crowd-out in its CHIP program.

In the context of CHIP and Medicaid, many children are eligible but not enrolled. Thus, in comparison to Medicare, which allows for near "auto-enrollment" for those over 64, children's caregivers may be required to fill out 17-page forms, produce multiple consecutive pay stubs, re-apply at more than yearly intervals and even conduct face-to-face interviews to prove the eligibility of the child. These anti-crowd-out procedures can fracture care for children, sever the connection to their medical home and lead to worse health outcomes.

Crowding Out Supply

Crowding out is also said to occur in charitable giving when government public policy inserts itself into roles that had traditionally been private voluntary charity.

Crowding out has also been observed in the area of venture capital, suggesting that government involvement in financing commercial enterprises crowds out private finance.

Complication of Public Provision

- In principle, the government could solve the optimal public goods provision problem and then either provide the good directly or mandate individuals to provide it.
- In practice, three problems emerge:
  - Crowd-out.
  - Measuring costs and benefits.
- Measuring future costs & benefits is even more difficult.
  - Determining the public's preferences.
- In some cases, the private market may already be providing a socially inefficient level of the private good.

Optimal Second Best Provision of Public Goods

- Suppose govt has decided to levy a tax and provide public goods based on some rule.
- Two complications arise when trying to get to Samuelson First Best level:
  - Interactions with private sector provision.
- Public provision may *crowd-out* some of the private provision–as the government provides more of the public good, the private sector provides less.
  - Government cannot finance public goods through lump sum taxation
- Must modify Samuelson rule to account for distortionary taxation.

The Problem of Crowd-Out

- Full Crowd out: Conditions
  - People care only about the total number of goods provided: there is no warm glow from giving.
  - Provision of public goods will be financed by charging equal amounts to each of them.

- The government provides no more public goods than were being provided privately beforehand.

- Then each unit of public provision will crowd out private provision one-for-one.

Public Goods with Endogenous Private Provision

- Interest in crowd-out began with Roberts (1984)
- Expansion of govt services for the poor since Great Depression accompanied by comparable decline in charitable giving for the poor.
- Inference government has grown tremendously without having any net impact on poverty or welfare
- Evidence mainly based on time series impressions.
- But theory underlying this claim very sensible, as subsequent work showed

Bergstrom, Blume, and Varian (1986) Model of Crowd-Out

Individual h solves:

$$\max_{X^h, G^h} u^h(X_h, G_h + G_{-h})$$

$$\text{s.t. } X_h + G_h = Y_h$$

$$\text{FOC}: u_x^h = u_G^h$$

Nash Equilibrium exists & is unique.

$\rightarrow$ G such that all individuals optimize given others behaviour.

Let G^* denote private equilibrium outcome.

Now suppose government introduces lump sum tax of t^h on each individual h. Revenue used to finance expenditure on public good $T = \Sigma t^h$

Individual optimization problem is now $\max u(X^h, G^h + G^{-h} + T)$

$\because G^h$ is private provision of public good.

$$\text{s.t.} X^h + G^h = Y^h - t^h$$

Let $Z^h = G^h + t^h$: Total contribution of individual h.

Then we can rewrite the above problem as:

$$\text{Max.} u(X^h, Z^h + Z^{-h})$$

$$\text{s.t. } X^h + Z^h = Y^h$$

This is isomorphic to the original problem.

$$\Rightarrow Z^* = G^*$$

Total public good provision unchanged!

Each person simply reduces voluntary contribution by t^h.

Private Responses to Public Provision: Partial Crowd-Out

- Full crowd-out is rare, though partial crowd-out is much more common and can occur when:
  - People who don't contribute to the public good are taxed to finance its provision.
- Contributors' effective income levels are higher than before.
- As a result of this income effect, contributors buy more if the public good is a normal good, offsetting the crowd-out to some extent.
  - Or when individuals derive utility from their individual contributions as well as the total amount of the public good provided.
- Warm glow model offsets crowd out effect.
- Suppose there are 2 individuals A&B. $\rightarrow$ A contributor, B $\rightarrow$ non contributor. Initially A contributes 10 unit, B nothing. Government imposed lump sum tax of 5 units each & provides 10 units. Now A gets 10 at the cost of 5. This is an effective increase in A's wealth.

Empirical Evidence on Crowd-Out

- Two empirical questions motivated by theory.
  - How large is the degree of crowd-out in practice?
  - What are the income and price effects on charitable giving?
- Two strands of empirical literature.
  - Field evidence (observational studies).
- How individual contributions respond to government spending: shows small crowd out. But they suffer from endogeneity problems.
  - Lab experiments.
- Lab experiments suggest crowd out is large.
- Lab experiments may not capture important motives for giving: warm glow, prestige

- Traditionally, lab experiments have been more influential but recent field studies may change this.

KINGMA 1989

- Studies individual contributions to public radio stations.
- Cross-sectional survey of individuals who listened to public radio. 3,500 individuals and 63 different radio stations.
- Research Design: OLS regression of individual contributions on government support.

$$D_i = b_0 + b_1 G_i + X_i + e_i$$

Di = individual contribution.

Gi = government support.

Xi = set of controls: individual income, individual education, age, price (tax bracket).

Summary Statistics For Public Radio Listeners				
	Contribution		Noncontribution	
	Mean	Standard Deviation	Mean	Standard Deviation
Contribution($)	45	52	0	0
Age(Years)	46	14	45	16
Income($)	48.074	27.586	37.582	24.818
Education(Years)	16.4	2.4	15.3	2.8
Listening(Hours Per Week)	10.75	11.25	6.00	8.00

D = -65.036 + .539(Income) - .010(R) - .015(G) – 15.014(Price)
(3.38) (6.49) (.94) (3.02) (.74)
+10.018 (Eductn) + .288 (Age)
(8.01) (3.26)

Kingma 1989

- Main result: *b1 = - 0.015 implies* crowd-out rate of 20% at the average.
- Significantly negative but much less than 1-1 prediction of theory.
- Identification Problem: government support might depend on individual contributions.
- E.g. non-contribution by individuals leads to govt provision.
  - Creates a spurious negative correlation between govt support and individual contributions.
- We need an exogenous shifter that affects government contribution without affecting individual contributions.
- E.g.: legislated reform that bans government support.

Hungerman 2005

- Studies crowd-out of church-provided welfare (soup kitchens, etc.) by government welfare.
- Uses 1996 Clinton welfare reform act as an instrument for welfare spending.
- One aspect of reform: reduced/eliminated welfare for non-citizens.
- Motivates a diff-in-diff strategy: compare churches in high non-citizen areas with low non-citizen areas before/after 1996 reform.

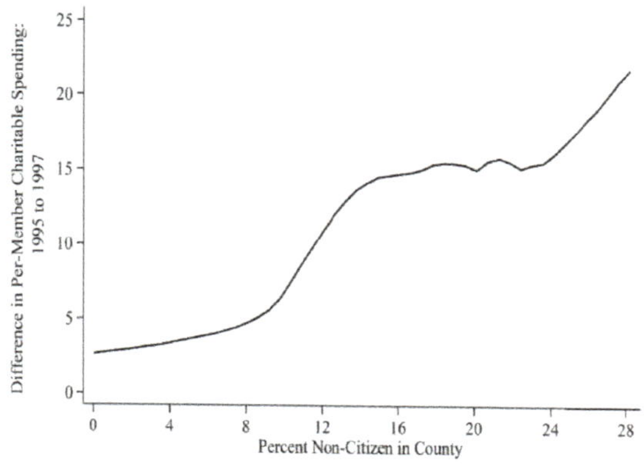

Source: Hungerman 2005

- Estimates imply that total church expenditures in a state go up by 40 cents when welfare spending is cut by $1.
- Exogenous variation make these estimates much more credible.

Andreoni 1993: An Experimental Test of the Crowding-Out Hypothesis

- Presents lab experiment to test if government contributions to public goods, funded by lump-sum taxation, completely crowds out voluntary contributions.
- A public good was provided by three subjects.
- Each subject was given a budget of seven tokens. Each subject could "play" from zero to seven of these tokens, with the payoff from any play depending on the number of tokens played by all of the group members. All subjects moved simultaneously.
- Two groups: no-tax and tax.
- Subjects in the "no tax group" were told that payoffs would be determined from the payoff matrix, where payoffs are denominated in cents. The matrix in Figure was generated from a Cobb-Douglas utility function where Gh is the number of tokens played by the individual, G = G1 + G2 + G3 is the total number of tokens played by the group.
- Each game repeated twenty times.
- Payoff from any play depends on the number of tokens played by all of the group members. (simultaneous move).

– {Payoffs determined by $U_h = (7 - Gh)^{1-a} G^a$ }

- The parameter A is chosen to meet specifications of the Nash equilibrium outcome, Pareto efficient outcome, equilibrium payoff levels, and concavity of utility.
- Tax group: A tax of two tokens on all subjects which is then donated to the public good. And can then choose G_h = 0, 1, 2, .., 5(pay off determined by matrix in Figure).
- Each game repeated 20 times.
- Voluntary contribution.

No-tax game:

- Turns out that Nash equilibrium is G_h = 3 but Pareto efficient outcome is G_h = 6.

Tax game:

- Nash equilibrium is G_h = 1(+2, involuntary) but Pareto efficient outcome is G_h = 4(+2, involuntary).

TOTAL INVESTMENT BY THE OTHER TWO GROUP MEMBERS	YOUR INVESTMENT 0	1	2	3	4	5	6	7
0	0	1	3	6	9	10	11	10
1	1	4	8	11	14	15	15	14
2	5	9	14	18	20	21	20	17
3	12	17	22	26	28	28	25	22
4	21	28	33	36	37	35	32	27
5	34	40	45	48	47	44	39	32
6	49	56	60	61	59	54	47	38
7	68	74	77	76	72	64	55	44
8	90	95	96	93	86	76	64	51
9	115	118	117	111	102	89	74	58
10	143	144	140	131	119	103	85	66
11	175	173	166	153	137	118	97	75
12	210	205	193	177	157	134	109	84
13	248	239	223	203	178	151	122	93
14	290	276	256	230	201	169	136	103

THE NO-TAX PAYOFF MATRIX

Source: Andreoni 1993

TOTAL INVESTMENT BY THE OTHER TWO GROUP MEMBERS	YOUR INVESTMENT 0	1	2	3	4	5
0	33	36	37	35	32	27
1	45	48	47	44	39	32
2	60	61	59	54	47	38
3	77	76	72	64	55	44
4	96	93	86	76	64	51
5	117	111	102	89	74	58
6	140	131	119	103	85	66
7	166	153	137	118	97	75
8	193	177	157	134	109	84
9	223	203	178	151	122	93
10	256	230	201	169	136	103

THE TAX PAYOFF MATRIX

Source: Andreoni 1993

Average Real Contributions to the Public Good Per Round for the No-Tax and Tax Conditions

Round	No-tax condition Trial 1	No-tax condition Trial 2	No-tax condition Average	Tax condition Trial 1	Tax condition Trial 2	Tax condition Average	Overall difference
1	2.94	2.83	2.89	4.05	3.66	3.86	0.97
2	2.66	2.55	2.61	3.72	3.72	3.72	1.12
3	3.33	2.61	2.97	3.38	3.72	3.55	0.58
4	3.11	2.38	2.75	2.77	2.77	2.77	0.02
5	2.72	3.33	3.03	4.27	3.61	3.94	0.91
6	2.72	2.72	2.72	3.44	3.38	3.41	0.69
7	2.88	3.05	2.97	4.11	2.94	3.53	0.56
8	2.72	2.66	2.69	3.22	2.88	3.05	0.36
9	2.88	2.55	2.72	4.05	3.55	3.80	1.09
10	3.22	3.11	3.17	3.77	3.11	3.44	0.27
11	2.88	2.83	2.86	3.61	3.22	3.42	0.56
12	2.61	2.55	2.58	3.00	3.00	3.00	0.42
13	2.77	2.83	2.80	3.77	3.33	3.55	0.75
14	2.61	2.66	2.64	3.44	2.83	3.14	0.50
15	2.77	2.61	2.69	3.27	2.94	3.11	0.42
16	3.05	2.72	2.89	2.94	2.88	2.91	0.02
17	3.27	2.77	3.02	3.50	3.61	3.56	0.54
18	2.44	3.05	2.75	3.72	2.72	3.22	0.48
19	3.05	2.38	2.72	3.38	2.83	3.11	0.39
20	2.11	2.38	2.25	3.16	2.83	3.00	0.75
Average:	2.84	2.73	2.78	3.53	3.18	3.35	0.57

Source: Andreoni 1993

Andreoni 1993

- Results:
  - Crowding-out is substantial: 71.5% on average.
  - But Crowding-out is incomplete and subjects who are taxed are significantly more cooperative. This is true even though the tax does not affect the Nash equilibrium prediction.
  - This result is taken as evidence that people experience some private benefit from contributing to public goods: warm glow effect.
  - Overall evidence on crowd out suggests that carefully targeted govt programs can still have considerable net impact.

References

- Downs, Anthony (1957). "An Economic Theory of Political Action in a Democracy". Journal of Political Economy. 65: 135–150. doi:10.1086/257897
- David M. Cutler & Jonathan Gruber (2 February 1995). "Does Public Insurance Crowd Out Private Insurance?". Ideas.repec.org. Retrieved 9 November 2014
- Husted, Thomas A. & Lawrence W. Kenny (1997). "The Effect of the Expansion of the Voting Franchise on the Size of Government Model". Journal of Political Economy. 105: 54–82. doi:10.1086/262065
- Gruber, Jonathan (2012). Public Finance and Public Policy. New York, NY: Worth Publishers. ISBN 978-1-4292-7845-4
- Holcombe, Randall G. (1980). "An Empirical Test of the Median Voter Model". Economic Inquiry. 18: 260–275. doi:10.1111/j.1465-7295.1980.tb00574.x
- Krehbiel, Keith (2004). "Legislative Organization". Journal of Economic Perspectives. 18: 113–128. doi:10.1257/0895330047735634 67
- Mas-Colell, Andreu, Michael D. Whinston, and Jerry R. Green (1995). Microeconomic Theory. Oxford University Press. ISBN 978-0-19-507340-9

- Rice, Tom W. (1985). "An Examination of the Median Voter Hypothesis". The Western Political Quarterly. 38: 211–223. doi:10.1177/106591298503800204
- Clinton, Joshua D. (2006). "Representation in Congress: Constituents and the Roll Calls in the 106th House", The Journal of Politics, 68(2): 397-409
- Congleton, Roger (2002). The Median Voter Model. In * C. K. *Rowley (Ed.); F. Schneider (Ed.) (2003). The Encyclopedia of Public Choice. Kluwer Academic Press. ISBN 978-0-7923-8607-0
- Husted, Thomas A. and Lawrence W. Kenny (1997). "The Effect of the Expansion of the Voting Franchise on the Size of Government", Journal of Political Economy, 105(1): 54-82
- Nisan, Noam; Roughgarden, Tim; Tardos, Eva; Vazirani, Vijay (eds.). "Chapter 10". Algorithmic Game Theory (PDF). pp. 246–252. ISBN 978-0521872829
- McKelvey, Richard D. (1976). "Intransitives in Multidimensional Voting Models and Some Implications for Agenda Control", Journal of Economic Theory, 12: 472-482
- Eckel; et al. (2005). "An experimental test of the crowding out hypothesis". Journal of Public Economics. doi:10.1016/j.jpubeco.2004.05.012. Retrieved 2014-11-07

Permissions

All chapters in this book are published with permission under the Creative Commons Attribution Share Alike License or equivalent. Every chapter published in this book has been scrutinized by our experts. Their significance has been extensively debated. The topics covered herein carry significant information for a comprehensive understanding. They may even be implemented as practical applications or may be referred to as a beginning point for further studies.

We would like to thank the editorial team for lending their expertise to make the book truly unique. They have played a crucial role in the development of this book. Without their invaluable contributions this book wouldn't have been possible. They have made vital efforts to compile up to date information on the varied aspects of this subject to make this book a valuable addition to the collection of many professionals and students.

This book was conceptualized with the vision of imparting up-to-date and integrated information in this field. To ensure the same, a matchless editorial board was set up. Every individual on the board went through rigorous rounds of assessment to prove their worth. After which they invested a large part of their time researching and compiling the most relevant data for our readers.

The editorial board has been involved in producing this book since its inception. They have spent rigorous hours researching and exploring the diverse topics which have resulted in the successful publishing of this book. They have passed on their knowledge of decades through this book. To expedite this challenging task, the publisher supported the team at every step. A small team of assistant editors was also appointed to further simplify the editing procedure and attain best results for the readers.

Apart from the editorial board, the designing team has also invested a significant amount of their time in understanding the subject and creating the most relevant covers. They scrutinized every image to scout for the most suitable representation of the subject and create an appropriate cover for the book.

The publishing team has been an ardent support to the editorial, designing and production team. Their endless efforts to recruit the best for this project, has resulted in the accomplishment of this book. They are a veteran in the field of academics and their pool of knowledge is as vast as their experience in printing. Their expertise and guidance has proved useful at every step. Their uncompromising quality standards have made this book an exceptional effort. Their encouragement from time to time has been an inspiration for everyone.

The publisher and the editorial board hope that this book will prove to be a valuable piece of knowledge for students, practitioners and scholars across the globe.

Index